THE MAKING OF
THE AUSTRALIAN COMMONWEALTH
1889–1900

THE MAKING OF THE AUSTRALIAN COMMONWEALTH

1889-1900

A STAGE IN THE GROWTH OF THE EMPIRE

BY

BERNHARD RINGROSE WISE

LONGMANS, GREEN, AND CO.
39 PATERNOSTER ROW, LONDON
NEW YORK, BOMBAY, AND CALCUTTA
1913

DEDICATED TO THE
71,965 ELECTORS OF NEW SOUTH WALES
WHO VOTED "YES" ON JUNE 3, 1898

PREFACE

THIS is not a *histoire documentée* of the movement towards Australian Federation,—(that should be the work of an Australian University),—nor another study of the constitution, nor a memoir ; but the record by an eye-witness of the making of the Commonwealth during the critical period from 1889 to 1900, which aims at giving to a later generation a more vivid picture of that time, and making intelligible the policy and passions of the contending parties, the personalities of the rival leaders, and the ebb and flow of popular sentiment which was the decisive factor in the great event.   It is a story, which is worth the telling, of a time when high ideals inspired men to effort, and may repeat itself sooner than we think in a struggle for the closer Union of the British peoples.

If the names of the actors be unfamiliar to English readers, let it be remembered that Galt, George Brown, Tupper, and John A. Macdonald were little known in England twelve years after the formation of the Dominion of Canada ; and, that all, who do work for the Empire, have a place in its history, whether they inhabit London, Ottawa, or Sydney.

And, if the narrative appear to Australians to move too much in New South Wales, they, also, need to be reminded that this was the pivotal Colony of the Australian group, and that in no other was there any serious contest.

B. R. WISE.

SYDNEY, AUSTRALIA,
Jan. 15, 1913.

CONTENTS

CONTENTS

THE MAKING

OF THE

AUSTRALIAN COMMONWEALTH

CHAPTER I

THE TENTERFIELD SPEECH

DURING the second and third quarters of the year
1889 there was a very remarkable lull in the politics
of the Australian Colonies. The New South Wales
Parliament had settled down, after a general election,
to a discussion of a 'non-contentious' Land Bill,
which occupied a Session of thirteen months ; while
in Victoria a coalition Government was enjoying the
first fumes of an intoxicating land-boom. In every
Colony, indeed, the political field was clear of the
old party issues, and the tide of public opinion
at the dead ebb. To Sir Henry Parkes, the Prime
Minister of New South Wales, such a time seemed
favourable to the consideration of constitutional
problems ; and the narrative opens with his unavailing
efforts to bring the other Premiers to his way of
thinking.

B

. I .

On July 9, 1889, he wrote confidentially to Mr. Duncan Gillies, the Premier of Victoria, suggesting that the time had arrived for creating ' a Federal Parliament and Executive, with complete authority, upon the lines of the Dominion of Canada.'[1] Mr. Gillies, writing on August 12, showed that he considered such a proposal to be both chimerical and unnecessary— chimerical, because he ' could see no present prospect of bringing it about,' and unnecessary, because 'the Federal Council already possessed the necessary machinery for concerted action.' His counter proposal was that New South Wales should join the Council, which ' then should be given a more representative character and might be clothed by the special authority of the various Legislatures with power to deal with the proposals of the larger Federation.'[2] Sir Henry Parkes let the matter rest and waited for another opportunity.

This came on October 9 of the same year, when the report of Major-General Bevan Edwards, who had been commissioned by the Imperial Government to inspect the defences of Australia, was given to the public. In this he recommended, among other changes, the fortification of several points of strategic importance and the organisation of the military forces of the several Colonies under one command as an Australian Army. It was clear that these recommendations

[1] The two letters containing this proposal are referred to in Mr. Gillies' letter to Sir Henry Parkes of August 12, 1889 (*Parl. Papers Leg. Ass. N.S.W.*, December 19, 1889). They are not known otherwise to the writer.

[2] As to the powers and origin of the Federal Council, from which New South Wales had stood aloof, see *post*, p. 18.

could not be carried out effectively except under some form of Union; and that there must be a single Australian Government for defence purposes, if for no other reason. Accordingly, on October 15, Sir Henry Parkes addressed a circular telegram to the other Premiers inviting them to a Conference to consider General Edwards' report. Again he met with a rebuff!

Mr. Gillies, who replied for all, once more objected that any conference which ignored the Federal Council would be barren of results, and that to create a new federal body to deal with defence alone would certainly seem strange, and would not increase Australia's prestige. He added, with a touch of sarcasm, that only the attitude of New South Wales caused a divided instead of a united Australia, and that this could be brought about at once instead of being postponed to a future day, and to other men, if only Sir Henry Parkes would join the Federal Council.

Sir Henry Parkes wasted no more time in correspondence; but on October 21, keeping his intention secret even from his colleagues, journeyed to Brisbane to consult with the leaders of both political parties— Mr. Boyd Morehead, the Premier, and Sir Samuel Griffith, the leader of the Opposition—and endeavour by personal persuasion to bring them and others to his view. The Queensland Cabinet (as one of its members has informed the writer) listened to him with polite incredulity; and, while not committing themselves to an approval, indicated their desire that he should take his own course.

Upon October 24, on his return journey, he reached Tenterfield, which is a border town between

New South Wales and Queensland, perched upon the Dividing Range, which runs along the coast from Carpentaria to Cape Howe. From its altitude it seems to overlook Australia; and, by reason of its situation, it is comparatively free from provincial prejudice. Thus it was a natural minaret from which to sound the trumpet-call, which stirred with life the dry bones of the Island Continent. There, on October 24, 1889, Sir Henry Parkes made the great speech, which, although its significance was not appreciated fully at the time, marks in decisive fashion the beginning of a new era in Australian politics. Others before him had advocated Federation; but he was the first who made his appeal directly to the patriotism of the people; so that, from this day forward, the desire for Union, which had floated before men's minds as a vague aspiration for many years, took definite shape.

Owing to the pains which he had taken to conceal his intention, his speech was not reported fully; but, fortunately, the novelist David Christie Murray, who was visiting Australia, happened to be in the audience and has recorded his impressions:—[1]

It was my good fortune [he writes] to be present at that now famous meeting at Tenterfield, at which Sir Henry Parkes chose to make his pronunciamento with regard to Australian Federation, and I shall not readily forget the enthusiasm his speech evoked. His utterance was plain, straightforward and convincing; and the speaker's sterling belief in the greatness of his theme and the propitious character of the hour was strikingly evident. The excellent choice of words, the masterly elaboration of phrases, which were obviously moulded whilst he stood there upon his feet, were in some contrast to the

---

[1] See *The Cockney Columbus*, p. 277.

manner of his utterance. The voice was a little veiled by fatigue and age. The massive shoulders were a little bowed ; but the huge head, with its streaming wave of silver hair and beard, was held as erect as ever. The rough homely features were as eloquent as the words he spoke ; and the instinct of a natural fighting man lit up the ancient warrior's eye. The mere aspect and manner would have been remarkable to a stranger anywhere ; but there, where for the first time the voice of an authoritative statesman gave soul and utterance to the aspirations of a people, it was truly remarkable and not without a touch of sublimity.

It is apparent, even from the condensed reports which appeared in the daily Press, that the speech confirms this estimate of the speaker's qualities.

. 2 .

After referring to the work of the Session and the political situation in New South Wales, Sir Henry Parkes called attention to the report of Major-General Edwards, dwelling particularly upon his recommendation that the forces of the various Colonies should be federated together for operations in union in the event of war, so as to act as one great Federal Army. To accomplish this it would be necessary to have one central authority which could bring all the forces of the different Colonies into one Army. The question was what this authority should be. Some ' Colonial statesmen ' had suggested that it should be the Federal Council :—

They must have heard something of the Federal Council, on which New South Wales had not yet taken a place, and which sat in Tasmania, and held Sessions which never appeared to interest anyone !

After this gibe he examined seriously the constitution of the Federal Council in order to see whether it was the proper governing authority :—

This Federal Council was not an elective body, but merely a body appointed by the Governments of the various Colonies. It was therefore necessarily weak, and, under the Imperial Act which appointed it, no such tremendous power was given as that of originating and controlling a great Australian Army. The Federal Council also had no executive power. It could propose but could not execute. He would like to know what was to become of an Army without a central executive to guide its movements.

Therefore, he declared, the great question for them to consider was, *whether the time had not now arisen for the creation on this Australian Continent of an Australian Parliament as distinct from a Local Parliament, and an Australian Government as distinct from a Local Government.*

He reminded them that they were almost equal in number to the Americans when they formed their Constitution :—

Australia had now a population of three and a half millions, and the American people numbered only between three and four millions when they formed the great Commonwealth of the United States. The numbers were about the same, and surely *what the Americans had done by war they could bring about in peace?*

Harking back to the question of defence, Sir Henry Parkes dwelt next upon the military necessity of a uniform railway gauge, and pointed out that this also required concerted action under some common government. He came then to the question ' as to the steps which should be taken.' Some persons had suggested a conference of railway authorities and Ministers ; but in his opinion they 'must take broader and more powerful action in the initiation of a great council.' They must

appoint a Convention of leading men from all the Colonies, delegates appointed by the authority of Parliament, who would fully represent the opinion of the different Parliaments of the Colonies. This Convention would have to devise the constitution which would be necessary for bringing into existence a Federal Government, with a Federal Parliament, for the conduct of great national undertakings. The only argument which could be advanced in opposition was that the time had not come! He believed, however, that the time had come. In the words of Brunton Stephens, the Queensland poet :

> Not yet her day! How long 'Not yet ?
> There comes the flush of violet!
> And heavenward faces, all aflame
> With sanguine imminence of morn,
> Wait but the sun-kiss to proclaim
> The day of the Dominion born.

He believed that the time had come, and if two Governments set an example, the others must soon of necessity follow, and they would have an uprising in this fair land of a goodly fabric of free government, and all great national questions of magnitude affecting the welfare of the Colonies would be disposed of by a fully authorised constitutional authority, which would be the only one which could give satisfaction to the people represented.

And he explained, then, that

This meant a distinct executive and a distinct parliamentary power ; a Government for the whole of Australia. And it meant a Parliament of two Houses, a House of Commons and a Senate, which would legislate on these great subjects. The Government and Parliament of New South Wales would be just as effective as now in all local matters, and so would

the Parliament of Queensland.   He had no fear but that the
Federal Parliament would rise to a just conception of the
necessities of the case.

He concluded thus :

*The thing will have to be done, and to put it off will only
make the difficulties greater which stand in the way.*

· 3 ·

Lapse of years has not weakened the force of this
appeal, which was at once a declaration of faith, lifting
Federation above the dust of party politics, and an ar-
moury of arguments which still hold good.   Critics of Sir
Henry Parkes have sneered at the speech as an 'appeal
to sentiment' ; but considerations, which depend upon
sentiment, are not the least of the practical influences
upon human affairs.   And only the sentiment of good-
will, to which this speech appealed, could have united
the discordant elements of the Australian Continent,
and overcome the provincial prejudices which, had
Union been delayed much longer, must have exposed
the Colonies to the risk of civil war after the fashion
of the South American Republics.   This, indeed, is the
final answer to the critics both of Sir Henry Parkes
and of the Federationists, that, had Union been
delayed ten years, in all human probability it could
not have been effected except under the pressure of a
foreign or domestic enemy.   Federation has been
justified, as much by the prevention of evils, as by its
direct benefits !   To men of a later generation the
argument of the Tenterfield speech proves itself.   Why
eleven years passed, before it carried conviction to the
people of New South Wales, will become intelligible,
only if the events of the time are looked at through

the eyes of a contemporary ; and then the cause of wonder will be, rather that Federation was achieved at all, and not that its advent was delayed ! The ultimate success was due to men of all parties, who heard the call of a larger patriotism, and perceived that, with the Tenterfield speech, a new spirit had been born into our public life.

CHAPTER II

HESITATION AND MISGIVING

IMMEDIATELY upon his return to Sydney, Sir Henry Parkes renewed negotiations with the other Premiers. For the moment he had gone upon his way, unheeding their objections, to which his Tenterfield speech had been a characteristic answer. But, although he might launch his proposals in isolation, it was impossible to take the next step without their co-operation. Accordingly, on October 30, 1889, he prepared a despatch, in the form of a letter to Mr. Duncan Gillies, a copy of which was sent with a separate covering letter to each Premier, in which he combated the objections to his proposals, and renewed his appeal for a larger and closer Union.

. I .

This letter is so characteristic an example of Sir Henry Parkes' method of treating political questions, that it deserves to be quoted textually :—

Colonial Secretary's Office,
Sydney, 30 Oct. 1889.

SIR,—Your telegram, explanatory of your views in favour of bringing the machinery of the Federal Council into operation in giving effect to the recommendations of Major-General Edwards for the federalisation of Australian troops, reached me last week in Brisbane. Being extremely anxious to meet your wishes, I lost no time in re-examining the provisions of the Federal Council Act ; and I regret that I cannot concur in your view that the Council possesses the requisite power to constitute, direct, and control an united Australian Army. . . . . For more than twenty years I have had the question of Australian Federation almost constantly before me, and I cannot be accused of indifference to it at any time, merely because I had become convinced from earlier examination, while others were adopting the scheme of the present Federal Council at a later period, that no such body would ever answer the great objects of Federal Government. Leaving the provisions of the Act as to the legislative capacity of the Council, we are at once precipitated upon an impassable barrier, in the fact that there does not exist in it or behind it any form of executive power. . . . The Federal Council has no executive power to act at all. The Imperial Parliament, on the application of the Colonies, could, no doubt, pass an Act to constitute the Federal Army under one command, and to authorise its operations in any part of Australia ; but the Colonies could never consent to the Imperial Executive interfering in the direction of its movements. Hence, then, this first great federal question, when looked at fairly, brings us, in spite of preferences or prejudices, face to face with the imperative necessity for a Federal Government. And why should we turn aside from what is inevitable in the nature of our onward progress ? It must come, a year or two later possibly, but in any case soon.

I hope I need not assure you that this Government is anxious to work in harmony with the Governments of the sister Colonies in the matter under consideration, and is desirous of avoiding subordinate questions coloured by party feeling or collateral issues. It is a question to be put to the mind and heart of Australia, and on which it is hoped all sections of the collective population will unite without regard to narrower considerations. Believing that the time is ripe for consolidating the Australias into one, this Government respectfully invites you to join in taking the first great step, namely, to appoint representatives of Victoria to a national Convention for the purpose of devising and reporting upon an adequate scheme of Federal Government. With much deference to the views of the other Colonies, it is suggested that, in order to avoid any sense of inequality in debate, or any party complexion, the number from each Colony should be the same, and should be equally chosen from both sides in political life ; and that, in the case of each Colony, the representatives should be elected by Parliament and receive commissions from the Governor in Council. . . .

The scheme of Federal Government, it is assumed, would necessarily follow close upon the type of the Dominion Government of Canada. It would provide for the appointment of a Governor-General, for the creation of an Australian Privy Council, and a Parliament consisting of a Senate and a House of Commons. In the work of the Convention, no doubt, the rich stores of political knowledge which were collected by the framers of the Constitution of the United States would be largely resorted to, as well as the vast accumulation of learning on cognate subjects since that time.

Although a great and pressing military question has brought to the surface the design of a Federal Government at the present juncture, the work of a national character which such a Government could, in the interest of all the Colonies, most beneficially and effectively undertake, would include the noblest objects of peaceful and orderly progress, and every year the field of its beneficent operations would be rapidly expanding. I devoutly hope that you will be able to take the view which I have briefly explained, of the necessity now pressing upon these Colonies to rise to a higher level of national life, which would give them a larger space before the eyes of the world, and in a hundred ways promote their united power and prosperity.

Permit me, in conclusion, to say that you place much too high an estimate on my individual influence, if you suppose that the accession of New South Wales to the Federal Council rests with me. In my judgment, there is no person and no party here that could persuade Parliament to sanction the representation of this Colony in the present Federal Council.

I have &c.,

HENRY PARKES.

This despatch, which won acceptance finally in every point from the wisdom and precision of its views, was not at first received with favour ; and it became evident that the Premiers would delay their replies until they had consulted together. Consequently, on November 4, Sir Henry Parkes wrote another circular despatch, in which he specified the practical steps by which effect could be given to his suggestion to assemble a Convention. The plan which commended itself to his judgment was that each Parliament should pass the Resolutions, of which he submitted a draft, subject to any alteration that might be considered better calculated to carry out the object. These historic Resolutions, which illustrate the gulf between his soaring policy and the stop-gap expedients of the politicians, were in the following terms :—

That this House is of opinion that it is expedient and desirable that a Convention should be held of the Australian Colonies, at a place and time to be agreed upon, for the purposes hereinafter stated :—

1. To consider and prepare a Bill to provide for the Federation of these Colonies, such scheme of Federation to include the appointment of a Governor General, and the creation of a Privy Council and a Judicial Court of Appeal, and the establishment of a Federal Parliament consisting of a Senate and a House of Commons.
2. To consider, define and recommend the functions and powers with which such Government should be endowed to effectually carry out the objects of the Federation.

3. To consider and devise and embody in such Bill the necessary safeguards for the preservation of the rights and the satisfactory working of the provincial Governments of the several Colonies in relation to the Federal Power.

4. To prepare an address to Her Majesty the Queen praying that Her Majesty will be graciously pleased to cause the Bill so prepared to be introduced into the Imperial Parliament, with the view to its being passed into law, and that such address be signed by the respective Presidents and Speakers for and on behalf of the Parliaments of the several Australasian Colonies.

5. That the Colony of   be represented in the proposed Convention by   members of this House, who are hereby elected members.

. 2 .

These arguments, however, were not of the kind to influence Mr. Gillies, between whom and Sir Henry Parkes there was an incompatibility of temperament, which, but for the tactful offices of Mr. Deakin, who was a friend of both, might have wrecked the federal movement at its outset.   No two men were less suited to work together.   The one was a ' pawky ' Scotchman, without imagination or enthusiasm, short, chubby, round-faced, with little twinkling eyes and a thin, rapid and precise utterance.   The other was big and hirsute, with the face and sleepy eyes of an old lion ; deliberate in speech and movement, yet possessed of daemonic eloquence and power when roused.   Unmethodical and impatient of detail, he dreamt dreams and saw visions, which self-confidence and an ambition, which was without pettiness, prompted him to translate into realities ; but which were foolishness to Mr. Gillies.   On this occasion, Sir Henry Parkes' proposal to ignore the Federal Council and make a fresh start in the federal movement seemed to the former to be prompted by pique and vanity. It was remembered that Sir Henry Parkes himself had proposed the establishment of the Council at an inter-Colonial conference in 1881, upon the express ground that ' the time had not come for the construction of a Federal Constitution with an Australian Parliament,' yet had refused to join it, when it was constituted in 1885 upon the lines of his own proposal! The machinery of the Federal Council was sufficient, it was urged, to create a Federal Army ; and, if other actions were desired in the common interests, the Council could obtain extended powers. All that was required was the adhesion of New South Wales to this nucleus of a Federal Parliament. A fresh start was not needed by the other Colonies ; although this might extricate Sir Henry Parkes from a false position, to his own glorification! Mr. Gillies had expressed this view very strongly, in a letter to Sir Henry Parkes of August 12, 1889 :—[1]

On the various occasions when I urged you to join in the Federal movement, and not leave the parent Colony of New South Wales in a position of isolation, it was with the idea that you might suggest some alteration in the constitution of the Federal Council which, if made, might make it possible for you to join. If that were brought about there is much that could be done for Australia's advantage. In the first place, we shall be united ; in the second place, we could proceed to consider several important questions which must be dealt with shortly, and which would well come within the province of the Council to deal with—as for instance, to determine on the united action to be taken in the matter of defence, and to legislate so that the forces of one Colony could be made available

[1] *Parl. Papers Leg. Ass. N.S.W.*, December 19, 1889.

for service in any other Colony ; to advise on the best settlement of the Western Australian difficulty. These and others could be effectively dealt with, much more so than by any Conferences.

It will be within your knowledge that steps are now being taken by the various Legislatures of the Colonies represented in the Federal Council to secure an increase in the number of the members, which will not only give more effective representation, but will also add weight to its deliberations.

In turning the whole question over in my mind, I cannot help being forcibly impressed with the thought that, through the Federal Council on its enlarged basis, we might be able to consider and formulate the proposals of the larger Federation, and certainly bring about, in a much shorter space of time than could otherwise happen, the accomplishment of the high purpose you have in view.

It must be borne in mind that, for the future, the Federal Council will not be represented (as it is now) nearly wholly by Ministers. It will naturally assume a more representative character, and therefore, if necessary, might be clothed by the special authority of the various Legislatures with power to deal with the question.

Now, why should you not join us to do this great work ? What is the difficulty ? Surely it would be a worthy ambition for you to adopt the best means at your disposal—in fact, at your hand—to unite Australia in a Federation, which would not only promote her material interests and strengthen her against aggression, but also powerfully aid in uniting and cementing together all parts of the great Empire of which she forms a part. No one at present can do the work but you. You can remove the Federation barrier which has been created by the isolation of New South Wales from all the other Colonies on the federal movement. New South Wales did put her hand to the plough and did draw back. It is for you to put your hand to the plough and not draw back. You have at your disposal the means, which I have suggested, if you wish to use them. My advice would be—spend no unnecessary time in trying new means, but make use of the agencies which exist, and which, when being used, will create no alarm in the minds of the timid.   What you may refuse to do to-day someone else will do to-morrow, and I should be pleased to see you take the pride of place.   My deliberate judgment is that by far the greatest hope that we can have of the larger Federation becoming a fact in the near future lies in working it by means of the smaller Federation which we have in our hands.

Now I have freely written what was in my mind to say.

Yours etc.,

D. GILLIES.

The Honourable Sir Henry Parkes, G.C.M.G., Sydney.

· 3 ·

Even the undiplomatic frankness of this remonstrance did not express the real cause of the unwillingness of Mr. Gillies and the other Premiers to co-operate with Sir Henry Parkes, which was not so much a constitutional preference for the Federal Council as a suspicion of his motives in proposing to supersede it.   The inconsistency of his present attitude was attributed to a vainglorious unwillingness to take part in any federal movement of which he was not himself the leader.

Echoes of these charges may be heard even at the present time ; and the belief that they rest upon fact lingers still among those who do not understand Sir Henry Parkes ; although those who, like Mr. Deakin, Mr. Barton, or Sir Samuel Way, could penetrate beneath the surface, never gave them credence.   That he had changed his opinion about the Federal Council is undoubtedly true.   But many good reasons may be advanced, why a statesman, who had believed, in 1881, that such a body would make Union easier,

c

should have come to the conclusion, in 1885, that it was in reality an obstacle to Union. It was a non-elective body, composed of two representatives of the participating Colonies,—Victoria, Queensland, Tasmania, and South Australia,—which met biennially in Hobart and was charged with legislative power over important matters of common concern.[1]   It was a body at once too ambitious and too timid.   Its legislative power was too great to be entrusted safely to non-elective members ; while the absence of all executive authority and of the power of taxation prevented its measures from being equal to its pretensions.   Federalists in New South Wales had held aloof from this mimic Parliament, fearing that, if it gained an accession of strength by the adhesion of the Mother Colony, an exercise of authority beyond its powers of execution might discredit altogether the idea of Union.

I am convinced [wrote Sir Henry Parkes] that the whole matter is wrongly based. It is impossible for any body constitutionally feebler than the Colonial Parliaments to stand any strain in legislation against any public feeling in any one of them. . . . The Federal Council is based upon the idea of initiating Federation ; . . . but, as it stands, it wants the elemental strength of election. It wants the strength of the highest authority, which is the authority of the people of

---

[1] The Council had original legislative powers over :
    i. The relation of Australia with the islands of the Pacific.
    ii. The prevention of the influx of criminals.
    iii. Fisheries in Australian waters beyond territorial limits.
    iv. The service of process.
    v. The enforcement of judgments beyond the limits of a colony.
It had also derivative legislative power over : (1) defence ; (2) quarantine ; (3) patent law ; (4) copyright ; (5) bills of exchange ; (6) marriage and divorce ; (7) naturalisation ; (8) other matters which any two or more Colonies might agree to refer to it.

the several Colonies. No Federal Council is capable of putting out its strength unless it is a Convention elected by the representatives of the people.

That Sir Henry Parkes did not perceive the validity of these objections in 1881 may reflect upon his judgment ; but that he should express them in 1889 will not justify the charge of insincerity, which contemporaries brought against him. Certainly no one, who lived in Sydney at that time, can entertain a doubt but that he expressed the opinion of New South Wales, and that even his great influence could not have brought that Colony into the Federal Council. Even the Ministers, who represented New South Wales at the Conference of 1883, when the Council Bill was framed, were unable to carry motions in Parliament approving of it, although they were supported generally by large majorities. The opposition to the Federal Council came not from Sir Henry Parkes, as the other Colonies believed,—in a misconception as to the opinion of a neighbour which is not infrequent even now after twelve years of Federation,—but from the people of New South Wales, guided by their Press ; and in this instance it would be difficult to deny the correctness of the popular instinct.

The charge that Sir Henry Parkes was actuated by vanity, like all aspersion of motives, is more difficult to meet. That he was vain, no one who knew him will deny. Yet his was not the fatuous and destructive vanity which stands in the way of self-knowledge, but the harmless vanity of an intensely sympathetic nature which, having been crushed by harsh treatment in youth, sought in later years assurances from others that his work was good. No visitor at his house will forget the almost childish happiness with which he showed the autographs and letters of distinguished persons whom he had met or corresponded with. In this there was no vulgar self-assertion, but a conscious pride that the self-taught Warwickshire peasant, living in a remote and small community, was recognised as an equal by the best spirits of his age.

I was thinking [he once said to a friend, after reading G. W. Russell's ' Life of Gladstone '] of a comparison between Mr. Gladstone's life and my own. When he was at Eton preparing himself for Oxford, enjoying the advantages of a good education, with plenty of money, and being trained in every way for his future position as a statesman, I was working at a rope-walk at fourpence a day, and suffered such cruel treatment that I was knocked down with a crowbar, and did not recover my senses for half an hour. From the rope-walk I went to labour in a brick-yard, where I was again brutally used ; and when Mr. Gladstone was at Oxford I was breaking stones on the Queen's highway, with hardly enough clothing to protect me from the cold.'

That Sir Henry Parkes had a noble ambition to consummate himself the Union of Australia, which for nearly forty years he had done his utmost to promote, may be conceded to his detractors. But that he was actuated by mean considerations of vanity in seizing with statesmanlike promptitude the opportunity, which circumstances offered, of broadening the basis of the Federal Union, will not be admitted by anyone who studies closely the considerations which governed his conduct on this critical occasion. It is significant that his sincerity was never doubted by his close associates, and that those, who made the charge, were unacquainted with his character.

· 4 ·

The replies of the Premiers to Sir Henry Parkes' despatches of October 30 and November 4 reveal in every line the timidity and doubt, from which the federal movement was lifted by the genius and conviction of Sir Henry Parkes. Mr. Gillies (November 13), although feeling 'grave doubts as to the success of a movement towards Federation at the present time,' as spokesman of the other Premiers, was willing, 'in order to ensure consideration' of such an important proposal, that 'representatives of the various Colonies at the Federal Council' should confer with representatives from New South Wales, 'to discuss, and, if deemed necessary, to devise and report upon an adequate scheme of Federal Government.' The appointment of representatives by Parliament appeared to him to be objectionable, because it 'would commit the Parliaments, without sufficient consideration, to the determination that the time was ripe to establish a Federal Parliament and Federal Government,' and it was desirable to leave them 'unfettered' in such a matter. In the meantime, he urged, New South Wales should meet the emergency of Major-General Edwards' report by joining the Federal Council; because, although that body did not possess executive authority, it could pass general measures dealing with defence which would 'enable the Colonies to do what they cannot do now, viz., act together in time of need. For this purpose the Council requires no executive authority.' Mr. Gillies admitted 'that a Federal Government, clothed with the authority of a Federal Parliament, could do much more and do it better,' but contended that the solution of the immediate difficulties by the Federal Council ' ought not to be rejected because we may not be able at present to obtain a better one.' He concluded by elaborating his contention that a Federal Army was unnecessary at present : all that was required was that the Federal Council should pass an enabling Act ' dealing with mobilisation and the direction and control of the local forces ' which, in an emergency, might be adhered to by each Colony.

Mr. Morehead, Premier of Queensland, adopted Mr. Gillies' suggestion that New South Wales' representatives should meet the Federal Council in conference, but expressed more sympathy with Sir Henry Parkes' larger views. He recognised also that Sir Henry Parkes could not induce New South Wales to achieve these through the Federal Council ; although he was himself ' persuaded that its supersession by a Dominion Parliament would be more advantageously brought about by a process of development than by an act of displacement.'

Mr. Fysh, Premier of Tasmania, considered that Sir Henry Parkes' proposals were ' evidently much larger than is necessary for purely federal defences ' ; but was willing to adopt Mr. Gillies' suggestion of ' a parliamentary talk,' although he believed that it would be possible to 'work through the Federal Council to the broader Federation,' and could not ' ignore the fact that a Federal Council exists.'

Dr. Cockburn, Premier of South Australia, answered according to the same tenor. ' The consummation of Australian unity ' seemed to him ' so much to be desired that he was not disposed to dispute as to the details of the mode of approach ' ; but it seemed to him that the right course was for New South Wales to join the Federal Council. Still, he would agree to a conference between that body and representatives of New South Wales.

Mr. Malcolm Fraser, Colonial Secretary of Western Australia, telegraphed his 'favourable and earnest co-operation in considering the question of Federation, and hoped that Sir Henry would accept the mode of action suggested by the Government of Victoria.'

A deadlock seemed to have been reached ; and the comment by the *Sydney Morning Herald*, which had appeared on November 7, when the tenor of the intended replies was known :—' It is not probable that the Convention proposed by Sir Henry Parkes will be held '—seemed justified abundantly by their text.

· 5 ·

The position, indeed, was more critical than the public knew. For the moment Sir Henry Parkes had lost heart, and doubted his capacity to lift the dead-weight of timidity and prejudice. The note of depression can be heard in a speech which he delivered on November 6, at St. Leonards, in which, after asserting his claim to be ' the oldest advocate of a genuine Federation of the Colonies,' and developing with noble eloquence his old contention that ' the time was not only near, but had already come for a complete system of Federal government,'—he expressed his willingness to 'give place to any other leader to-morrow, if one could be found with better attributes for the post than he could lay claim to.' A correspondence preserved by Lord Carrington,[1] at that time

[1] Now the Marquis of Lincolnshire.

Governor of New South Wales, contains proof that this was no rhetorical self-depreciation, but a genuine expression of discouragement.   In one letter Sir Henry declares his inability to overcome his difficulties, and his intention to leave the consummation of Australian Union to someone whose position would be less misunderstood.   Lord Carrington—a politician and man of the world—did more than restore Sir Henry Parkes' confidence.   Regardless of precedent, he opened a correspondence with the Colonial Office and the other Governors, which had considerable influence in creating a more just appreciation of the new situation.   Sir Henry Parkes always recognised his obligations to Lord Carrington, whose unsuspected services to the cause of Union would be revealed, if the correspondence which he has preserved were published.

But Sir Henry Parkes was always roused by opposition ; and when his despondent mood had passed away the fires of his indignation burst forth afresh in a reply to Mr. Gillies' despatch of November 13.

Colonial Secretary's Office,
Sydney, 19th November 1889.

SIR,—Your despatch of the 13th inst. in reply to my communication of the 29th October, on the subject of the Federation of the Australian Colonies, presents several aspects of the question and submits suggestions which deserve the fullest consideration, and I propose to deal with these at some length in a separate letter.   In the meantime, it seems necessary from the personal interest which has been attracted to my course of action on this important question, chiefly by your own public utterances, though to some extent by past events, to say a few words in explanation of the position which I at present occupy.   In the first place, as I have repeatedly explained, I had satisfied myself after careful examination and

...ome time before the assembling of the inter-Colonial ...ention of November 1883, that the scheme for promoting union between the Colonies, as afterwards embodied in the Federal Council Act, would not, and could not, work effectively for federal purposes.

At the time when the Convention sat I was in England, and had no opportunity of expressing an opinion on the proceedings of that body, but on my return I took the first opportunity to state my views in Parliament, and record my vote in accordance with the deliberate conviction I had formed.

Coming to the present movement and my part in connection with it, it was after my course of action, as I explained above, that you repeatedly appealed to me to take the lead in the cause of Federation.

Sir Henry Parkes quoted several passages from speeches of Mr. Gillies in support of this assertion, and continued :—

I hope you will pardon me in expressing my regrets that you should have used the words with any reference to my proposals that the ' members of the Federal Council were being discredited and intentionally thrown aside ' ; and again, that the Federal Council was ' a quarter hitherto somewhat despised.' Most certainly I do not desire to speak of the members of the Federal Council, many of whom I personally know and sincerely respect, in these terms ; nor can I consent to be understood as taking any contemptuous view of the Council, because I cannot believe in its adequacy. In the great historical transactions which resulted in the lasting Federation of the United States, proposal after proposal, expedient after expedient, and organisation after organisation had to give way before solid ground was discovered ; but I have never heard that any such feeling as you indicate was allowed to interfere in moving from good to better, and from better to best.

I have, etc.,

HENRY PARKES.

The defiant note broke out again on November 22, at a meeting Leichardt :—

When it became his fortune to take a prominent this movement, he was quite prepared for everything tha. since taken place ; he was quite prepared for persons wh. could not see beyond the range of their immediate interests to misrepresent what was aimed at in the movement of Federation. He was by no means sure that he was not quite prepared for the opposition that had been assumed by some men, who certainly ought to have known better, in raising all kinds of collateral issues in this great movement. He had proposed to obtain the sanction of the several Parliaments to meet to confer together. He did not believe they ought to meet without the sanction of the highest authority of the land. For his part, he would be unwilling to take part in any Conference which had not the stamp of parliamentary approval. He sought to enforce his views on no one. He only invited a consultation fairly representing the whole of the Colonies.[1]

. 6 .

Fortunately Lord Carrington's correspondence with Sir Henry Loch (then Governor of Victoria) had produced its intended effect ; and Mr. Gillies, writing on November 22, replied in very friendly terms. He withdrew none of the utterances quoted by Sir Henry, whom he still regarded as ' the leader and head of the federal movement,' Nor was he wedded to the Federal Council :—

[1] *Sydney Morning Herald*, November 18, 1889. One other passage from this speech should be quoted. ' It was not true, as had been stated, that the only question which had awakened Federation was the military question. No doubt that had acted, as it were, as the key to the others ; but there were a vast number of large questions deeply affecting the progress of the country.'

I did not then, and do not now contemplate that we are to be satisfied with the Federal Council, and there can be no difference between us in the opinion that nothing short of a fully organised Federal Government could answer the high purposes of a Federal Australia.

This letter would be received by Sir Henry Parkes upon November 23. Parliament was to meet upon the 26th, when the fateful decision must be declared. The situation had improved materially since November 7, and Sir Henry Parkes determined to go forward. A paragraph accordingly was put into the Governor's speech in these terms :—

Circumstances have lately presented the ground for raising a question of nobler magnitude than any other which can possibly engage the intellect or enkindle the patriotism of the Australian populations—that of the several Colonies occupying Australian territory rising and uniting in the formation of one powerful Australian nation. The Government has opened negotiations with the other Australian Governments with a view to this momentous step in national life being taken at no distant date ; and you will be glad to learn that, with such difference of opinion as to modes of procedure as were reasonably to be expected, the most friendly disposition towards the one great object is manifested in all the Colonies. The birth of a nation is an epoch which can have no succeeding parallel, and the national sentiment awakened in the parent Colony is a sure presage of the august time which is approaching in their fortunes. There is every prospect of the Colonies cordially meeting in consultation on such preliminary steps as may be deemed advisable, and no reason to doubt but that the intercourse will lead to patriotic agreement.

The confidence which this paragraph breathes is a measure of Lord Carrington's success in influencing opinion in the other Colonies. Sir Samuel Way, Chief

Justice of South Australia, had also been active in creating a better understanding of Sir Henry Parkes' motives and position ; while he had been foremost also among personal friends in urging him to persevere.

· 7 ·

After Mr. Gillies' declaration that 'nothing short of a fully organised Federal Government could answer the high purposes of a Federal Australia,' the difference between him and Sir Henry Parkes ceased to be vital, and the question became one as to the method of arriving at agreement. As to this also Mr. Gillies had provided a middle course which did not escape the quick perception of Sir Henry Parkes. Speaking of the Federal Council in his despatch of August 12, he had described its members as 'representatives of the various Colonies' and, again, as 'representative public men who possess the confidence of their respective Colonies.' It is possible that Mr. Gillies intended to draw a distinction between the Council as a governing body and the members who composed it ; but, if this be so, it is curious that the distinction should not have been noted either by Mr. Morehead or Dr. Cockburn, whose views he was also expressing. Sir Henry Parkes, however, recognised that the phraseology would allow New South Wales to meet the members of the Council as 'representatives' of their respective Colonies, and yet leave her free from the embarrassment of recognising the Council by taking part in its deliberations. Accordingly, on November 28, he penned a third despatch to Mr. Gillies, in which, without abandoning his position, he agreed on behalf of New South Wales to meet 'the members of the existing Federal Council as "representative public men" to discuss the whole question of Federation.' The despatch is in these terms :

Colonial Secretary's Office,
Sydney, November 28th, 1889.

SIR,—In reply to your letter of the 22nd instant, and in further reference to your previous despatch of the 13th, I beg to state that I wished to be understood in last writing to you as anxious to make clear my position as an individual in relation to the Federal Council ; and I again assure you that the action of New South Wales in remaining aloof from the Council, so far as I can form a correct opinion, has never in any material degree rested with me. . . .

It does not, however, appear to be necessary to enter into any further discussion on the circumstances affecting the attitude of New South Wales in 1883 and the intervening years. She now offers her hand to the other Colonies, without reserve and without stipulation for any advantage to herself, and invites them to meet on equal ground in the great cause of Australian Union, which she believes represents the soundest sentiments and the highest interests of the Australian populations.

This offer was accepted by the other Colonies, and it was agreed that the Conference of 'Representatives' should meet in Melbourne in the following February. Thus, through Sir Henry Parkes' wise tenacity of purpose, the tide of public opinion was set in the direction of a Federal Union, instead of being deflected by the counsels of timidity toward a strengthening of the Federal Council.

CHAPTER III

ELEMENTS OF DISCORD

THE real significance of the Tenterfield speech lay (as has been shown) in Sir Henry Parkes' determination to press his arguments to their conclusion, and accept no half-hearted counsel of compromise. His aim was to establish a fully organised Federal Parliament and Executive, and he would be satisfied with nothing less ; although it was plain already to every observer that such a resolution would antagonise the Colonies which belonged to the Federal Council, whose co-operation was essential to the success of his great enterprise. Nor was his own Colony of New South Wales, although in full agreement with his objections to the Federal Council, free from misgivings as to the sincerity with which he made these large demands. The state of local politics was such that the suspicion was widespread that he had raised this new issue of Federation deliberately for party purposes. Thus, at the time when he required to have the confidence of the other Colonies and his own, both withheld this from him, although for different reasons ; and cross currents of opinion were set in motion, which not only deposited obstacles in his path, but also swayed the federal movement in many of its later stages. The situation bristled with difficulties, and demanded a courage and perspicacity which posterity can appreciate better than contemporaries.

. I .

In his Tenterfield speech Sir Henry Parkes had appealed to Australians, that the demon of party discord should be exorcised from the federal movement ; but a man of his experience could hardly have expected a response. The leader of a party, who proposes a new policy, will be criticised by his opponents from their own standpoint ; and, if the time chosen for the new departure coincide with the waning fortunes of his party, his motives will be suspected.

Now it happened that towards the end of 1889 Sir Henry Parkes appeared to be losing ground both in and out of Parliament. For twenty years, except for two brief intervals, he had shared the government of New South Wales with a single rival—Sir John Robertson. Both these leaders, differing in their temperament and methods, had the same veneration for parliamentary government. As a parliamentarian, who ranks with Peel, Gladstone, and Sir John A. Macdonald, Sir Henry Parkes' strength lay in an almost intuitive perception of constitutional propriety, according to the underlying principles of Responsible Government. Sir John Robertson, more brusque in manner and less tolerant of forms, aimed, with an equal sincerity, at moulding our Parliament after the model of Great Britain. It is true that performance often fell short of the ideal ; because the conditions of a young country do not favour a system which presupposes considerable reticence and magnanimity, and depends for its successful working upon a nice balance between what is lawful and what is expedient. Yet, on the whole, under the influence of these two leaders, parliamentary usages were held in great respect, and constitutionalism was in the ascendant.

The general election of 1880, which was as notable in its consequences as the entry of the Labour Party into politics eleven years later, changed the spirit of the Legislature by replacing the veterans, who had been trained in the English tradition, by younger men, of Australian birth, for whom the word ' unconstitutional ' possessed no terror.[1] The new men came into power in 1883 under Sir Alexander Stuart, after a general election had scattered the remnant of the Parkes-Robertson coalition ; and, although Sir Henry Parkes regained office in 1887 upon the issue of Protection or Free Trade, he never regained his former supremacy. In Parliament he was as a voice crying in the wilderness to young men, who regarded his constitutionalism as pedantry ; while, in the constituencies, he had antagonised the Catholics by his Education Act, and his ancient fame was unknown to the younger generation of voters, many of whom were recent immigrants. Thus, by the end of 1889, it was manifest that his power was tottering. The general election, held earlier in the year, had given his Government a majority of only two ; and it was so clear that the Protectionists were the growing party, that eager aspirants to Office were calculating the date of their migration to the Government benches. The general perception of these facts explains the charge of insincerity, which, in New South Wales, as in the other Colonies, proved

[1] See Parkes' *Fifty Years in the Making of Australian History*, vol. ii. p. 38.

to be most hampering to the federal leader. ' Impossible,' it was argued, ' that so artful a politician as Sir Henry Parkes should not see the writing on the wall ; and what was more likely to stave off defeat, than the confusion of his opponents by a new issue ? '

That these misgivings did not unite the New South Wales Opposition against Federation was due to the influence of Mr. Barton, who thus performed the first of his great services to the cause of Union.

. 2 .

Mr. Barton,[1] whose judicial temperament had been matured by a three years' occupancy of the Speaker's Chair, although counted among the Protectionists because he had been Attorney-General in the short Administration of Mr. Dibbs (January–March 1889), was at this time breaking slowly with his early attachment to the doctrines of Free Trade, to which, like many of his generation, he had given an unreflecting adherence. In any case the fervour of his Australian patriotism would have been stronger than his fiscal leanings. The day after the Tenterfield speech he wrote a warm letter of congratulation to Sir Henry Parkes, and a week later (November 3) made a public and unequivocal declaration in favour of Federation at a meeting of the Australian Natives' Association in the Town Hall. From this time forward Mr. Barton was Sir Henry Parkes' first lieutenant in the federal struggle ; until the old man upon his political death-bed in 1891 entrusted him with the

[1] Now the Right Hon. Sir Edmund Barton, G.C.M.G., and a Justice of the High Court.

succession to the leadership.   Those Protectionists who, like the late Mr. J. P. Garvan and Sir Joseph Abbott, put Union before Party, followed Mr. Barton's lead at once ; but the majority adhered at this time to their official leader, Mr. Dibbs—some out of loyalty, and some from a genuine belief that Federation was a stalking-horse against Protection.   The precarious position of Sir Henry Parkes appeared to justify an expectation of immediate office ; so that the disappointment was keen, when it appeared that the party was not agreed upon the wisdom of setting up a local tariff, while there was the prospect of a federal tariff coming shortly into operation.   The anti-Federalists were numerous enough, however, to make it impossible to maintain a political armistice.   One leading Protectionist, Mr. David Buchanan, a barrister and member of the Assembly, of considerable parts to which he seldom did justice, twitted Sir Henry Parkes in the *Sydney Morning Herald* (January 21) with being a convert to Protection, and drove home his arguments with unholy glee :—

Sir Henry Parkes sees that if he maintain his Free Trade principles as a condition precedent to Federation, Federation can never be brought about ; and therefore he is prepared to purchase Federation by throwing overboard his Free Trade principles.   But let Sir Henry Parkes stand as true as steel to his Free Trade principles, or refuse to federate unless Free Trade is made the policy of the Federated Colonies, it would avail the Free Trade party nothing. Federation would be carried over their heads by the Protectionists, and Protection declared by the Federal Parliament to be the policy for evermore.

Even Protectionists, who, like Mr. Barton, imputed

no dubious motive to Sir Henry Parkes, were forced to declare their fiscal views at the risk of appearing to acquiesce in the misgivings of the anti-Federal section of their party. Thus, Mr. Barton at Glen Innes on January 22 affirmed his fiscal faith to be as strong in favour of Protection as Sir Henry Parkes had declared his to be in favour of Free Trade. Mr. Lyne was present at this meeting and there declared that unflinching hostility to any form of Federation in which he never wavered, until Lord Hopetoun commissioned him, unexpectedly, to form the first Federal Ministry !

· 3 ·

The Government or Free Trade party was split at once by the same division as the Protectionist ; and with more reason, because of the probability that a common Australian tariff, which would be the first fruits of Federation, would reflect the Protectionist views of the other Colonies rather than the Free Trade view of New South Wales. Mr. McMillan, the Colonial Treasurer—a spokesman for the soft-goods houses, which at that time dominated Sydney politics—voiced these misgivings on the day after the Tenterfield speech. ' Federation ' (he said at a meeting at Waverley) ' would be intolerable except upon the basis of Free Trade with the whole world.' The party as a whole, however, refrained from public disapproval—some of its members from a robust faith in the triumph of their views in the wider arena of the Federal Parliament, and others because they refused to put ' Free Imports ' above the Union of Australia.

The Free Traders, indeed, were in a difficult

position. While it might be urged [1] that Victoria was the only Colony which had adopted Protection deliberately as its peculiar policy, and that the other Colonies, being concerned with tariffs only as a means of raising revenue, would be at liberty to support the New South Wales Free Traders in the Federal Parliament,—yet it was plain that industries were growing up in every State under the indirect protection of the tariff, the preservation of which would be a matter of concern to its representatives. South Australia, in particular, was at the moment, under the leadership of Sir John Cockburn, developing a Protectionist policy for her own manufactures. And, even if Tasmania and Queensland returned a body of Free Traders, it was not certain that the supporters of Protection would be in a minority.

Nevertheless the Free Traders, who supported Federation, did not believe entirely without reason that their views might prevail in the larger arena of federal politics. At this time the border districts were the stronghold of Protection, because they suffered from the border duties. They were Retaliationists first, and Protectionists because Protection was the weapon of Retaliation. It was thought probable that, when inter-Colonial Free Trade had removed the cause of irritation, they would return to the Free Trade faith. Again, Australia was becoming very rapidly an exporter of food-stuffs ; and it was argued that, when this happened, the farmers would not consent to protective duties on the articles they bought, which would give them no advantage in respect of the articles

[1] See speech of Sir Henry Parkes at Manly, *Sydney Morning Herald*, January 4, 1890.

they sold. It seemed, therefore, that the first result of Federation would be the detachment of the farmers' vote from the Protectionists. These were vain anticipations ! The farmers, recognising the value to themselves of a secure Home Market, continue to be the strongest supporters of a protective tariff. Another formidable difficulty stood in the way of the Protectionists !

How would it be possible [it was asked] to frame a tariff which would suit all the Colonies ? Victorian manufacturers bought their raw materials in the open markets of the world. Would they be content to buy them from the contracted limits of the other Colonies or would not they insist upon a wider choice ? [1]

It is possible that these forecasts might have proved correct, if Federation had been brought about in 1890. Ten years later, when each Colony, except New South Wales, had moved further towards Protection, and the conditions of the world's commerce had changed, owing to the growth of trusts and the organisation by governments of land and sea transport, they had lost their basis. The argument, then, took a different form, which was anticipated even in these early days, in an address by Dr. Garran, LL.D., at the annual meeting of the Liberal and Free Trade Association (January 31, 1890), which ought to be reprinted in any documented history of the federal movement, both for its intrinsic merits and because it marks the definite separation from the federal movement of the official Free Trade party in New South Wales. A Liberal of the mid-Victorian days, Dr. Garran, who was at this

[1] See speech by Mr. Wise at a meeting of the Liberal and Free Trade Association of Redfern, *Daily Telegraph*, February 25, 1890.

time editor of the *Sydney Morning Herald*, had complete
faith in Representative Government, and regarded all
attempts to impose restrictions on the popular will as
inconsistent with freedom. Since the Federal Parliament would be elected by the people, he was prepared
to trust its decisions, and regarded the preliminary
demand of conditions as inconsistent with the exercise
of its proper functions. ' To put freedom in fetters
and call it Federation is a burlesque ; and those who
propose to do this are forgetting altogether what
self-government means,' was one phrase of a notable
Address, which was quoted many times as the struggle
proceeded. He saw, too, that Federation was impracticable, if each Colony insisted upon its own
terms ; and that, while the advantages of Union
were great, the danger was greater of ' creating
vested interests in disunion.' To the Free Traders
he urged that a common tariff, by abolishing border
duties, would mean the opening of a wider area to unrestricted trade. Also, Free Traders could still contend
for their principles in the Federal Parliament ; and,
in any case, Union was of more importance than any
fiscal system !

Unfortunately the sentiment of nationality is
alien to the cosmopolitan creed of the Free Trader,
whose belief in *laissez-faire* renders him hostile or
indifferent to the organisation of political power.
Therefore, just as English Liberals to-day put Free
Imports into Great Britain above the Union of the
Empire, so the Liberals of New South Wales in 1890
put Free Imports into Sydney above the Union of
Australia. Resolutions were moved at once by Mr.
Neild, whom we shall meet again in association with

Mr. G. H. Reid, ' deprecating any form of Federation calculated to imperil the Free Trade policy of New South Wales,' and recommending that ' the support of the Association shall be given only to those candidates who should give a first place to the advocacy of Free Trade.'

After a discussion which extended over nine meetings, these resolutions were carried (February 22) by a majority of two to one; the numbers being, For 29, Against 19. The significance of this vote was not lost upon Mr. G. H. Reid. Henceforward the official organisation of the Free Trade party was directed against Federation.

CHAPTER IV

ELEMENTS OF DISCORD (*continued*)

IT was the fate of those, who championed the cause of Australia through the ten years which followed the Tenterfield speech, always to be opposed by extremists, who had no single bond of sympathy except hostility to Federation, and whose opposition was not the less bitter because their arguments were mutually destructive. In 1890 this curious combination of opposites was between ' Imperialists ' and ' Republicans,'—the one asserting that Federation would destroy the Imperial tie, the other that it was a device for destroying local autonomy in the interests of ' Imperialism.' The Republican element in this alliance soon vanished from the political scene ; but the other remained dangerous to the last.

. I .

The sentiment of Nationality was such a potent influence in the final triumph of the federal cause that it is hard to realise that, at the outset of the movement, it threatened a formidable hostility. This was due to a misconception of the meaning of Nationality, which was not surprising in a community isolated by distance from the centres of thought, and without leisure for continuous study. Political and philosophical ideas often become popular in a young country, just as they are going out of date in Europe. Thus, it was not recognised generally in Australia in 1889-90 that the separatist doctrine of indifference to Imperial interests, which, under the influence of the Manchester school, had dominated English politics in the middle of the century, had become discredited by the consolidation of German power in 1870 and the new situation which this created. True, the doctrine of the Manchester school had never been accepted by Australians, because it was repugnant to the instinct of Empire, which is at the root of all successful colonisation. None the less, these teachings had produced their effect ; so that, when the annexation of New Guinea was disavowed and British interests in other parts of the Pacific (*e.g.* Samoa) were ignored, men were driven, as a counsel of despair, to look on Independence as a possible destiny. Certainly the thought of separation did not originate in Australia, but with the pedants in Great Britain, who for two generations controlled the State. All of these might not express their views with the same directness as Cobden :—

It is customary to hear our army and navy defended as necessary for the protection of our Colonies—as though some other nation might otherwise seize them. Gentlemen, where is the *enemy* that would be so good as to steal such *property* ? *We* should consider it quite as necessary to arm in defence of the National Debt ! ' [1]

but all held and promulgated the idea that the separation of the Colonies from Great Britain was inevitable and desirable.

The few courageous men, such as Froude and Lord

[1] See *Political Addresses*, p. 242.

Beaconsfield, who fought against this doctrine of disruption, were unable to make much impression on public opinion until the publication of Professor Seeley's ' Expansion of England ' in 1883, which marks a turning point in the growth of Imperial sentiment. The re-action, as was natural, went too far. Few of those, who still had faith in the future of the Empire, were acquainted with its constituent parts ; and the time was not ripe for any definite scheme for closer Union. Consequently vague language was used, especially by members of the Imperial Federation League, which seemed to imply a desire to limit the self-governing powers which the Colonies already possessed. For it was not yet realised that, the only sound basis of Imperial Union is the development of each Dominion along its own lines of national growth. The very phrases ' Imperial Federation,' ' Imperial Partnership ' forced those, who interpreted them literally, to make an unwilling choice between Independence and Absorption.

In this distracted state of public opinion the direct advocacy by *The Bulletin* of an Australian Republic gained many converts from the ranks of those whose Australian sympathies should have predisposed them to the cause of union. How this Republic was to be maintained without a navy or army was not explained. It is possible that the brilliant editor, Mr. J. F. Archibald, from his French origin and American experience, had a pious belief in a republican form of government ; but it is more likely that his journalistic instinct perceived the advantage for a paper, which lived by stinging criticism, of flouting thus the most ' respectable ' sentiment in the community ! Whatever the motive, many young men, who had learnt to trust *The Bulletin* as an organ of Australian sentiment, were persuaded by its articles, in the earlier stages of the movement, to look on Federation as a step towards a form of Imperial Union, which would deprive Australia of Autonomy. In a cartoon, which appeared on February 22, 1890, Australia was depicted as a kangaroo leaping into the open mouth of the British lion. And such sentences as ' Go slow ' : ' There is no popular demand for Federation ' : ' Beware of Imperialism,' appeared in every week's issue.

This is foolish talk to our ears ; but it must be remembered that Australia was then very immature. Extreme youth is always self-conscious ; and the supercilious interest of the British tourist inspires even less affection than the *hauteur* of the remittance man ! The young men of *The Bulletin* were blowing off ! Even to-day, it is sometimes forgotten that always singing ' Rule Britannia,' and always waving the kangaroo, indicate the same imperfect type of citizenship ! Moreover, the demand for independence was an acceptance of the often tendered advice of British Liberals, as well as an emphatic answer to those who were believed (erroneously) to desire the absorption of Australia in Great Britain. Fortunately, this kind of opposition soon died away ; and, in the later stages of the struggle, *The Bulletin* rendered such pre-eminent services to the cause of Union, that its earlier vagaries are only remembered by the historian.

. 2 .

Mr. Jebb, in his ' Studies in Colonial Nationalism,' —a work which may be said to have explained the

British Empire, which Professor Seeley re-discovered,—
has pointed out the slow transition from the old spirit
of ' Colonial ' dependence on Great Britain to the self-
respecting ' Nationalism,' which bears its part, as an
equal, in the burdens of the Empire.   In 1890 the
Imperial spirit was at a low ebb ;   and the same
doctrines of *laissez-faire* and Separatism, which
Australian republicans accepted at their face value,
inspired another class of Colonists with a passionate
determination to remain within the Empire, and even
to exaggerate their loyalty.   Mr. Froude in his ' Oceana '
reports a conversation with Mr. Dalley in 1885, in
which the latter explained that his unwillingness to
further Federation was due to his misgiving as to its
ultimate goal ;   and it is certain that there lurked at
the back of the minds of many of the best Australians
the fear, lest Federation were a step towards a separation from the Empire.   Mingled with this Imperial
patriotism was an intense local patriotism,—natural to
men who had seen Victoria and Queensland split off
from New South Wales,—which refused to recognise
the equal *status* of the other Colonies with the Mother
Colony, of which they had once formed part.   As the
struggle proceeded, local prejudice, rather than Imperial
sentiment, became the driving force of the provincial
opposition ;   but it would be unfair not to recognise
that this provincialism always had a better side, or to
blame its advocates unduly, because they did not
perceive at once that Nationalism, which makes Union
possible on equal terms, and not Colonialism, which
implies the domination of an inferior by a superior,
gives the only sound basis of the Imperial tie.

The leader of the Colonial party—nicknamed later

the ' Geebung ' party[1]—was that picturesque personality of the past, Sir John Robertson, of whom it is as
hard to convey a true impression to a later generation
as it was for a contemporary, who had not come
under the spell of the enchanter, to appreciate the
adoration of his friends.   In 1889 he had retired from
active politics.   But his long experience of affairs and
keen insight into character made him still the political
oracle of a large circle ; while his chivalrous loyalty,—
(he once resigned office rather than vote to condemn
a supporter for political corruption),—attached with
the closest ties all who came under his influence.   His
presence was strikingly handsome—the features clear-
cut, flowing white hair and agile figure—while a
natural gift of profanity and an uncompromising
directness of speech, expressed in husky tones—(he
had no palate)—have enriched our annals with many
pleasant anecdotes.[2]   Nurtured in the traditions of
Colonialism, his outlook from New South Wales was
towards Great Britain ; while, having spent his life
in the service of the Mother Colony, the separation
from her of Victoria and Queensland, and the claim
put forward by the former for the Riverina, remained
in his memory as unforgivable ingratitude.   At first,
he refused to treat Sir Henry Parkes' proposals as
intended sincerely :—' Federation was just Sir Henry's
fad.'   Later, when speaking to a young follower, he

---

[1] The ' Geebung ' is a small berry, which grows near Sydney, and is
much relished by children.

[2] One of the most fit for publication is of a young and pretty girl,
who, in an outburst of enthusiasm, told him that she had seen a picture
of him in a newspaper which was so like that she had kissed it.   ' And
did it kiss you back ? ' he asked.—' No ! '—' Then it could not have
been much like me ! '

asked :—' Why should we —— well close our gates to all the world in order to trade with those —— fellows across the Murray, who produce just the same as we do ; and all they can send us is —— cabbages ? [1] Mr. Charles Lyne recalls in his ' Life of Sir Henry Parkes' another characteristic, though bowdlerised, outburst :—

The Governors—they send out boys now—are supporting Parkes ! The fools ! They think there will be Imperial Federation ; and they will find a United States of Australia and separation. Then, see, if Federation should come about, what a howl there will be when the seat of Government is removed to Melbourne, as it certainly will be.

It is only by realising that such utterances, which were the germ of many articles and speeches in later years, expressed sincere convictions, in language which was generally approved, that posterity will understand why the inevitable Union of Australia was delayed so long, and only achieved, imperfectly, after eleven years of bitter contest. Naturally, Sir John Robertson became the leader of the Anti-Federalists, and the Reform Club their headquarters.[2] Thence came the impulse and direction—later through Mr. J. H. Want, Sir John's devoted political son—to those strangely assorted allies who, as this narrative will tell, all but succeeded in preventing union.

[1] To Sir John Robertson Victoria was always ' the cabbage garden.'
[2] Sir John Robertson was President of the Reform Club. At one annual meeting, when the accounts disclosed a deficit, he told the members ' they must drink the —— club out of debt ! ' Next year there was a credit balance ! Sir Henry Parkes never belonged to a club.

· 3 ·

Another ebullition of hostility, noticeable because it was the first definite expression of a reasoned dislike to the federal form of government, came from Mr. Julian Salomons, Q.C., who, speaking at a Mayoral banquet on January 27, declared Sir Henry Parkes' proposals to be 'fraught with great danger,' and protested against 'giving up our independent government and becoming a provincial power and part of a Federal government.' Sir Julian Salomons (as he became later) was too large-minded to be a mere parochial patriot ; and in fiscal matters was a Laodicean, who regarded both Free Trade and Protection as political expedients, which were legitimate or illegitimate according to circumstances. His unceasing opposition to Federation was due to a reasoned dislike of the inconveniences of the federal system.

The scene shifts now to Melbourne and is concerned with the proceedings of the Conference.

CHAPTER V

THE MELBOURNE CONFERENCE

THE Conference of Ministers, which it had required so much diplomacy to bring together, met at Melbourne on February 6, 1890. Sir Henry Parkes and the Colonial Treasurer (Mr. McMillan) represented New South Wales, and Mr. Gillies (Premier) and Mr. Deakin (Chief Secretary) Victoria. Queensland and South Australia had joined to their Ministerial Representatives —Mr. Macrossan (Queensland) and Sir John Cockburn (South Australia)—the leaders of their Oppositions, Sir Samuel Griffith and Mr. Playford. Tasmania sent her Attorney-General, Mr. A. Inglis Clark and Mr. Stafford Bird (Treasurer). Sir James Lee Steere (Speaker) represented Western Australia, and Captain Russell (Colonial Secretary) and Sir John Hall (ex-Premier), New Zealand. It would have been impossible to assemble a more representative gathering, or one more competent to form and direct public opinion.[1]

Many Conferences of Ministers had been held before ; and each had removed some cause of irritation. But the Melbourne Conference was very different from anything of the kind yet known in Australia. Its meetings were open to the public ; and for the

[1] Mr. James Service (Victoria) and Mr. Barton (N.S.W.), being out of Parliament at the time, were not eligible as members of the Conference.

first time men saw the problem of Federation as a whole, and realised that the Union of the Colonies was an aim to be sought after for its own sake, and not only to meet the accident of some urgent need. Each speaker presented the question in a different light,—Sir Henry Parkes was supremely confident, Sir Samuel Griffith cautious, Mr. Playford critical and dubious,—yet all agreed that Union was both desirable and possible. Such a declaration forced Federation upon public attention, and was fatal to the old provincial isolation. The speeches at this Conference, accordingly, deserve to be re-called as the first decisive utterances of the movement, and because of the temper, knowledge, and ability which they display. Also they are new to the present generation.

. I .

A banquet held on the eve of the opening of the Conference is memorable for two great speeches, one by Mr. James Service, the other by Sir Henry Parkes. Mr. Service, a veteran fighter for the Union of Australia, was a merchant of large views and fine culture—at once a scholar and a man of business,—who, having led the squatting and Free Trade party in Victoria for many years, coalesced with Sir Graham Berry in 1882, in order to give rest and peace to a distracted colony. In 1890 he was no longer in public life, although his influence on opinion had not diminished. No one more suitable could have been selected to express, with wisdom and discrimination, the hopes of Australian patriotism for a successful outcome of the Conference's deliberations.

Beginning with a grateful recognition of the interest

in Federation—'the idea of which had permeated the whole of society and all classes of society. It had touched the imagination of the people and been approved by their judgment,' he hinted skilfully at his main theme—'they had many things federal, but still no federal Custom House,' and proceeded to review the previous stages of the federal movement, in which, although he made no mention of it, he had himself played no small part. Discussing the Federal Council, he recognised that it had failed, 'because the people of New South Wales refused to join it.' 'This,' he continued, 'should be a warning that we should be prepared to sacrifice our individual opinions and desires—to give and take—to make up our minds to one thing only, namely, that whatever the majority of the Colonies decide upon as the best method of working together, that method must be adopted by every other Colony.' Discussing, next, the 'difficulties in the way of a complete Union,' which, in his opinion, were not insuperable, he used a phrase in reference to the tariff, which became historic :—

The first question and probably the most difficult is that of a common fiscal policy. . . . I have no hesitation in saying that this is to me the lion in the path ; and I go further and say that the Conference must either kill that lion or the lion will kill it. . . . To my mind a national government without a uniform fiscal policy is a downright absurdity.

Mr. Service concluded his speech by a further reference to the Federal Council :—

If it should be found impossible at the present time to arrive at the goal of our wishes, a complete Union, I think this might still be reached later through the Federal Council.

Such a suggestion from one so ardent in the cause of Union as Mr. Service, is a measure of the strength and greatness of Sir Henry Parkes. The speech in which the latter replied to the toast is one of the finest examples of his eloquence.

The speeches of all orators, who make use of words to stir or convince an audience, and not as literary artists, necessarily lose much of their distinctive character and power in being read. The tones of the speaker are not heard ; his measured utterance, the massive dignity of his appearance, the contagious enthusiasm of the audience—everything is lacking, except the words. And, in the case of Sir Henry Parkes, the force of the words depended rather upon the flow of a rich stream of lofty diction, than upon the nice selection of apt phrases.[1] His sentences, too, although never involved, were often rugged ; and were impressive, rather from their force than from their beauty. On this occasion, however, he coined a phrase of true poetry, which is enshrined among the beauties of the English language—' The crimson thread of kinship runs through us all.'—He had been speaking of the separation of Victoria and Queensland from the Mother Colony of New South Wales.

We know [he said] that it is a wise dispensation that these

[1] ' He had the power,' says the writer of his obituary notice in *The Times*, ' developed to the point of perfection of which he was capable, of lifting a subject to the highest plane on which it could be treated. He had that breadth of sentiment and glow of imagination which enabled him often to breathe a living soul into what previously and in other men's hands had seemed mere clay. He seized principles and discoursed upon them in an elevated strain ; while others chattered about separate and—in their separateness meaningless—details. He loved great themes and great occasions ; and seldom failed to catch their inspiration.'

large Colonies sprang into existence, and we advised them when they were fighting their own battles independently of New South Wales ; but the time has now arrived when we are no longer separated. *The crimson thread of kinship runs through us all.* Even native-born Australians are Britons as much as those born in the City of London or the City of Glasgow, We know the value of our British origin ; we know that we represent a race, which for the purpose of settling new Colonies never had its equal on the face of the earth.

The tension of the audience reached its limit ; and the speech was interrupted by vociferous cheering.

Sir Henry dwelt on this note a little longer in order to emphasise his belief that Federation was no step towards separation but a ' mark of the unity of the Empire.' Then he passed to the question, which was in the minds of all.

This was his fashion of dealing with the ' lion in the path ' :—

What stands in the way of a Federal Constitution ? A common tariff ? National life is a broad river of living water. Your fiscal notions—and I am a Free Trader remember— your fiscal notions on one side or the other are as planting a few stones or cutting sandbanks to divert the stream for a little, in order to protect your own interests. This question of a common tariff is a mere trifle compared with the over-shadowing question of living an eternal national existence. For Free Trade or Protection, all must admit, is to a large extent but a device for carrying out a human notion ; but there is no human notion at all about the eternal life of a free nation. I say then—I speak for my Colony, which is as great as the rest of you—we are prepared—and I will answer for the Parliament and the people of the country I represent—to go into this national Union without making any bargains what-ever, without stipulating for any advantage for ourselves but trusting to the good faith and justice of a Federal Parliament.'

. 2 .

At the first meeting of the Conference Mr. Gillies was elected chairman ; and it was resolved, upon the motion of Sir Henry Parkes, that the Conference should frame its Resolutions in private, but that these should be debated in public. The brief discussion on this motion revealed a difference of opinion as to the scope and purpose of the Conference. Sir Henry Parkes regarded it as ' a deliberative body to debate questions rather than enter into minute consultation as to the particular form of Federation,' and, while willing that ' any matter of a disputatious character, admitting of new views and explanations ' such as arise in Committee, should be considered with closed doors, he thought that ' when the business was by a stated Resolution from the Chair, the public should be admitted.' Sir Samuel Griffith agreed, but with hesitation. He thought that the object of the Conference was 'to exchange ideas as to how far Federation is practicable at the present time. . . . Some members might think that a perfect Federation was possible now ; others that it was not practicable, and they might feel it their duty to point out the difficulties. And those difficulties would have to be met.' Mr. Playford was even more dubious ; yet was prepared to admit the Press, although this was unprecedented, 'in order that the public might thoroughly understand the ground on which they had come to certain conclusions.' He protested, however, against the idea that the Conference should not discuss the details of Federation. ' Nobody would know what they meant, if they just passed a bald resolution that they were ripe for Federation. They must go further and show to what extent they

were prepared to federate.' Mr. McMillan answered
Mr. Playford. He urged that the Conference was only
preliminary to a more representative and authorised
gathering. Their function was to come to an agreement
that Federation was within the region of practical
politics. Therefore ' their Resolutions would declare
that the time was ripe for Federation and then ask the
Colonies to send delegates to a Convention to discuss
the question in all its bearings both generally and in
detail.' He advocated therefore the admission of the
Press because, in his view, ' the discussion was to be, on
broad public lines, upon the question, Whether public
opinion has advanced so far that we proceed to the
formation of a Convention.'

This view prevailed ; and before the Conference
adjourned Sir Henry Parkes gave notice of his Resolution : ' To test what he thought must be tested, viz. :
the feeling of the Conference as to the time being ripe
for Federation,' in these terms :—

That, in the opinion of this Conference, the best interests
and the present and future prosperity of the Australasian
Colonies will be promoted by an early Union under the
Crown ; and, while fully recognising the valuable services
of the members of the Convention of 1883 in framing the
Federal Council, it declares its opinion that the seven years
which have since elapsed have developed the national life
of Australasia, in population, in wealth, in the discovery of
resources, and in self-governing capacity, to an extent which
justifies the higher act, at all times contemplated, of the
Union of these Colonies, under one legislative and executive
government on principles just to the several Colonies.

· 3 ·

The Debate upon this Resolution was maintained upon a high level. The speeches have a two-fold interest, the one arising from the essential similarity of all federal problems, and the other historical, due to their influence in shaping the issue of the struggle which came later. Nor is it only the trend of the argument, which has a bearing upon questions of the day, but also the very modern character of its particulars. The same difficulties, misgivings, prejudice and timidity, which delay the Union of the Empire, faced the Representatives of the Australian Colonies at the Melbourne Conference, and were expressed in almost the same words as those which may be heard to-day in any discussion upon Imperial relations. It will be well, therefore,—in so far as this is possible with due regard to space,—to express the views of the speakers in their own words.

Sir HENRY PARKES, who opened the Debate, began with a tactful reference to the labours of his predecessors and drew attention particularly to the report of a Select Committee (of which his friend Sir Gavan Duffy [1] had been a member) of the Victorian Legislative Assembly, dated September 8, 1857, 'less than a year after the introduction of Responsible Government.' From this he read some short passages. The first was as follows :—

Of the ultimate necessity of a Federal Union, there is but one opinion. Your Committee is unanimous in believing that the interest and honour of these growing States would be

[1] Of 'Young Ireland' fame, and the friend of Carlyle. His distinguished son—Mr. Frank Duffy—is now a Judge of the High Court of Australia.

promoted by the establishment of a system of mutual action and co-operation among them. Their interest suffers and must continue to suffer, while competing tariffs, naturalisation laws, and land systems, rival schemes of immigration and of ocean postage, a clumsy and inefficient method of communicating with each other and with the home Government on public business and a distant and expensive system of judicial appeal exist.

The next passage, which Sir Henry Parkes quoted from this report, was peculiarly consonant with his manner of dealing with political questions :—

The honour and importance, which constitute so important an element of national prosperity, and the absence of which invites aggression from foreign enemies, cannot perhaps in this generation belong to any single Colony in this southern group, but may—and we are persuaded would—be speedily obtained by an Australian Federation representing the entire group.

Then he quoted one sentence from the Report of this Committee which expressed a whole chapter of political philosophy : 'NEIGHBOURING STATES OF THE SECOND ORDER INEVITABLY BECOME CONFEDERATES OR ENEMIES.'

'We have proved this,' said Sir Henry Parkes, 'unhappily to be true, and who can doubt but that, had the Colonies acted upon this Report thirty-three years ago, many things savouring of enmity, at all events of something more than rivalry, would have been avoided ? ' He referred, next, to the Convention of 1883, which was the parent of the Federal Council, and reminded the Conference that Mr. Service had intended always that this should be a step towards a closer union. He praised the work of this body in developing a public opinion in favour of Federation, and pointed out the great development since 1883 'in industry, education, refinement in social manners and in the estimates of moral life, until Australia was now in a condition that it might be contrasted favourably with some of the wealthiest States in the world, not only in respect of its enterprise, its skill and its industrial vigour, but also in the higher walks of life.' He quoted figures in support of these statements and concluded this portion of his speech with this inquiry :—' If, then, we were fit in the year 1857 to enter into a Federation, how much more are we fit now ? And if we are not fit now, with the elements of strength which I have very cursorily pointed out, when shall we be fit ? . . . If it is said that we are not ripe for complete Federation now, then when shall we be ripe ? Will it be to-morrow or this day twelve months, or this day five years ? In what degree shall we be better off than we are now ? '

He then made pleasant fun of Mr. Service's 'lion in the path' :—

The other night a gentleman, the most striking feature of whose character is his practical common sense, told us that there was a lion in the path, and that this Conference must either kill the lion or be killed by it. Well ! the fabled lion is most frequently presented to us as a foreign monster, as a thing directly opposed to the person who is pursuing the path— that has the most opposite notions to the end that person has in view. The lion is supposed to be an enemy that will tear him to pieces. I have never seen the fabled lion presented to the world under any other circumstances ; and thus interpreted there is not and cannot be any lion whatever in our path. *There is no obstacle in the path before us except impediments which we have created ourselves.* Nature has created no obstacle. That principle of Divine Goodness—call it what you may—which exists and overrules the world, has created this fair land of Australia, situated as it is, wisely created it for a grand experiment in human government, and there is no lion, and no natural difficulty before us. The path is plain and bright with the genial sunshine of our own blue heavens, with no impediment in it whatever.

Then, changing his tone from one of encouragement to one of warning, he continued :—

If we are only wise, and can only agree among ourselves ; if we acknowledge that bond which unites us as one people, whether we will or no ; if we acknowledge frankly that kinship from which we cannot escape, and from which no one desires to escape—if we acknowledge that, and if we subordinate all lower and sectional considerations to the one great aim of building up a power which, in the world outside, will have more influence, command more respect, enhance every comfort and every profit of life amongst ourselves—if we only enter into the single contemplation of this one object, the thing will be accomplished, and accomplished more easily and in shorter time than any great achievement of the same nature that was ever accomplished before. But let there be no mistake ! *We cannot become a nation and still cling to conditions and to desires which are antagonistic to nationality. We cannot become one united people and cherish some provincial object which is inconsistent with that nationality.*

[Would that these words of warning had been taken to heart during all the first twelve years of Federation !]

Speaking next of the material advantages which might be expected from Federation, Sir Henry Parkes instanced among other things the ' improvement by the power of a Central Government of our means of communication,' little dreaming that it would be counted a mark of statesmanship, by those who came after him in New South Wales, to deny to the national Government control over the national railways. He referred also to the risk of war, which no nation could escape, however peacefully inclined, and pointed out the necessity for military training for defence under a Central Government. 'Therefore,' he said, 'the Federation Government must be a government of power. It must be a government armed with plenary power for the defence of the country.' Such a government might be established gradually with the concurrence of the States, but, in that case, it 'should be in design from the very first a complete legislative and executive government, suited to perform the grandest and highest functions of a nation.' At the same time, the functions of the States must not be invaded wantonly; because it was the duty of the whole of the delegates to have a jealous regard for the rights and just privileges of the Colonies they represented. It would be impossible for any Federal Government to expect to give satisfaction, unless its powers—which he still contended must be sufficient for its high purposes—were in harmony with what was justly due to the several Colonies.

His conclusion was that, in their own interests and in the interests of future generations, it was their 'duty to ask the Parliaments of the different Colonies to consider whether or not the time for Federation was come.'

· 4 ·

Sir SAMUEL GRIFFITH, who followed Sir Henry Parkes, was the only member of the Conference who had taken part in the Convention of 1883. He was also Chairman of the Federal Council. A special importance attached therefore to his assurance that he, like Mr. Service, ' went to the Convention of 1883 with the expectation that the various Parliaments would go much further in the direction of Federation than they actually did.' However, they had done then ' all that they could see to have been practicable and desirable.' Circumstances now were altered. Now, he had no doubt of it being desirable, and he believed practicable, to do more. How much more was a very difficult question to answer ; and upon that opinions might differ. For himself he desired a complete Federal Parliament and Federal Executive, one Dominion with no rivalries,—no Customs rivalries, at any rate, amongst themselves. How far then could they go ? There were some things, such as defence and external affairs, which it was quite clear the separate provincial Governments could not do properly or efficiently, although they might do them in some sort of a way. Yet it must be remembered that through long separation the several Colonies had become ' practically sovereign States ' and this ' absolute freedom to manage their own affairs ' might prove a difficulty. Many people, although they were favourable to the idea of Federation in the abstract, yet would hesitate to give up any of the rights which they had been in the habit of exercising. The advantages of Federation, like everything else, would have to be paid for : they could not be got without giving something in return, and every power, which might be exercised by the Federal Government with greater advantage than by the separate Governments, involved a corresponding diminution in the power of the separate Governments and Legislatures. That was the first objection with which they would be met. But there was an answer to it. There were some things which the separate Parliaments and Executives could not do. And he instanced defence, external affairs, and fiscal union. As to the latter he said :—

There must be some day a fiscal union. Whether it can be brought about just now or not is a matter upon which opinions must differ very much. I think, for my part, although I admit freely that Federation without fiscal union would be unsatisfactory, that its absence would not be an insuperable obstacle. . . . Suppose we had a central Government for defence, uniform laws, the regulation of trade and commerce externally, the post-office, the sea-fisheries, etc., and the Colonies still had separate tariffs, we should be so much the better off, by reason of the regulation of the things I have named by a central Government, and, as regards fiscal matters, we should be no worse off than we are. . . . It is no use disguising the fact that the protective duties of many of the Colonies are designed quite as much with a view to protect the Colonies against their neighbours as to protect them against the outside world—indeed a great deal more so. Moreover, in some of the Colonies the revenue raised by tariff duties imposed upon their neighbours' products forms a very large proportion of the income of the Government ; and when the great question of *cui bono* comes to be asked in the Parliaments, these Colonies will require a satisfactory answer as to what they are going to gain by surrendering their protective duties.

[It was well, perhaps, that prosaic considerations of profit and loss should bring Sir Henry Parkes' soaring eloquence to earth ; and speakers must not be considered to have been indifferent to the grandeur of his dream, because they emphasised the difficulties in the way of its realisation. Yet no one, except Sir Henry Parkes, perceived,—and this is the measure of his influence—that these difficulties could never be resolved by negotiations and arrangement, until there had been first what, in religion, is termed a 'change of heart,' widening the outlook of Australians and bringing home to them the conviction that for 'One People' there must be 'One Destiny.']

Sir Samuel Griffith then enumerated the matters which could be dealt with better by one Parliament and one Executive, much as they appear in the fifty-first section of the Constitution,[1] and pointed out that the 'work left for provincial Parliaments would still be large and important.' After dwelling further upon the difficulties to be overcome, he urged that the delegates should not be deterred by any fear of not being able to do everything, but should do the most they could, remembering the old saying that 'half a loaf is better than no bread.'

Even after twelve years of Federal Union the ignorance of one State of the affairs of the others is very great. In 1890, when the means of communication were few and inconvenient, this seemed to Sir Samuel Griffith to be one of the great obstacles in the way of Union, as it is to-day an obstacle in the way of Union of the Empire :—

Another difficulty [he said], which will meet us, has reference to the want of knowledge, which one Colony possesses of another. If, for instance, the Legislature of a country is asked to surrender its great powers of legislation to another body, people will naturally want to know of whom that body is to be constituted, and whether the members of it would consider their interests as well as they would consider them

[1] See Commonwealth of Australia Constitution Act, 63 & 64 Vict. cap. 12.

themselves. I would counsel all public men, during the two or three years which must elapse before any definite result can be achieved from our labours,—

[No one at this time imagined that ten years would pass before this consummation]—

to take every opportunity, both in public and private life, of making themselves acquainted with the different powers of Australasia, and of making the different powers of Australasia acquainted with them. Let us endeavour as far as possible to distinguish between means and ends. The end we have in view is the establishment of a great Australian nation. . . . Matters such as those of fiscal policy are, after all, only means, not ends, in themselves. Whatever conclusion may be arrived at in regard to such matters, it is our business not to lose sight of the one great end in view —the establishment of a nation.

And then the mantle of the prophet fell upon Sir Samuel Griffith also :—

The moral effect upon the people of Australia of the accomplishment of such an object will be very great indeed. Look how much wider will be the field for the legitimate and noble ambition of those who desire to take part in the affairs of a great nation—as it will be—a nation practically commanding the Southern Seas. The energies of men are cramped when they are confined to matters which, although of considerable magnitude in themselves, are nevertheless, to a great extent, local in their character. . . . I shall be deeply disappointed if, as the result of this Conference, there are not laid the foundations of a real, strong, permanent, and complete Federal Government by Australasia.

· 5 ·

Mr. PLAYFORD, ex-Premier, and at the time Leader of the Opposition in South Australia, continued the debate. ' Honest Tom ' Playford was a burly giant, who, entering politics late in life, had never lost a rustic bluntness of speech, which was excused by all who knew his natural amiability. A practical man of affairs rather than a student, he was antagonistic by temperament to Sir Henry Parkes, whose idealism he regarded as fanciful and his methods as devious. The clash between these two masterful men was the dramatic feature of the Conference, and was the more striking because each was a son of the soil, who revealed his origin by the doggedness, caution and unexpected versatility, which are the hereditary qualities of the English peasantry of ancient lineage.[1]

At the outset he objected to the ' baldness ' of Sir Henry Parkes' Resolution. Everyone (he said) was agreed that Federation was desirable ; the real difference was as to the powers to be given to the Federal Parliament. The Conference should have been discussing these, because that was what the people wanted to know. The misfortune was that Federation had been taken up by the leading states-men of the various Colonies, and as a consequence —or as a fact—the question had not been taken up by the people, who were not, so far as South Australia was concerned, educated sufficiently upon the question that they could be said either to be unmistakably in favour of Federation, or to know how far they were willing to go in that direction. Mr. Playford then referred to the efforts of leading men in the past to create an interest in Federation, and their failure to induce the people to take up the subject heartily. For his part, he thought that the difficulties

---

[1] Sir Henry Parkes believed he could trace his descent from Faul-conbridge.

in the way of Federation were greater than those which any other country had faced ; and he illustrated this opinion from the history of the United States and Canada, showing how, in each of these cases, Federation had been brought about by the presence of foreign countries. To his mind Sir Henry Parkes' 'statement of the glorious progress' of the Colonies was an argument for those who were opposed to Federation. 'If they were the wealthiest people in the world without Federation, and the best-governed and most prosperous communities that existed at the present time without Federation, " Why on earth," would say the opponent of Federation, " should they go in for Federation ? " ' The better policy, he thought, for Australia, was 'to build up slowly and carefully a public opinion in favour of Federation.' This had been Sir Henry Parkes' view in 1881, when he moved a Resolution affirming that the time was not ripe for Federation. Then he turned on his opponents :—

I believe it is said that harmony is sometimes improved by inserting a little note of discord now and again into the music. Perhaps I shall insert one or two notes of discord regarding the Colonies of New South Wales and Victoria. I do not wish to do that in any offensive manner, or with any other object than that of enabling me to answer questions which have been asked and will be asked again in South Australia. In the first place I would like to ask Sir Henry Parkes how was it that, after he had introduced the Federal Council Bill in 1881, the Colony of New South Wales refused to come into the Council when it was formed, and how was it that he himself opposed its coming in ? I do not know the reason, and I should like to know it.

Sir Henry Parkes : I will tell the honourable gentleman now, if he thinks well.

F

Mr. Playford : I don't know which is the better course. I will appeal to the President.

The President : It is a mere matter of convenience. If the honourable gentleman thinks that it would assist his argument he can hear the explanation now.

Mr. Playford : No ! It would perhaps be well to give Sir Henry Parkes time to consider the question.

Sir Henry Parkes : There is not much consideration required.

Mr. Playford : Possibly not. I put the question in good faith, because it has been put in our Colony and it will be put again by the enemies of Federation. I should like to be able to give a straightforward, honest answer to it.

Sir Henry Parkes : You had better have the explanation now. It will only take a few minutes.

Mr. Playford : No, it will come better in the proper order. Sir Henry Parkes will have the right of reply.

Next, Mr. Playford accused Sir Henry Parkes of failure to redeem a promise given at a late Conference of Premiers to introduce a Bill for the restriction of Chinese immigration, and asked whether ' this conduct showed that sincere desire for Australian unity which we were led to suppose, from the speech he delivered to-day, actuates him ? '

The last charge was the most galling, namely, that

during the whole of Sir Henry Parkes' address he did not say a single word about our relations with the Mother Country. Whatever happens I intend to remain loyal to the Mother Country, and so does the Colony I represent. No matter how affairs are managed, we intend to continue to belong to that great Anglo-Saxon people whose home is Great Britain.

Mr. Playford then directed his attention to Victoria. This Colony, he said, had been the greatest sinner in building up a tariff wall between the Colonies. She had in fact ' created the necessity to federate, in order to pull down the barriers she had chosen to erect.' Would Mr. Deakin explain this change of front ? What reason had Victoria for first building up these barriers and wanting now to pull them down ?

Is she not actuated by self-interest in some form ? The answer is, say the people in South Australia, that Victoria, having been the first in the field with Protection, having built up her manufactures, established her industries and got her skilled workmen around her, does not fear competition now with any of the Colonies. She can now compete successfully against them, and by breaking down the barriers she will gain an advantage over the neighbouring Colonies ; by adopting that course she will reap the greatest benefit and pocket the most ' tin.'

Returning to the main argument, Mr. Playford declared himself hostile to any Federation on the Canadian plan, and insisted that the residue of power should remain with the several Colonies as in the Constitution of the United States :—

Although unity is a grand thing, it is not everything. As far as local Legislatures are concerned, I contend it will be the wiser course to leave to them all the power we possibly can, apart from such powers as they cannot exercise individually. . . . The general Parliament should have its powers and duties clearly and specifically defined, everything else to be left to the local Parliaments.

The only matters which, in Mr. Playford's opinion, should be left to the Federal Parliament were 'such as related to Customs duties, the Marriage laws, and a Court of Appeal.' For his part he would vote for the Resolution, but he wanted to ' point out to the Conference the difficult problem which beset

F 2

it.' He feared that they might go too far, and by endeavouring to secure a Dominion like Canada lose all, and so put back Federation to a future generation.

. 6 .

Mr. DEAKIN, who followed, congratulated Mr. Playford on his 'frank, forcible, and extremely vigorous speech,' which he took to be ' as complete an adhesion as is necessary to the principle embodied in the Resolution.' He continued, in a passage which may stir the complacency of those who argue that, since all is well with the Empire to-day—at least upon the surface,—there is no need to seek an improvement in its organisation :—

One of Mr. Playford's difficulties is that we have no difficulties. He considers that one of the misfortunes of the present Conference is that it meets without a sufficiently great occasion ; without that force of circumstances, such as existed in Canada and the United States, which might compel us to form a Union *nolentes volentes*. . . . (But) will the honourable gentleman venture to advance the opinion that he can do nothing, see nothing in the future possibilities of this Continent which may compel Federation ? Will he not admit, if he view the situation frankly, that, so far from being unlikely, it is practically a matter of certitude that, sooner or later, we too shall be forced into circumstances which, with or without our will, will force us into alliance ? How much better then, if, recognising this as one of the inevitable future events of our history, we face the question in a time of peace and quiet, and without any severe external compulsion. . . . Instead of being forced into partnership by a crisis, it will be far better for us to be united before the crisis arrives, that we may face it with a bold and unbroken spirit.

Yet that Mr. Deakin was alive to the difficulties, which were occasioned by the want of pressure from without, was made clear later in his speech, when he quoted the saying of Alexander Hamilton that, ' The establishment of a Constitution in time of profound peace, by the voluntary consent of a whole people, was a prodigy to the completion of which he looked forward with trembling anxiety.' Continuing, Mr. Deakin, after questioning whether Mr. Playford had not been in error in assuming that the differences between the Colonies were greater than they really were, dealt with the assertion that ' all great reforms spring from the people.'

That [he said], is perfectly true. They spring from the people when they are ripening for execution. It does not follow that the idea springs from the many; but, rather, it must of necessity take its birth in the mind of one, or at all events in the minds of a few.

Speaking for Victoria, he could assure Mr. Playford that the people were moved by a desire for Federation ; and a large body of them were prepared to make sacrifices for Federation. His answer to Mr. Playford's doubt as to the motives of Victoria in advocating now the removal of border duties, applies with equal force to the arguments of those who consider that the fiscal independence of the Dominions is an insurmountable obstacle in the way of Imperial Union :—

Certainly Victoria imposed protective duties with the idea of self-benefit, and without considering the interests of her neighbour in the slightest degree—(other Colonies acted in the same way). And why is it thus ? Because you have created in these Colonies a series of centres of independent life, and each of these centres of independent life will seek to maintain and multiply itself without regard for, and in more or less hostility to, the others. . . . The one remedy, if you desire a remedy, for the present condition of things is to create another centre of national life, which shall so far absorb these minor centres as to give the people of the several Colonies one common interest instead of antagonistic interests. You cannot by any means short of Federation modify the present independent lives of the Colonies so as to develop a national force to which all individual forces shall minister.

Then, coming to close quarters, he continued :—

If Mr. Playford asks whether this proposal is not made at the present time by Victoria from self-interested objects, I say ' Yes ! Most assuredly.' Do I believe that it is to the interest of Victoria that there should be a Federation of the Colonies ? Certainly I believe it ! If I did not believe it I should require stronger arguments than I do now to convince me that the Federation movement is one to be supported. If he asks the equivalent question, ' Do I believe it to be to the interest of the other Colonies of the Australian group that there should be Federation ? ' I answer, with equal frankness, that ' I believe it to be just as much to their interest as to the interest of Victoria.'

Passing next to ' fragmentary and rather supplementary ' comment on the Resolution, Mr. Deakin referred to ' some of the difficulties of Union which must be taken into account,' the first of which was what Sir Henry Parkes had called ' the something more then rivalry ' between the Colonies. His words may be quoted in the hope that the time may come soon when they will have a purely antiquarian interest :—

I believe there is a feeling existing between the different Colonies of Australasia at the present time—that is, between some people in one Colony and some in another—which is of an entirely regrettable character. One has only to observe the comments which appear, even in the best newspapers of one Colony, upon events taking place in another Colony, to see that there is not a generous spirit of kinship exhibited by the critics. Representative journals even rejoice over the difficulties experienced by another Colony, perhaps because it may suit the political policy of the paper to do so, but sometimes apparently without that cause, and for no other reason than that there is a kind of rivalry existing between the Colonies. This is an unfortunate factor and one the existence of which should not be disregarded. We cannot be sure that circumstances might not fan these latent oppositions into something far stronger and more difficult to cope with. They are too strong already ; and it belongs to us to provide such measures as shall prevent them growing stronger. We must direct much of the loyalty which is now attached to individual Colonies to a central ideal of the national life of Australia, so that our countrymen shall exhibit their loyalty to the nation and the nation only, and shall feel that what transpires in any part of the Colonies has as much interest for them as events occurring in the particular spot in which they dwell.[1]

Mr. Deakin dealt next with the facts 'which pointed to the timeliness of Federation,' instancing the examples of Canada and the United States, the unsettlement and danger of foreign aggression in the Pacific, the need for a Representative in London to express Australian views, the necessity of providing for the administration of

---

[1] In May 1912 the Victorian Government issued a circular to the depositors in the State Savings Bank, advising them not to invest in the Commonwealth Bank because the funds would not be spent in Victoria, but in building the transcontinental railway and other investments outside of Victoria ! At the same time the Government of New South Wales refused to give the Commonwealth sufficient control over a small portion of the shores of Jarvis Bay to enable it to establish a naval training college in that locality. Also the railways on the borders of New South Wales and Victoria still stop at a dead end a few miles from the frontier ; while the distance between the Queensland and New South Wales railway stations at Murwillumbah is a quarter of a mile ! The Government of New South Wales in 1912 refused to provide a residence in Sydney for the Governor-General, unless the Commonwealth would pay for this. Such facts as these are a striking commentary on Mr. Deakin's words.

New Guinea and the Northern Territory, and the pressing need of united action for defence purposes. It is interesting to observe that, at this time, even so strong a Federalist as Mr. Deakin contemplated the retention by the States of their railways, telegraphs, and post offices ; although he would have given to the Commonwealth control over external means of communication such as mail and cable lines.

He dealt lightly with the question of the tariff, ' knowing that this subject will have to be thrashed out by the Convention ' ; but his few remarks contained this pregnant reflection on the suggestion of Sir Samuel Griffith that Federation might be possible without a common tariff :—

If this suggestion be adopted, the position in which the Federal Government would find itself would be the rather uncomfortable one of a government without any great source of revenue, unless it be specially endowed with some new powers of taxation, the operation of which would hardly introduce it in a favourable light to the inhabitants of this Continent.

The bearing of this upon the proposal of Sir Gordon Sprigg for an Imperial surtax on all Customs duties to be applied for Imperial defence purposes is very significant. Then, glancing at what proved to be later the almost insoluble problem of finance, Mr. Deakin continued :—

If the local tariffs are to be maintained for a period of years, it will be absolutely necessary that their collections should, from the first day of the formation of a Federal Government, be undertaken by the officers of that Government, even if the revenue has to be afterwards paid over into local Treasuries. There should from the first be a federal control over all the ports of Australasia by Federal Customs and officers. It will be necessary for the Federal Government to have the means of maintaining itself. It must receive the Customs revenues and deduct what it is authorised to deduct, paying back to the several colonies the surplus there would be over the small expenditure upon such a form of government. . . . A common tariff is a *sine quâ non* of national life. There can be no true union which does not include a Customs union. I will not yet admit that it is necessary that it should be even postponed.

Mr. Deakin's next theme was the Federal Judiciary, with functions which should be similar to those of the Supreme Court of the United States. Such a Judiciary, with a Federal Executive and a Federal Legislature, would be the ' organ of a Sovereign State, which would not be a figment or shadow, nor exist only on the sufferance of the local Parliaments, but would draw its authority straight from the people of the different Colonies, obtaining from them the plenary powers to be exercised by it within certain limits . . . It would act directly through its judiciary, and in other ways, upon every citizen within its borders.'

It followed from this view of the sovereignty of the Federal Government that the people of Australia should establish Federation for themselves :—

All that is possible for this Conference or a Committee to do is to present to the Australasian people a means by which they can, if they so please, transform themselves and their separate segments into a great and united nation.

He ' did not fear the result of an appeal to the people.' Another gain to which he looked from Federation was an improvement in the type of legislator :—

We shall, I believe, bring into the field of federal legislation a large body of trained political intelligence and also a number of minds not at present employed upon political issues, and we shall enable these to place at the service of the Union an ability and culture which shall be capable of conducting the business of the nation in a manner befitting its powers and its promises.

Finally, he reminded the Conference that no Constitution shaped by the Convention would be final :—

Let that Constitution be what it may, if in any respect it fails to meet the wishes and needs of the people of Australia, they will still have the right, and certainly should be specially endowed with the power, of moulding it from time to time more and more into harmony with their needs and desires.

And he recalled the fact that the Constitution of Victoria had been amended four times since its grant in 1855. The last words of a peroration of great power and eloquence were an expression of confidence in the ultimate triumph of those who were now entering upon the hour of their labours and their trial.

The Conference adjourned until next day.

· 7 ·

Mr. A. INGLIS CLARK, Attorney-General for Tasmania, who was prevented by an untimely death from serving the Commonwealth which he had helped to form, was more American than the Americans in his admiration of American institutions. During a visit to Boston he had made friends with the best type of educated American, at a time when the heroic tradition of Lincoln and the Civil War threw the darker features of American life into obscure shadow, so that the dazzled eye saw nothing of the coming conflict between rich and poor, in which the tyranny of unscrupulous wealth was to establish itself, under the forms of freedom, by reason of the rigidity of the

Constitution and the opportunities this offers to political corruption. No one in Australia, not even excepting Sir Samuel Griffith, had Mr. Clark's knowledge of the constitutional history of the United States ; and, when knowledge of detail is combined with zeal, its influence on a deliberative body becomes irresistible. That our Constitution so closely resembles that of the United States is due in a very large degree to the influence of Mr. A. I. Clark. His speech at this Conference, when he followed Mr. Deakin, is interesting as containing the germ of the ideas which dominated the Convention of 1891.

Mr. Clark began his speech by a literal acceptance of Mr. Playford's doubt as to the willingness of South Australia to accept Federation. If this view were well-founded he was willing, for his part, that the four contiguous colonies of Victoria, Tasmania, New South Wales, and Queensland should federate among themselves.[1]

Mr. Clark next disputed the accuracy of Mr. Playford's assertion that it was the pressure of foreign enemies which forced the United States into Union, and quoted from Daniel Webster's argument in *Gibbons* v. *Ogden* that ' The Constitution had its immediate origin in a conviction of the necessity for uniformity or identity in commercial regulations . . . The prevailing motive was to regulate commerce.'

Turning, then, to the matters with which the Conference was concerned more immediately, he pointed out that all the financial difficulties, including that of

[1] Sir Henry Parkes, it will be observed, was the only representative who kept before him steadily the idea of a complete Union, and refused to consider the possibility of any other form.

Customs duties, would disappear, if the Commonwealth took over the debts of all the States, as the Dominion Government of Canada had done.

Mr. Clark, as he informed the Conference, was at this time a Free Trader, and, as such, appealed to Mr. Playford not to increase the difficulties in the way of Federation by delaying it until the South Australian tariff had become higher.   As a Free Trader, he resented the injury done to Tasmania by the Victorian tariff ;   but Federation would prevent a recurrence of this.   Then he declared himself upon the kind of Federation he desired :—

For my part I would prefer the lines of the American Union to those of the Dominion of Canada.   In fact I regard the Dominion of Canada as an instance of amalgamation rather than of Federation ;   and I am convinced that the different Australian Colonies do not want absolute amalgamation. What they want is Federation in the true sense of the word. . . . I believe that, if the American Union were now constituted on the lines of Canada, there would be far more danger, dissension, irritation and disunion than exists at present.

At the same time Mr. Clark thought that the Central Government ' might have some few more powers than are possessed by that of the United States ' ;   and he disagreed with Mr. Deakin's suggestion that the posts and telegraphs should be under local control.   He strongly supported the proposal to create a Federal Judiciary which should also be a Court of Appeal from the State Courts.   Then he pointed out the impracticability of advancing any further stage towards Federation by the agency of the Federal Council :—

If we take another step and attempt to add to the powers and increase the numbers of the members of the Federal Council, we shall immediately be faced with the problem of the taxing power. If you are going to increase that body, and to give it greater power and dignity and larger functions, you must inevitably give it a revenue and an executive ; and, if you are going to give it a revenue, you will immediately be met with the questions as to the proportion of the representation of the various Colonies. Are you prepared to give equal representation to all the Colonies in a single Legislature possessing taxing powers ? I am afraid the larger Colonies would object to this ; and if there is unequal representation with taxing power, it is likely that the smaller Colonies would think they stood in danger of being swamped and outvoted. The only solution of the problem is the adoption of the bi-cameral system. But, if it is once determined to go in for a bi-cameral Legislature with taxing power and an executive of its own, all other questions would be matters of such detail that they would not be worth while reserving. The partial measure of Federation, which some people talk about, has been already taken in the formation of the Federal Council. That is the full extent to which a partial Federation can practically go, and immediately you attempt to go further you must go the whole distance.

The concluding portion of Mr. Clark's speech was devoted to the support of Federation ' upon sentimental grounds,' and is of general interest on account of the light which it throws upon the much-abused word ' Nationalism ' :—

Perhaps [he said], I value the sentimental side of the question more than I do the practical side. . . . I remember very distinctly once reading an article in the *Princeton Review* by Professor E. A. Freeman, entitled ' The Sentimental and Practical in Politics,' and with that wealth of historical illustration which he has at his command, and which he uses so skilfully, he demonstrated—at least to my judgment—that what had been in the early stages of every political question derided and ridiculed as its sentimental aspect afterwards proved to be its real practical aspect. I believe it will be the

same with regard to Australian Federation.   After all, sentiment is more than one half of human life.   We are sometimes
asked what we mean by a nation and by national life.   I
believe a nation, as was stated by Sir Henry Parkes, is, first of
all, a sufficient aggregate of population. . . . But that population to be a nation must be localised.   It must be located
within certain physical limits, and must be responsive to all
the influences of its physical environments . . . There will
(thus) be produced a distinct type of life, and, in the case of
nations, a distinct type of national life.   I believe that the
physical environments of the French, the Italian, the Spaniard
and the English, combined with the inter-action of the units
composing those people upon one another, have produced the
several distinct types of manhood found in those countries.
In Australia we have a population which is encircled by definite
physical environment, with a climate, soil, and other physical
components peculiarly its own ; and human nature in Australia
is not going to be an exception to human nature all over the
other parts of the globe.   It will be influenced by its environment ; and it will, undoubtedly, in time produce its definite
national type in response to the environment. . . . But I
believe that the distinct type of national life, which is produced
by the causes I have attempted to describe, will never come
to perfect fruition, will never produce the best results without
political autonomy.   We are asking now for the political
autonomy of a United Australia, in order that that national
life, which we believe will exist under those conditions, may be
produced and may bear the best fruits.

   I believe this national life can exist without political independence, and without political autonomy, as a germ, or even
more than a germ.   But it will never be satisfied, it will never
do that which it ought to do, until it obtains political autonomy.

. 8 .

   Sir JAMES LEE STEERE, who followed Mr. Clark,
adopted Mr. Playford's hesitating tone.   He was critical
of the generality of Sir Henry Parkes' motion, 'which

was a kind of blank shot fired across our bows to make us show our colours.' As representative of a small State, he feared any Federation like that of Canada ; and he thought still that, if the members of the Federal Council were made elective, this body could do all that was desired.

Captain RUSSELL, who spoke for New Zealand, held out little hope of that Colony joining in a Federation with Australia :—

It has many interests in common with Australia, but it was probable that it could not at once submit itself to a Government in which it would have so unimportant a part. The native question, for instance, which was peculiar to New Zealand, could not be dealt with at present by a Federal Government. Still he was unwilling that the door should be closed upon New Zealand, and would like that Sir Henry Parkes' Resolution should be amended by the addition of words entitling the remote Australasian Colonies to admission to the Federation later upon terms to be agreed upon.

Dr. COCKBURN, who spoke for South Australia as its Premier, expressed the misgivings of his Colony with more diplomacy than Mr. Playford. As an uncompromising Protectionist he warned the Free Traders in the Conference against hugging the delusion that ' Federation would prove to be a vindication of the principles of Free Trade ! ' Rather it would be ' the institution of a more complete system of Protection— the apotheosis of a strong protective policy.' South Australia, for instance, had framed her tariff ' as a protective tariff and not at all in the spirit of raising revenue.' Therefore South Australia would ' want some little time ' before she joined the Federation which would expose her manufacturers to competition.

He, for his part, agreed with Sir James Lee Steere that Federation ought to be brought about slowly by a development of the Federal Council.

Perhaps the most valuable portion of Dr. Cockburn's speech was his historical account of the reasons which led to the establishment of the Canadian Dominion, from which he drew the conclusion that the facts which made centralisation desirable in Canada did not exist in Australia, and were of a kind to render that precedent undesirable for us to follow. Nor did he think we ought to copy slavishly the Constitution of the United States, because that was incompatible with the practice of Responsible Government.

This—which was only a reference by the way— was the first mention in the history of the Conference of that which was to prove one of the most difficult parts of the federal problem. Mr. Clark, by an inter-jection showed his slight appreciation of the British system ; but his views found no support.

Dr. Cockburn unkindly pointed out that

The very points on which the framers of the American Constitution prided themselves, those forms which they them-selves invented, are the very parts of their system of govern-ment which have proved to be failures ; while, on the contrary, those they adopted from England, which were the growth of centuries, have been found to be successful.

The speech was one of the most interesting in the debate, and well repays study ; but extracts cannot do justice to a close argument from history.

The third day's session was opened by Mr. Mc-Millan, who made a good debating speech in support of Sir Henry Parkes' Resolution. Recognising that it was too late in the discussion to make new suggestions, he gave a skilful summary of the speeches which had been made already, steadily keeping before the Conference his own view in favour of a complete Union, upon lines independent of the Federal Council. Later, he touched a note which was to sound above all others in the controversy of later years. Speaking of the necessity that each Colony should give and take, he said :—

No really great effort of patriotism was ever yet unattended with enormous sacrifices. I may say, without egoism, that the sacrifices made by New South Wales in this union of the Colonies will be greater than the sacrifices of any other Colony in the group. . . . We are now a Colony which could be, if we wished, independent of all the other Colonies. If we desired to impose heavy protective duties along our borders as against the outside world, we would be better able to carry out such a plan than any other Colony of the group. No other Colony could stand as we could stand.

Then, as was befitting a Colonial Treasurer, he dwelt upon the savings which might be effected by a consolidation of the State debts. He was not, however, in favour of the Central Government taking over the railways, which represented the greater part of the security for that indebtedness. The immediate and most important of the gains which he anticipated from a closer union was a strengthening of Australian defences. Yet even this was a detail, which would be discussed more appropriately in the Convention, which he was confident would follow upon this Conference.

Mr. McMillan was followed by another Treasurer, Mr. STAFFORD BIRD, of Tasmania. Like his colleague, Mr. A. I. Clark, he emphasised ' the strong feeling and deep interest which existed in Tasmania in favour

of Federation ; ' but, ' while wishing almost to forget
for the time that he was a Tasmanian, and to feel that
he was an Australian,' he could not conceal from the
Conference that Tasmania, small Colony as she was,
' had individual and sectional interests in connexion
with her producing and commercial pursuits, which, in
her measure and in proportion to her population, were
as great as those of any other Colony.'   Tasmania,
too, had suffered much from the Victorian tariff, yet
no ill-feeling need remain.   A Customs Union was
a *sine quâ non* of Federation.   He was not prepared
to agree that New South Wales would make the
greatest sacrifices ;   because he thought that those
Colonies which had the heaviest protective duties
would necessarily suffer most in loss of revenue by
the   establishment   of   inter-Colonial   Free   Trade.
Even if one Colony did lose more than another,
yet the advantages of Union to each would be well
worth even considerable sacrifice.   The increase in the
volume of commercial transactions would be one such
compensation.   In his view, the Federal Government
should aim at getting control of the Pacific—' the
New Hebrides, Fiji, and the rest of the islands which
are the natural adjuncts of an Australian Empire.'
For this reason he would regret that New Zealand
should stand out.   Like others, Mr. Bird would have
attained Federation through the Federal Council ;   and
still indulged the hope that New South Wales would
join that body, if its constitution were amended.

The speech of Sir JOHN HALL, who followed Mr.
Bird, is memorable chiefly by the phrase in which he
summed up the objections of New Zealand to unite
with the Australian Colonies :—

Nature has made 1200 impediments to the inclusion of New Zealand in any Australian Federation, in the 1200 miles of stormy ocean which lie between us and our brethren in Australia.

Still he did not give up hope that, at some later date, circumstances might render possible the adhesion of New Zealand.

· 9 ·

After Sir John Hall had ended, the Conference listened to what many have considered the best speech delivered during its Debates.

Mr. J. M. MACROSSAN, of Queensland, who followed Sir John Hall, was, during the few remaining years of his life—(he died in 1891, while the Convention of that year was in session)—the second figure in the federal movement next after Sir Henry Parkes. It is questionable, indeed, whether he did not overshadow Sir Henry Parkes at the Convention of 1891. Mr. Deakin once said of him, in conversation with the writer, that ' on the floor of the House he was almost Sir Henry's equal, while, in Committee, he was the superior.' For he joined to Sir Henry's enthusiasm and breadth of view a quick perception of detail, which the latter lacked, and a power of presenting details in an attractive form. He was, perhaps, the only member of the Conference who sympathised fully with Sir Henry Parkes, and was willing to go the whole length in the establishment of Federation. A summary of his speech will show both the extent and the precision of his view.

He began by approving the ' vagueness,' as it had been termed, of Sir Henry's Resolution, which, in his opinion showed a 'wise discretion,' because, 'if he had proposed a motion more precise and definite, we probably should never have arrived at a unanimous decision upon it.' Little had been left by other speakers for him to say, still he 'would advance some arguments which might have a bearing on the subject.' 'At the outset' he would declare his belief in Federation :—

I believe in Federation complete and simple. I believe we shall do no good in Australia until we have complete Federation.

In a few words he would state what he meant by 'complete Federation,' by enumerating some of the subjects which the Dominion of Canada could deal with exclusively :—

First, there is the public debt and the public property ; second, the regulation of trade and commerce ; third, the raising of money by any mode or system of taxation ; and fourth, the borrowing of money on the public credit ; next there was military and naval defence and service.

'The control of these matters,' he said, 'is indispensable to a complete Australian Federation.' Many other subjects of legislation might be spoken of. He would confine himself to those enumerated. First as to taking over the debts. He considered that the Commonwealth, by converting the State debts, could save in interest between one and two millions a year. The money to pay the interest could be raised by the Commonwealth by any form of taxation without loss to the States. Mr. Macrossan developed this argument at some length ; but, since the figures upon which he relied are out of date, the story is not advanced by extracts from this portion of his speech. Taking over the debts implied that the Commonwealth should take over the railways. The argument on this point is as apt to-day as when it was used first :—

If the Federal Government takes over, as it must, the whole of our debt, it will, of course, take over the property on which that debt has been contracted. This naturally follows in any matter of State business. Some objection may, perhaps, be raised in reference to the management of the railways by the federal authorities, who may not be so conversant with local wants and requirements as the present Governments. In order to meet that objection I would point out that in three of the Colonies I know of, and perhaps in the fourth, railway Commissioners have been appointed for the control and management of the various railways. All that the Federal Government will have to do, in a case of this kind, is to make the railway Commissioners federal officers, and the management will remain the same as at present. A system of this kind will have the advantage of still further removing the management of the railways from that political influence, the existence of which was the chief reason why Commissioners were first appointed.

Nor could the result be anything but advantageous :—

If the management of the railways is left entirely and solely under the control of the different local Governments, the same wars of tariffs will go on in the future as they have done in the past, . . . but, if we place the management under the control of a Federal Executive, we shall be relieved from any apprehension of a federal railway war, whilst the railways will be managed as well as they are now by people who will be as conversant with local requirements as they are at present.

It is scarcely to be doubted but that the time must come when both the public debt and the railways of Australia will be under the control of the Australian Government. Well indeed would it have been for Australia had Mr. Macrossan's views found favour with the Conventions of 1891 and 1897-8.

Mr. Macrossan would have gone even further ; and would have endowed the Commonwealth, certainly with the waste lands of the Continent, and probably with all the public lands. The United States had given the Federal Government full control of the public lands ; and no one could deny that they had been well managed. In Canada, on the other hand, the Dominion Parliament left the control to the local Parliaments. Which was the better system was a matter for discussion. Speaking, next, of the fears of the smaller Colonies lest the abolition of inter-State duties should disorganise their local finances, Mr. Macrossan pointed out that if this result should happen, which he questioned, the Commonwealth would have power to subsidise the injured Colony to whatever extent was necessary. This was done in the United States and in Canada. As to the fears of South Australia lest her industries should suffer by the competition of Victoria, he doubted if this would be the case. At any rate, ' although Victoria no doubt will have a slight advantage after the throwing down of the Customs barriers, she would not have that advantage very long.' And, since inter-Colonial Free Trade must follow Federation, South Australia could lay her account with that, in the knowledge that she would be protected from the competition of the outside world.

Next he spoke of some of the difficulties raised by other speakers, referring particularly to Sir Samuel Griffith :—

One of his objections is that the people of the different Colonies are not prepared to go the length that we, the delegates in this Conference, are prepared to go. . . . Now, sir, I believe that the people of these Colonies are far more ripe in the cause of Federation than some honourable gentlemen give them the credit of being. I thoroughly believe that, if the question were put to the Colonies to-morrow, as certain questions are sometimes put in Switzerland and in other countries under what is called the Referendum, the majority of the people of Australia would vote for Federation as against no Federation. And I believe also that they would give their votes intelligently, knowing what Federation meant, what sacrifices would have to be made by the local Legislatures ; knowing also that it would mean the establishment of a Federal Executive and Federal Parliament with which they would have very little or no intimate connexion. . . . Why should we, then, who believe so thoroughly in Federation, be afraid to raise the standard of Federation which we feel ought to be raised, but which seemingly we are too timid to raise for fear of offending the susceptibilities of timid, conservative people ?

Coming back to a discussion of the powers which he thought should be conferred upon the Federal Parliament he spoke of the waste lands of the Continent :—

We must, I think, give to the Federal Parliament the full control of the waste lands of the Crown. I have said before that I am in doubt whether I would give the Federal Parliament the control of all the Crown lands ; but there is a large amount of waste lands of the Crown, almost outside of civilisation, which I think the Federal Parliament should also have full control of ; and the Federal Parliament should also have the same control over the territorial jurisdiction of such outside parts as portions of Western Australia, and the Northern Territory, for the formation of new States.

He foresaw the danger to the Commonwealth from the large size of the Colonies ; and would have given power to the Central Government to divide them, as population increased. [Mr. Macrossan, it will be remembered, represented Northern Queensland, where there was a strong agitation for separation from Brisbane.]

I believe also that power should be given to the Federal Parliament—as it is given to the Imperial Parliament—to cut up, if it is thought necessary, the different existing Colonies of Australia and form them into smaller States.   I consider that the Colonies of Australia are too large for good government.

Speaking, next, of the constitution of the Federal Parliament, he advocated a bi-cameral system, with the Senate ' a representative body in some way representing the Colonies as separate sovereignties.' He would not give the Governor-General the power of vetoing legislation, which was possessed by him in Canada ; and he thought that the State Governors ' ought to be elected by the people of each Colony.' He denied that the difficulties in the way were as great as those in the United States or Canada. ' The only real difficulty we have is the fiscal one.'   There might be a difficulty, if members of the Conference were too timid ; therefore he recalled Washington's appeal to the Convention which framed the Constitution of the United States :—

' If to please the people we offer what we ourselves disapprove, how can we afterwards defend our work ?   Let us raise a standard to which the wise and honest can repair ; the event is in the hand of God.'

. 10 .

The next day—the fourth sitting of the Conference —Sir HENRY PARKES replied on the debate. The wrath of the gods was in his heart ! He had been charged with insincerity and disloyalty by Mr. Playford ; and Sir James Lee Steere had questioned his conduct ! The scene lived long in the memory of all who witnessed it :—How the old man ' savaged ' Mr. Playford and heaped ridicule upon Sir James Lee Steere ! But no good purpose can be served now by transcribing the angry words. Enough that, as the provocation, so was the chastisement ! Nor is this the place to re-state Sir Henry Parkes' account of his change of opinion with regard to the utility of the Federal Council. The change was patent. Those who wish to see an improper motive will not be convinced of the opposite by more asseveration.

The most interesting new matter in the speech was the reading of a hitherto unpublished letter from Professor Lecky, expressing an opinion with reference to the revolt of the American Colonies, with which few will disagree, and yet few will take to heart.

The historian of the eighteenth century, writing to Sir Henry Parkes, pointed out that, if the British Colonies in America had been federated, in all probability they would have remained in the Empire :—

The taxing policy of Grenville which caused the revolt was adopted [he wrote] only from the wish that these Colonies should have an army for their own protection ; but there was then no single body which could represent them all, and it was the extreme difficulty of obtaining the concurrence of a great number of separate Legislatures that induced him to adopt his fatal plan of taxing them by means of the British

Parliament. If America had been constituted as Australia would be upon your plan, no difficulty would have arisen, and it is totally certain that British taxation would never have been proposed.

Sir Henry Parkes then forecast the future of the Empire in words, which are memorable as one of the earliest recognitions that national equality is the only basis of Imperial unity[1] :—

My whole being trembles with an unuttered prayer that the whole of the British possessions may remain for ever forming parts of one beneficent Empire, such as the world has never seen. I can see no permanent obstacle to such a consummation. I see no reason, why the Australians should not become a Federal Dominion—a result, which we are all, I hope, trying to bring about. The North American Colonies will, I think, become more completely a Federal Dominion by some reform of their present constitution. Our South African possessions may with great care—and great care will be necessary—become also a cluster of States ; and I can see no reason on earth why this comparatively great independent congeries of States should not unite with the Mother Country in forming an Empire such as has never yet been formed, which would carry our language, our laws, our social habits, our literature, our great stores of science to all parts of the habitable globe. My prayer is that wise counsels and unforeseen beneficent influences may bring this about. But it may be otherwise ; it may be, as many respectable and reputable citizens dream, that we shall form a nation by ourselves. But, whatever is the future destiny of Australia—whether it is the grand destiny of forming part of this new Empire that ought to rule in the interests of peace the whole world, or whether it becomes a separate nationality—what we are attempting to do now is commended by wisdom, commended by foresight, commended

[1] The writer had expressed a similar view in an article which appeared in *Macmillan's Magazine* in 1885.

by every principle of national morals, and will be equally beneficial to the people whatever course events may take.

This reference to the possible alternative of independence has a strange sound to modern ears. But it must be remembered that, in 1890, Mr. Chamberlain had not directed the Colonial Office; nor had the essential unity of the Empire been revealed by the South African War, which is the British parallel to the War of Secession in the United States. The concept of *imperium et libertas* was beginning to inspire some men of ' light and leading ' ; but the separatist doctrines of the Manchester school still dominated British thought. Only six years earlier (1885) Lord Blachford, who, as Mr. Frederic Rogers (' the man Rogers ' of Chief Justice Higginbotham's sarcasm) had been the real ruler of the Empire from his Under-Secretary's chair,[1] had written a survey of his political life in which occurs the following passage :—

I had always believed—and this belief has so confirmed and consolidated itself that I can hardly realise the possibility of any one seriously thinking the contrary—that the destiny of our Colonies is independence, and that in this point of view the function of the Colonial Office is to secure that our connexion, while it lasts, shall be as profitable to both parties, and our separation, when it comes, as amicable as possible.[2]

Compare with this Cobden's ideal, as expressed in a letter to his brother in 1842 :—

The Colonial system, with all its dazzling appeals to the passions of the people, can never be got rid of except by the

---

[1] He resigned his position as Permanent Under-Secretary for the Colonies in 1871 ; but continued, as Lord Blachford, to exercise considerable influence in Imperial matters.

[2] *Letters of Lord Blachford* (John Murray, 1896), at pp. 299-300.

indirect process of Free Trade, which will gradually and imperceptibly loosen the bands which unite our Colonies to us by a mistaken notion of self-interest !

Fortunate, indeed, it has been that Englishmen, outside of England, have never lost faith in their Imperial destiny !

Sir Henry Parkes' speech might have ended with this confession of faith ; but he had still to defend his Colony against the charge of lukewarmness, and renew his assurance that, Free Trader as he was, he would even risk that policy for the sake of Union.

After this speech Mr. GILLIES, as President, tried to heal the breach between Sir Henry Parkes and Mr. Playford ; and again defended the Federal Council, through which, in his opinion, Federation could be obtained most easily, provided that New South Wales would become a member. The speech was not otherwise notable.

Mr. Playford added a few words of protest against Sir Henry's attack, and the Resolution was carried with the substitution of the words ' Australian ' and ' Australia,' for ' Australasian ' and ' Australasia.'

Captain Russell then moved ' as a corollary ' :—

That to the union of the Australian Colonies, contemplated by the foregoing Resolution, the remoter Australasian Colonies shall be entitled to admission at such times and on such conditions as may be hereafter agreed upon.

And this was carried without dissent.

The Resolution that :—

Members of the Conference shall take such steps as may be necessary to induce the Legislatures of their respective Colonies to appoint delegates to a National Australasian Convention, empowered to consider and report upon an adequate scheme for a Federal Constitution.

was moved by Mr. Deakin, whose speech was devoted to a useful explanation of the purpose and working of a constituent Convention, which, although in general use in the United States, was a novelty, at this time, in Australia.

A discussion followed as to the time and place of meeting. Finally, it was agreed to leave the place of meeting to be settled later, and to add to Mr. Deakin's Resolution that the Convention should meet ' during the present year.' The number of representatives for each Colony was fixed at seven. Before the Conference closed Mr. Deakin made a last effort to extend the powers of the Federal Council. His motion was in these terms :—

That, as some time must elapse before a Federal Constitution can be adopted, and as it is desirable that the Colonies should at once take united action to provide for military defence, and for effective co-operation in other matters of common concern, it is advisable that the Federal Council should be employed for such purposes so far as its powers will permit, and with such extension of its powers as may be decided upon, and that all the Colonies should be represented on the Council.

In face of the opposition of Mr. McMillan and Sir Henry Parkes this motion was not pressed to a division. Sir Henry Parkes stated his own position very effectively :—

If honourable members accepted my explanation that I had convinced myself, before I was called upon to take any step in consequence of the Convention of 1883, that the Federal Council scheme, instead of being a promoter of Federation, would be a stumbling block in the way of Federation, I don't see how it can possibly be expected that I, as an individual, could consent to urge New South Wales to enter the Federal Council now.

The Conference closed by the adoption of an Address to the Queen, expressive of loyalty.

CHAPTER VI

THE MELBOURNE CONFERENCE AND PUBLIC OPINION

THE speeches at this Conference have been summarised with considerable fulness, not only because they are the first memorable public utterances in the history of the movement initiated by Sir Henry Parkes ; but also because, from their intrinsic merit, they deserve a better fate than burial in a Blue Book. A reader must be struck by the anticipation of all the points, which became the subject of controversy in later years. On the one side are ranged Sir Henry Parkes and Mr. Macrossan, representing the whole-hearted Federalists, —those who were called later ' the Federalists at any price '—and advocating the subordination of the local Legislatures to a strong Central Government. On the other side were Mr. A. I. Clark and Mr. Playford, representing the extreme State Righters, who looked for national development through the friendly rivalries of independent Legislatures, and would have confined the powers of the Central Government within the narrowest limits. Between these two extremes stood those who, like Sir Samuel Griffith, were doubtful of the possibility of Union, but were prepared to accept it on such terms as the States might agree upon, provided that the power of the States were not curtailed too much. This diversity of aim and temperament is apparent in every point of difference.

. I .

First, was the time ripe for Union ? Should there be delay, until the people of Australia understood the question better, and until the States were on the same level of industrial development ?   Or was it true, as Sir Henry Parkes insisted, that it would never be more easy to federate than at the present time, and that the obstacles would grow larger by delay ?

Secondly, what form should the Union take ? Should there be a central elective Legislature ; or should they hasten slowly, and enlarge the powers of the Federal Council ?

Thirdly, if the Federal Council should be superseded, what powers should be entrusted to the Central Government ?   Should it be confined to doing those things which the Colonies could not do, while separated, such as making provision for defence and external affairs, or should it have general legislative authority over all matters of common interest ?

Fourthly, how were these powers to be defined ? Should they be granted specifically, and by way of limitation, to the Central Legislature, as in the United States ; or should the Canadian example be followed, in which the powers of the State Legislatures were enumerated, and the undefined residue given to the Parliament of the Dominion ?

Fifthly, there was the question of finance, which by general consent was the crux of any arrangement ! Should unlimited power of taxation be conferred on the Central Government ; or should each State be permitted to adopt its own tariff ?

Sixthly, if it were conceded that there should be a common tariff, how was the loss of revenue from duties on inter-State goods to be made up to the several States ? Should this be by grants in aid ; or should the Central Government be given power to relieve the States by taking over their debts ? And, in that case, should the railways and public lands, which were a security for the State debts, pass also to the Federal Government ?

Seventhly, could any Colony afford to surrender any portion of its taxing power without guarantees against loss ? Yet, if this were made a condition precedent to any Colony agreeing to the Union, and if each Colony insisted upon its own terms, there could be no Union !

Finally, what was to be the constitution of the new Parliament ? If there were to be equal representation of the States in the Senate, what powers ought that Chamber to have over finance ? How, too, would it be possible to work Responsible Government, when each of the two Houses of Parliament had equal power ? Was it possible to frame a Constitution which at the same time would recognise the equality of the States and secure the larger States against being ruled by a minority of voters in other parts of the Continent ?

. 2 .

Such difficulties, considered separately, appeared insuperable ; but the discussion of them all together had shown that differences of opinion might be softened almost into unanimity under the influence of a common aim. The Conference of 1890 served its purpose. It educated its members and helped to educate the people in a matter imperfectly understood. It pointed

H

the way to action and gave the signal for advance. Yet, at the time, it seemed to have exercised little influence upon opinion ; because no attempt was made to circulate a report of its proceedings, and newspaper reports of speeches are difficult to follow and soon forgotten. Those, however, who looked beneath the surface, saw that the federal movement had made a great step forward, and that things could never be again, as they were before the Conference met. Sir John Robertson was among these men of clearer vision ; and he set himself at once to criticise and oppose. In a characteristic letter to the Press (February 17, 1890) he denounced a contemplated attack upon the territory and liberties of New South Wales :—

Cannot a blind baby [he wrote] predict that in the event of the boundary between us and Queensland, between us and South Australia, between us and Victoria, coming under vote, we shall assuredly go to the wall ! And so with every liberty and right which we possess. At present we are the freest country in the world. Let us keep so. The only excuse put forward for our self-abasement is that a travelling soldier said that our army (save the mark !) would be more under control and that we might require *assistance* from Victoria and South Australia ! As if in time of war they would not have more than enough to do to protect their own shores ! . . . If necessary let us add to our fleet. . . . Does Sir Henry Parkes forget that we already belong to the greatest and most beneficent Federation the world has ever seen—the Federation of the British Empire ? Talk about the ' birth of a nation ' was high-flown nonsense ! . . . What has all this talk about the United States to do with New South Wales ? Is George III going to be King and Lord North his Minister ? If so, federate with the Evil One if you will, or with anyone ! But Queen Victoria is our Queen and Sovereign, and Ministers and the people of England have been our most loving friends. Why, then, are we called upon to ignore them ?

But, while attacking in this way Sir Henry Parkes' proposals, Sir John Robertson would not listen to any disparagement of his old rival and colleague,—' the loyalest colleague man could ever have ' he once described him to the writer,—although he might regret that he should ' run away with the bit in his teeth at times.'

Our neighbours [he wrote] may affect to laugh at the great speeches delivered by our chief, but there is not another man in Australia who could approach them for ability or for the amount of information they contain. I recommend our young men to preserve the report of them for reference.

Next day, however, his indignation forced him to a less complimentary outburst. He had read the passage in Sir Henry Parkes' reply, in which he claimed to speak for the whole of New South Wales in advocatng Federation ; and this was too much for his old friend. After repudiating Sir Henry's right to make this claim, he questioned the latter's motives :—

Doubtless [he wrote on February 18], the question of Free Trade and Protection should be fought out fairly and honestly, fought out as of yore. But surely it is not right to drag a herring across the line, as is being done by this accursed Federation, which will endanger every interest and be of no use but to swell the importance of one man ?

It is necessary to repeat that, if we would understand the story of the fight for Union, we must recognise that these views and this language, now so strange to us, reflected accurately the sentiments and taste of a very considerable section of New South Wales opinion, which grew stronger, as the fight progressed, under the encouragement of Mr. Want and Mr. Reid.

· 3 ·

After the Conference, interest in the movement appeared to subside. Sir John Robertson's letters aroused no controversy; and Federation was pronounced by his friends to be ' as dead as Julius Cæsar.' An attempt was made, on the suggestion of Mr. Wise,[1] to establish a periodical for a scientific discussion of federal problems; and an editorial committee was formed in Sydney, of which the members were Mr. Justice Windeyer, Mr. Barton, Professor Pitt Cobbett, Mr. O'Connor, Mr. W. P. Cullen, Mr. Henry Gullett (who had been recently sub-editor of the *Daily Telegraph*), Mr. J. W. Hill and Mr. Robert Thompson (two of the many private persons who rendered service to the federal cause without reward or fame), Mr. Alex. Oliver (parliamentary draughtsman), Mr. J. P. Garvan, Sir Joseph Abbott, and Mr. Wise.

A circular letter was written on behalf of this Committee (July 9, 1890) to leading men in the other Colonies explaining the proposal, from which a few passages may be cited:—

It is proposed to establish a monthly periodical under the title of the *Australian Federalist*, which should be open to persons of all parties, and be devoted exclusively to a detailed scientific criticism of those aspects of Federation which do not readily lend themselves to popular discussion. It is hoped by this means to bring together in a connected and permanent form a mass of information and criticism that may be

---

[1] *Sydney Morning Herald*, May 24, 1890.

of considerable service to all those, who will be called upon hereafter to explain in detail to the voters of Australasia, whether in Parliament or through the Press, the precise nature of the issues upon which the votes of the people must finally be cast. . . . It is the intention of the editorial committee to select beforehand the subject for discussion in each month's number; and they will invite contributions upon it from all persons who are interested in the movement towards Australian unity. The first number will be devoted to a critical comparison of the Constitutions of the United States and Canada. In the second, it is proposed to invite a historical and critical discussion of types of Confederate and Federal Unions. Among other subjects which will be from time to time discussed may be mentioned :—

The comparative merits of the American and Canadian systems of Federation.

The advantages or disadvantages of creating a Federal Capital.

The unity or separation of the Executive and Legislative departments.

The admission of new States.

The provisional government of unsettled territory.

The sources of federal revenue.

The nature of an ultimate controlling authority in the event of disputes between the Federation and the States.

The constitution and the functions of a Supreme Court.

The apportionment of the public debts of the States.

The joint control of railways and other public assets.

The comparative merits of the uni-cameral or bi-cameral system of legislation.

The possibility of adopting the principle of the Referendum.

Although this project was taken up warmly by such leading Federalists as Mr. Deakin, Sir Samuel Way, and Sir Samuel Griffith—the latter opining that ' the great difficulty will be in New South Wales, where such

articles would do great good,'—only two numbers of
the *Australian Federalist* appeared—the first on January
26, 1891, and the other on March 2.[1] There were not
enough men of leisure in the community who possessed
the requisite knowledge ; while the general public,
as Sir Samuel Griffith wrote, 'wanted to know,—as
unfortunately they do in most cases—what money is
there in it, and beyond that it was of no interest to
a majority.' Nevertheless, the project is worth re-
calling as evidence of a very clear appreciation of the
nature of the federal problems ; and, although it failed,
others, later, took up the work. Mr. W. P. Cullen, now
Chief Justice of New South Wales, published a critical
examination of the Swiss, American and Canadian
Constitutions ; Mr. Wise analysed in parallel columns
the American and Canadian Constitutions, and Mr. Just,
on the order of the Tasmanian Government, published
a useful account of the earlier movements towards
Australian Federation under the title ' Leading Facts
about Federation.'

The battle was to be fought, however, not in the
study, but at the polling booths.

[1] This periodical must not be confused with a weekly newspaper
of the same name which appeared in 1897. This latter was a commercial
venture, brought into existence at the time of the first Referendum to
advocate the views of the supporters of the Convention Bill. It is
invaluable to the historian as a record of speeches and contains many
extracts from the country press. It continued in existence for about
two months.

CHAPTER VII

CONSTITUTING THE CONVENTION

THE debate upon the Resolutions, by which Sir Henry Parkes invited the concurrence of Parliament (May 7, 1890) with the recommendation of the Conference to hold a National Convention, reflected accurately the cross-currents of opinion, which have been described in earlier Chapters.[1] The extreme party men on both sides were dubious or hostile,—the Protectionists from a fear lest their triumph should be deferred, the Free Traders lest their cause should lose. The Republican sentiment was expressed by Mr. Dibbs and Mr. Traill, who at that time was connected with *The Bulletin*, both of whom hailed Federation as a step towards separation from Great Britain. Sir Henry Parkes and his two Ministers, Messrs. McMillan and Bruce-Smith, spoke as the whole-hearted advocates of an Australian Parliament, with full powers over finance and tariffs; but only two Free Traders (Messrs. Frank Smith and Vivian) were prepared to go so far. Mr. J. H. Want and Mr. Crick voiced the provincial opposition to Union in any form; and Mr. G. H. Reid was friendly in profession, but hostile in argument and action. The speeches, however, were very inferior to those at the Conference; and few of them have any value, except as a record of contemporary opinion.

[1] See *ante*, Chapters II and III.

The question was too large for those who were unfamiliar with constitutional problems, and whose outlook was confined within the limits of their own Colony. The very qualities, which fitted members for the party politics of a province, were hindrances to an impartial discussion of Federation ; and it is a tribute to the power of the federal sentiment that, under such conditions, so strong an effort was made to keep the question out of party politics.

. I .

Sir Henry Parkes' speech—although he writes of it himself with complacency : ' My speech in support was received with much approbation '[1]—contained little that was new and was marred in tone by the personal note, which was introduced by his omission of Mr. Dibbs from the list of proposed delegates, ' for the plain reason ' (as he has explained)[2] ' that Mr. Dibbs had recently declared himself in the broadest terms hostile . . . . so that it never occurred to me that he would or could consent to sit in a Convention to promote the Union of the Colonies.' The reason may be ' plain ' ; but it is allowable to those, who knew Sir Henry Parkes, to see a spice of mischief in his action, without attributing to him anything out of harmony with his character ! Certainly it would have been magnanimous to pay a compliment to an opponent ; and Sir George Dibbs was a gallant figure at all times.[3]

Speaking next after Sir Henry Parkes, although

[1] *Fifty Years in the Making of Australian History,* vol. ii. p. 276.
[2] *Ibid.* vol. ii. p. 277.
[3] A very characteristic letter from Sir George Dibbs to Lady Dorothy Nevill has been published by her in *Under Five Reigns,* p. 234.

smarting under his ungenerous treatment, he denied
any hostility to Federation ; but made it plain
that this opinion must be taken *sub modo*. The
Federation Mr. Dibbs desired was ' a federation of
everything in common, under which our boundaries
would be removed and the questions of railways,
lands, education and every form of law would become
common to the whole country,'—in short, not Federation but Unification ! And this single government of
Australia was not to be ' under the Crown ' but
independent ! It does no injustice to the memory
of Sir George Dibbs to point out that these ideas
were crude. He was an administrator rather than a
constitutionalist ; and his mind was not systematic.
If he had ever considered the problems of Federation,
which may be doubted, his was a temperament to cut
the knots instead of unravelling them. At bottom
he sympathised with Sir John Robertson, and shared
the provincial prejudices of the old Colonialism ;
so that, although his inclination would be for strong
government, his advocacy of an impracticable Unification was regarded, at the time, as evidence, rather of a
dislike of union, than of a desire to make it closer.
Later, in 1894, he elaborated a detailed scheme of
Unification, which will be mentioned in its place.

Even Mr. Want, who followed, criticised Federation
rather as a Free Trader than as a provincialist. ' I
am certain that you cannot play more completely
into the hands of the Protectionists of this Colony
than by bringing about Federation.'

He was careful, however, not to declare himself
explicitly against Federation ; although his arguments
led to no other conclusion :—

New South Wales has everything to lose and nothing to gain. . . . South Australia will get Broken Hill and our silver mines. Victoria will get Riverina. Queensland will take our sugar lands, and we shall be left with a ridge of mountains and nothing else to govern.

Two members, representing border constituencies, the one adjoining Victoria, the other Queensland, Mr. R. B. Wilkinson and Mr. Thomas Ewing, although they held opposite views upon the fiscal question, agreed in a vigorous protest against these provincial sentiments. The speech of Mr. Ewing was a particularly powerful and eloquent appeal to the members of his own party not to place themselves in opposition to the national sentiment in order to gain a temporary political advantage :—

I have no fear [he said] of Australia's death from natural causes ; but I have great fear for her future, when I find so many, who hold high political positions, telling us that we are too good to federate with our Australian brothers ; when I find them so sceptical of the good and genuine intentions of the other Colonies of Australia. That is when I see the evidence of that egoism and scepticism which must eventually destroy any people.

He concluded with a fine reference to the great explorers who had crossed mountains, rivers and deserts, in order to widen the confines of Australia, and whose work was thwarted by the perpetuation of the boundaries of rival Colonies.

The perverted view of Nationalism, which, influenced by the separatist doctrines of English Liberalism, saw no future for Australia save in independence, was expressed by Mr. Alexander Brown and Mr. Copeland, two personal friends of Mr. Dibbs. This view gave place so soon to a truer conception of nationality within the Empire that it is sufficient here merely to note its existence.

. 2 .

Whilst the debate was in progress, Sir Henry Parkes met with a serious accident, which proved to have disastrous consequences to the success of the federal movement. On Sunday, May 18, he was thrown out of a runaway cab, and broke his right leg. He was within a few days of his seventy-sixth birthday, and never recovered entirely from this shock : ' I never recovered,' he writes,[1] ' the buoyancy of life, which I had enjoyed up to the unfortunate hour of this occurrence.' His enforced absence from Parliament led to difficulties with his colleagues, which have been described by himself in his political biography,[2] and left the Federal party without a leader at a critical time. When he returned to Parliament four months later, he seemed to lack the nerve to deal effectively with an accumulation of difficulties ; and, at the end of the following year, his weakened health became a welcome excuse for a retirement from public life, which unexpectedly brought Federation to a standstill. Allowing for the obstacles of the Maritime Strike in 1890 and the suspicions of the Labour Party during 1891–3, it is probable that, but for this accident, Federation would have been accomplished seven years earlier. Still, it may be that delay was inevitable ; and that the men had not yet been fashioned, who could be the instruments of a great movement.

[1] *Fifty Years in the Making of Australian History*, vol. ii. p. 283.
[2] *Ibid.* vol. ii. pp. 280–6.

· 3 ·

The debate continued in a desultory fashion and with repeated adjournments during Sir Henry Parkes' absence ; but the only speech which deserves attention is that of Mr. Reid, because it is the first pronouncement on the question of Federation of a man who, in the years which followed, was regarded by one section of the public as its real father and by another as its arch-enemy ; and who, in either view, became a conspicuous figure in the movement.

Brought up in Sydney, when Sydney was a very small place, and now in his forty-fifth year, Mr. Reid's admirable social qualities had gained him popularity in every circle. Beginning as a clerk in the Treasury and at the age of thirty-five admitted to the Bar, he had entered Parliament as one of the ' new men ' [1] in 1880, having gained a medal from the Cobden Club for an essay in defence of Free Trade ; but, although he had held office as Minister of Public Instruction under Sir Alexander Stuart (1883-5), he was not yet (1890) regarded as a serious politician. His indifference to party was notorious, and his attendance in Parliament irregular. Except during his tenure of office, it had been his habit to leave the Chamber, after making a prepared speech, at an hour which would ensure a report in next morning's papers ; and no one, at this time, suspected that underneath a mask of genial banter was concealed a Scotch tenacity of purpose. Free Trade seemed to be his only settled political

[1] See *ante*, p. 32. Readers must bear in mind that this work aims at reproducing contemporary opinion, and not at estimating judicially the actions of the rival leaders, which almost certainly were misjudged in the heat of party conflict. Thus, the writer must not be supposed to be passing judgment upon Mr. Reid, or Mr. Barton, because he states the facts which caused the struggle to centre finally in the rivalry between them.

conviction. Yet, even his belief in Free Trade was subordinate to his dislike of Sir Henry Parkes, who had slighted him in the Treasury, and against whom he felt a generous indignation, because of an injury which he believed him to have inflicted upon one of his friends. Thus, Free Trader as he was, in 1887 he had moved a vote of censure against Sir Henry Parkes for putting Free Trade before Local Government ; [1] and now (June 1890) he was to censure the same leader for putting Federation before Free Trade ! Yet his speech, critical as it was of Sir Henry Parkes' proposals, did not condemn the federal principle ; although his criticisms were so pungent that the protestations of sympathy seemed out of place. His opposition probably was the natural impulse of a man of his temperament and surroundings ; but it is impossible to forget that, if Sir Henry Parkes had failed to carry his proposals, the succession to his leadership would have been open ; and that Mr. Barton, who was always Mr. Reid's rival, had declared himself unequivocally upon the other side.

The terms of his speech will be the best explanation of these comments.

His first words were by way of caution and warning. The burden of proof, he contended, lay upon the Federalists, 'who wished to change the current of their national growth, to discard their existing con- stitutions, to turn their back upon experience, upon actual prosperity, and to engage in irrevocable political experiments.'

---

[1] Namely, by proposing as the first business of that session the removal of the Dibbs-Jennings *ad valorem* duties, which had been denounced throughout the country by Mr. Reid and others as ' a sneaking in of Protection.'

He proceeded, then, to trace the history of the movement, declaring that the impulse towards it was 'not an impulse of brotherly love. Not that sort of outpouring of fraternal affection which might bring brothers together. It was the old story—"At the heart of this movement is the military spirit."' The same impulse (he admitted) had brought about the federation of the United States and of Canada. Still, 'whilst they must not disregard military questions, whilst they must remember the danger to which they were exposed, they were not called upon, thank Heaven, to legislate in a panic.' For instance, so long as Australia remained under the flag of England there was no risk that 'we should be exposed to serious dangers from naval attack. China was our only possible enemy by land,' and our Chinese legislation showed that 'we feel strong enough to defy the powers of China.' Therefore he concluded :—

Let us forget all about the Chinese ; let us think of Australia ; let us think of our own interests.

At present they were in

the oratorical and rhetorical stage of the movement when people were moved early to applause. Soon they must come to business ; and, then, the Australians would be found to be the keenest, 'cutest and most difficult men in the world to deal with.

Referring to the recent Conference, he regretted that its members

mistook so much eloquence for information . . . and showed a disposition to suppress a consideration of the difficulties in the way . . . .The average man, the ordinary man, travels slowly towards ideals. He cannot jump at conclusions. When you talk to him about precipitating us into a nation, his shrewd common sense tells him that you are pretty much telling him to take a leap in the dark. It is the fashionable way of inviting you to shut your eyes and open your mouth and you will get something very nice.

Mr. Reid, next, quoted from speeches at the Conference ' as showing some of the views of some of the ablest leaders of public opinion.' ' Sir Samuel Griffith,' for instance, had urged that the Federal Government should manage ' the public debt and property ; the regulation of trade and commerce ; the raising of money by taxation ; and the borrowing of money upon public credit.' On these points he expressed no opinion of his own, remarking merely ' these are some of the knotty points of this question.' Quoting next from Mr. Deakin's speech, he described the Victorian leader as ' talking business,' and the Victorians as ' the best, keenest diplomatists in the Australian colonies, who had always been too clever for New South Wales.' Mr. Macrossan's remarks at the Melbourne Conference[1] aroused his indignation :—

I want to know what is left for us if his scheme is carried out. All our revenue will be gone ; all our railways will be gone ; all our lands will be gone ; and then we shall be a nation !

Returning to the substance of the Resolutions, he thought that ' they ought to know what is to be the scope of the legislative powers of the Federal Parliament, and whether it was to be constituted on Canadian or American lines.' After explaining the difference between these two forms of union he declared :—

[1] See *ante*, pp. 83–88.

I have no hesitation in saying that I will never be a party to any Constitution which is framed on Canadian lines.

but added, as if with prescience :—

Perhaps I should not say that I shall never be a party to it, because in the course of time you do not know what changes may take place.   This is a world of change.[1]

His next expression of opinion was :—

I will be no party to the adoption of any form of Constitution whatever which will interfere with the Constitution of this country without a direct appeal to the people.

Therefore, he thought that any Convention Bill ought to be submitted to Parliament, not for its ‘approval’ but for its ‘consideration.’   And that, then, the opinion of the people should be tested at a General Election, when

If the Constitution as a whole was thought advisable to adopt, the Government would succeed in their appeal to the people.

Next, Mr. Reid examined the subjects ‘which would come within the scope of the Federal Parliament.’ The first was defence.   So far as naval defence was concerned he would rely upon the British Navy, and although Federation might strengthen the military defences of Australia, yet it should not be forgotten that ‘even after Federation each Colony would want to keep its own soldiers within its own boundaries.’

Finance seemed to him an insoluble problem.   Unless the Federal Government took over the State debts there would be ‘a financial crisis in every Colony’; and the railways would have to go with the debts.   But no one would be inclined to hand over

[1] See *post*, p. 275, footnote.

the railways. The site of the Capital was another difficulty ; unless Parliament met in the several capitals in rotation.

The 'most important question' was that of a uniform tariff. Mr. Reid's language on this subject is familiar to modern ears ; for, in Australia in 1890, as in Great Britain to-day, the belief in Free Trade was the real obstacle to Union. Mr. Reid was unwilling to support any Federation 'which would drag New South Wales into the mire of Protection'; and he would never federate 'until he had a better and more rational idea that his principles would not be sacrificed. He believed too strongly in freedom to hand over the destinies of his Colony to men who would fetter its people and injure its commerce. And even if he stood alone, he would oppose the scheme; because "only a madman" could believe that Free Trade would continue under Federation.'

The conclusion of this remarkable speech was an advice 'to hasten slowly to put an end to the independence of New South Wales.'

It was not easy for Federalists to regard the maker of this speech as being on their side. If words had any meaning, it was a declaration of a determination to put provincial Free Trade before Australian Unity, and it breathed in every sentence mistrust of the other Colonies.[1]

The debate occupied fourteen sittings, and the Resolutions were carried on September 10 with the substitution of Mr. Dibbs for Mr. Garvan as one of the delegates.

[1] For Mr. Reid's own explanation of his position at this time see *post*, pp. 271–2, and pp. 319–20.

· 4 ·

The brunt of the debate in the Legislative Council, which was the citadel of the old Colonists, was borne by Messrs. Barton and O'Connor, and Dr. Garran. Their opponents harped on variations of the same theme—the danger and ignominy of giving to the other Colonies a voice in the direction of the affairs of New South Wales. The appeal was both to prejudice and self-interest. The policy of New South Wales, for many years, had been to concentrate the trade of the Colony in Sydney ; and the railway system was organised to this end. Preferential rates in favour of Sydney drew the produce of the interior past other ports or towns, which might have become competing centres of commerce under other conditions ; and unprofitable railways were driven into the border districts, in order that cheap carriage might counteract the tendency of their trade to seek an outlet in Victoria, South Australia, or Queensland, which, geographically, were their natural markets. Clearly, Federation was a menace to this centralising and unfriendly policy. The freedom of intercourse, which was a postulate of Union in any form, meant, not only the removal of customs barriers, but that the State railways should be used no longer as weapons in a commercial war. Those, who thus championed Sydney against Australia, became known, at a later date, as ' Prudent Federalists.' Their leader was the Hon. Louis Heydon, a Sydney solicitor in large practice, and the title was assumed for the first time in this debate. ' This House,' he said, ' ought to be more *prudent* and less dominated by ideas and enthusiasm than the other House ' ; and the reason for the necessity for *prudence* was expressed, quite bluntly, to be the fear of a reversal of the

policy of aggrandising Sydney :—' If we break down
the barrier between us and the other Colonies we
shall lose territory and the trade of territory to them.'
Victoria, South Australia, and Queensland all had
a grievance against the railway policy of New South
Wales :—

Was it then ' prudent ' for a rich man [New South Wales]
to go into partnership with three plaintiffs in a big action
against him. .... The majority will settle what is to be done ;
and of course they will help one another at our expense.

To men of this school it was all-important that
Sydney should be the titular capital of any Federation ;
and no appeal to a larger patriotism would induce them
to forgo that demand :—

A small piece of vanity is appealed to [said Mr. Heydon
in this connection] in order that the ruin of Sydney and the
loss of autonomy by this great Colony may be smoothed over.

Although the debate extended over ten sittings
the discussion was half-hearted. Mr. Barton had
pointed out that the question before the House was not
as to the terms of a Constitution, but merely as to the
appointment of delegates to a Convention ; and that
the occasion for debating the Constitution would come
later. Mr. Barton's speech was noteworthy for a
pronouncement, (which Mr. O'Connor had made also),
that he preferred the United States form of Federation
to that of Canada, and would not support a Constitution
on the lines of the latter. The delegates to the Convention were chosen by ballot,—Mr. Barton, Sir
Patrick Jennings, and Mr. W. H. Suttor, who represented the Government in the Chamber.

Everything was now ready for the meeting of the
National Convention.

CHAPTER VIII

THE CONVENTION OF 1891

THE first National Australasian Convention met in Sydney on March 2, 1891, ' empowered to consider and report upon an adequate scheme for a Federal Constitution.' The delegates had been chosen in each Colony from either side of the House, and all were men of high position in public life.

It was beyond all dispute [1] the most august assembly which Australia had ever seen. The majority of its members were men who yielded to none of their compatriots in their fitness to do the work which had to be done. They had all risen to positions of eminence in their respective countries, by their own merits and force of character, without any of the aids of fortune ; and their number included all the Prime Ministers of Australia and nine others, including Sir George Grey, Mr. Gillies, and Sir Thomas McIlwraith, who had held the office of Prime Minister in former Governments. They had been elected by all the Parliaments of the Colonies, and therefore, in a constitutional sense, they represented all the people of Australia. 'It is difficult,' writes Sir Henry Parkes, ' to see what democracy could desire, if this was not a democratic gathering.' And yet, as will be seen, this body, for reasons which

[1] See *Fifty Years in the Making of Australian History*, vol. ii., p. 366.

Sir Henry Parkes did not appreciate, was out of touch with popular sentiment.

. I .

The official banquet, which, in those days, was an inevitable incident of all political gatherings, took place in the Town Hall on the evening of March 1, and is memorable for the title of the Toast, proposed by Sir Henry Parkes—' One People, One Destiny '—which became later the motto of the Federal party. In his speech Sir Henry Parkes broke no new ground, but was content to re-state the arguments in favour of immediate Union with his accustomed vigour and enthusiasm. Sir Samuel Griffith, while repeating his warning not to be too sanguine, indulged in one flight of practical sentiment.

I am tired [he said] of being called a Colonist. The term is used no doubt at the other end of the world without the slightest intention of using a disparaging expression, but unconsciously as a term of disparagement. The Colonist is really regarded by the usage of the term as a person who is in some respects inferior, who does not enjoy the same advantages and is not quite entitled to the same privileges as other members of the Empire.

Has the average Englishman yet shed this mental attitude ? Or does he not still regard Colonials as doubtful people, with accents, but without manners ?

Mr. Playford spoke also and showed that he had advanced far since the Melbourne Conference. His reply to those, who said that Federation would destroy their liberties, struck directly at the true significance of this kind of opposition. ' The people,' he said, ' will lose no power. The local Legislatures may lose a little. But the people will have larger powers than before.' The remark was prophetic of the future struggle between the people and the politicians.

. 2 .

When the Convention opened next day Sir Henry Parkes was elected its President, as being both Premier of the Colony, in which the Convention sat, and the 'immediate author of the present movement.' On March 4 he submitted Resolutions, which it is unnecessary to quote in full, which laid down clearly the fundamental principles of a Federal Union, viz., inter-Colonial Free Trade, a common tariff, federal defence and the preservation of provincial rights in provincial matters ; and suggested, as a machinery for carrying out these principles, a complete National Government with legislative, executive and judiciary departments : a Parliament of two Houses (one representing the Nation, the other the States) and the British system of Responsible Government.

In the debate upon these Resolutions, which occupied six days, the contest was renewed between the advocates of a larger Union and the minimising supporters of 'State rights.' The issue, however, was never in doubt. Sir Henry Parkes, deprived of the assistance of Mr. Macrossan, who died while the Convention was sitting, was matched unequally against the learning of Sir Samuel Griffith and Mr. A. I. Clark. Even the Resolutions which he proposed were a compromise and did not go so far as he himself desired. Their first draft, as he records in his 'Fifty Years in the Making of Australian History '[1] had been submitted

[1] Vol. ii., p. 358.

by him to an informal meeting of the New South
Wales delegates, but failed to win acceptance.   They
differed from those, which he proposed, in several
points, which still are of interest.   Thus, instead of
the clause reserving to the several Colonies their
' powers, privileges, and territorial rights,' he proposed
originally the appointment of a commission, to devise
' an equitable scheme for the distribution of the public
lands and the satisfying of existing territorial rights,
such scheme keeping in view both the necessary
strength of the National Government and the just
claims of the respective provinces.'   Had such a
clause been adopted, not only would the Central
Government have been provided with a permanent
and increasing revenue from the unoccupied lands of
Northern Queensland, and the Northern Territories of
Western and Southern Australia, which would have
made it independent of the custom-house, but machinery would have been set up for the division of the
existing Colonies into smaller areas, which would have
equalised the distribution of political power and thus
saved the Federation from many difficulties.   It is
not unlikely that the next great constitutional reform
will be in the direction of Sir Henry Parkes' rejected
proposal.

Having thus secured the financial independence
of the Central Government and safeguarded its powers
against the predominance of a large State, Sir Henry
Parkes originally had proposed two other Resolutions
for protecting the independence of the provinces :—
First, that the local Parliaments should have a voice
in the disposal of the Customs revenue ; and, secondly,
that the Senate or State House should not be restricted

in the exercise of its legislative powers in matters of finance. As has been mentioned, the other delegates from New South Wales refused to agree to any of these proposals.

It is noteworthy that Sir John A. Macdonald also was thwarted in his desire to give fuller powers to the Central Government of Canada, because, like Sir Henry Parkes, he was unable to convince his fellow delegates :—' If we could have one Government and one Parliament legislating for the whole of the people, it would be the best, cheapest, and the most vigorous and strongest system of government we could adopt.' The opposition of Ontario and the Maritime Provinces prevented the realisation of this ideal. Like the smaller Australian Colonies, these were prepared for Union but not for Unity. Both Sir John A. Macdonald, therefore, and Sir Henry Parkes had to be content with a compromise, which was designed to combine the strength of a Legislative Union with the sectional freedom of a Federal Union, in which local interests were protected.[1]

· 3 ·

In proposing the adoption of these Resolutions Sir Henry Parkes described the spirit, in which they should be approached, in terms, which apply to any movement, which may yet be made towards a larger Federation of the British Empire.

I venture, before entering upon a discussion of these special resolutions, to appeal to every Colony and to every delegate representing every Colony to meet the work which we are

---

[1] See on this question an interesting article by Mr. J. A .R. Marriott in the *Fortnightly Review* of September 9, 1912.

now about to begin in a broad federal spirit. We cannot hope for any just conclusion—we cannot hope reasonably for any amount of valid success—unless we lose sight, to a large extent, of the local interests which we represent at the same time as we represent the great cause. There can be no Federation if we should happen, any of us, to insist upon conditions which stand in the way of Federation; there can be no Federation, no complete Union of these Governments, of these communities, of these separate Colonies, unless we can so far clear the way as to approach the great question of creating a federal power as if the boundaries now existing had no existence whatever. I think it is quite consistent for every one of us to disburden his mind of our local—I will not say prejudices—but of our local inclinations, without in any way impairing our patriotic resolve to preserve the rights of each of the Colonies we represent. It does seem to me in the highest degree necessary that we should approach the general question in the most federal spirit that we can call to our support.[1]

Speaking next to the second Resolution he defined it to be

an absolutely necessary condition of anything like perfect Federation that Australia should be free in its trade and intercourse; that there should be no impediment of any kind between one section of the people and another; but that trade and general communication should flow from one end of the continent to the other with no one to stay its progress or call it to account.

As to the tariff, he declared that, whether it were Protective or Free Trade,

it will be the duty of every loyal and patriotic citizen to cheerfully submit to the decision of the Parliament, and of those who hold an opinion different from that which may be in the ascendant, to fight the battle out in the Federation.

[1] *Convention Debates*, pp. 23-4.

· 4 ·

The discussion, which this speech initiated, turned mainly on the relative powers of the two Houses over Money Bills, and on the possibility of adapting Responsible Government to a federal system. As Sir Samuel Griffith pointed out, federation involved the principle, absolutely new in the British Empire, that ' every law should receive the assent of a majority of the States as well as of a majority of the people.' The problem was how to secure ' a deliberate and not a coerced concurrence of both Houses.' The only solution in his opinion was that there should be ' an equal number of representatives from each State in the Senate or State House, and that this Chamber should be a continuous body, periodically renewed by the vacation of office of a portion of its members.' But, if this were conceded, it appeared to him to be ' quite inconsistent with the independent existence of the Senate as representing the separate States that that Chamber should be prohibited from amending Money Bills . . . To give the Lower House alone a practically uncontrolled authority over expenditure was irreconcilable with the principle, which required the assent of a majority of the States to all legislation, and such a restriction upon the co-ordinate authority of the State House must cause friction, and in the final result a deadlock.' He pointed out, also, that the principle of equal State representation in a House of equal authority with the people's House, which he considered to be ' the fundamental principle of a federal system,' created new and unprecedented conditions in the working of Responsible Government.

Nobody has ever tried the experiment of a government depending upon one House, and the machinery of the State equally depending on another.

Then turning to the question of Responsible Government, he asked this pertinent question :—If both Houses had equal authority—(and unless the State House had the power of vetoing every legislative proposal they would be departing from the fundamental principle enunciated in the first Resolution, viz., that they were only surrendering to the general government what was absolutely necessary for the benefit of the whole of Australia, leaving to the several States their autonomy . . . 'To which House must Ministers be responsible ? Or must they be responsible to both ? And, if so, how ? '

Mr. Hackett (Western Australia) put the dilemma later in the debate :—

Either Responsible Government will kill Federation, or Federation will kill Responsible Government.

Sir Samuel Griffith's solution was to permit the problem to work out its own development, only providing in the Constitution that the Executive *might* —not *must*—sit in Parliament.

Mr. Playford (South Australia) and Sir Thomas McIlwraith (Queensland) expressed similar views on behalf of the 'small' States. The former declared that these 'must be protected against being ridden over rough-shod' by the States, which had the preponderance of population ; and asked pointedly :— ' Why, after they had been offered equal representation in the Senate, the right to be considered a unit in the Legislature was to be taken away.' Mr. Barton was on the same side, considering that the power to 'amend' was equivalent to a 'veto in detail,' which ought to be permitted to a Chamber, to which a general power of veto had been given already.

Mr. Deakin put the question from the other side :— 'It is quite conceivable that immense majorities in the large States might be neutralised by small majorities in the small States,'—and suggested the compromise, which was adopted later, giving the Senate power to 'suggest' amendments to the other House, but not itself to make them.

The reply of Mr. Kingston (South Australia) on behalf of the small States was logically unanswerable :—

You—the large States—command a majority in the Assembly which ought to be sufficient for all practical purposes.

Mr. Munro (Victoria) : Not if it is checkmated in the other Chamber.

Mr. Kingston : There must be a check and a substantial check ; and if the smaller States are only going to be offered something, which is nominally a check and which will not stand the test of time and use, it appears to me difficult to suppose that there will be any disposition on their part to enter into an alliance, by which they practically subordinate their powers and interests in any federal question to the decision of the majority in the National Assembly. . . . Any House which does not possess the power of amending or vetoing Money Bills in detail can be subjected to disadvantages, which practically render it powerless.

It was the same difference of opinion which had been foreshadowed at the Melbourne Conference, with the difference that the interval for reflection only seemed to have hardened the Delegates in their con-

flicting views. The battle was renewed, when the
Convention went into Committee of the Whole to
consider the Resolutions in detail (March 13). Two
proposals were submitted, the one by Sir John Downer
(South Australia), giving the Senate power ' to reject
in whole or in part ' a Money Bill, the other by
Mr. Wrixon (Victoria), permitting the Senate to affirm
or reject such measures but not to amend them, and
providing, as a protection to this House, that it should
be unlawful to ' tack ' anything to the annual Appropriation Bill. ' The debate became warm ; neither
side seemed inclined to give way, and hints were
thrown out that the delegates might as well " pack up
their portmanteaux." At last, however, the spirit
of compromise was successfully appealed to, and,
although no basis of compromise could as yet be found,
it was agreed not to press the matter to a vote at
that stage, but to withdraw both amendments and let
the decision stand over ' [1] until the Drafting Committee submitted their proposals.

On March 18 three Committees were appointed ;
one consisting of three members from each Delegation
to consider constitutional machinery ; a second consisting of one member from each Delegation to consider
finance, taxation, and trade regulations ; and a third,
also of one member from each Delegation, to deal with
the judiciary. The two latter Committees were to
report to the Constitutional Committee, which was
charged with the duty of preparing and submitting
to the Convention a Bill for the establishment of a
Federal Constitution. The preparation of this draft

---

[1] Quick and Garran, *Annotated Constitution of the Commonwealth*,
p. 128.

devolved upon a sub-Committee consisting of Sir
Samuel Griffith, Mr. Kingston, Mr. Barton, and Mr.
Inglis Clark. Thus, the long discussion of principles,
although it had led to no agreement on the critical
questions, had prepared the way sufficiently for the
submission of detailed proposals. The proceedings
of all the Committees were private; and the drafting
sub-Committee did its final revise from March 27–29
on board the Queensland Government yacht *Lucinda*,
at the mouth of the Hawkesbury river. It may be
explained, at this distance of time, by one who assisted
at this conclave unofficially, that the occasional
missing of the happiest turn of phrase by these
distinguished draftsmen may have been due to
the sea-sickness, which followed the surreptitious
heading of the steamer out to sea, and the rise of
a wind before she could return to harbour! One
wonders if the much respected 'Fathers of the
American Constitution' were always grave in their
deliberations!

· 5 ·

On March 31, Sir Samuel Griffith brought up the
report of the Constitutional Committee together with
the draft Bill to constitute the Commonwealth of
Australia, which was accepted by the Convention
without material alteration. Since it is not the
purpose of this work to discuss constitutional
questions further than is necessary for the understanding of events, it will be sufficient to explain
those provisions of the Bill which came later most
into controversy.

The provisions relating to the powers of the Senate, which became known as ' The Compromise of 1891,' must be mentioned first ; because the battle raged round these right up to 1900. Accepting the equal representation of the States in the Senate, as an essential condition of the Federal Union, the drafting Committee had to find some formula, which would admit the equality of the Senate with the House of Representatives, and, at the same time, retain the power of the purse in the popular Chamber. The compromise arrived at was exceedingly ingenious. The Senate was given equal power with the House of Representatives over all legislation, except Appropriation and Taxation Bills. These, it was provided, must originate in the Lower House and could not be amended by the Senate, although they could be rejected. The Senate was forbidden also to amend a Bill ' in such a manner as to increase any proposed charge or burden on the people.' Appropriation Bills were defined as Bills ' appropriating the necessary supplies for the ordinary annual services of the Government.' As compensation for these restrictions, the Senate was given a power, which had been proved to be effective in South Australia, to ' suggest ' amendments to any Bills, which it might not amend. That is to say, it might at any time return such a Bill to the House of Representatives ' with a message requesting the omission or amendment of any items or provisions therein.' Mr. Deakin had proposed this device during the debate upon the Resolutions. As a further guarantee to the Senate, the House of Representatives was prohibited from including more than one kind of taxation or any other matter except taxation in a taxing

measure. The 'tacking' of any measure to an Appropriation Bill (*i.e.*, the putting of a disputed provision
into such a measure), was forbidden also.[1] These
provisions, it was thought, safeguarded the federal
character of the State House ; while they secured,
also, that the majority of the people of Australia, who
elected the House of Representatives, should not be
thwarted in their wishes by the sectional interests of
a minority. The Convention of 1897-8 added another
precaution against a failure to attain this object
by provisions to secure the supremacy of the people's
House, in the event of the two Chambers coming to a
deadlock.

. 6 .

The solution of the other great problem of Federation—the compatibility of a federal system with the
practice of Responsible Government—was less definite.
Mr. Inglis Clark, in the debate upon the Resolutions, had
expressed a frank preference for the American practice
by which Ministers are excluded from Parliament ; and
Sir Samuel Griffith, while preferring executive responsibility, questioned its universal applicability, and
thought that circumstances might arise, under which
some other practice would be more useful. Accordingly
the Bill indicated the practice of Responsible Government without adopting the principle expressly. Thus,
it provided for a 'Federal Executive Council' ; that
Ministers should hold office during the Governor's
pleasure ; that they should sit in either House of
Parliament, and be members of the Executive Council,

---

[1] The 'tack' of Payment of Members to the Appropriation Bill
of 1865 had brought Victoria to the brink of civil war.

—all of which provisions are essential to the working of Responsible Government. They did not exclude, however, a modification of that practice ; because they left it possible (although this was not probable in Australia) for Ministers to hold office without having seats in Parliament. And that this was intentional had been admitted by Sir Samuel Griffith.

The compromise with regard to the tariff is thus described by Messrs. Quick and Garran : [1] 'It was obviously out of the question for the Convention to frame a tariff, or even to fix the principles on which the Federal Parliament should frame a tariff. Yet the Victorians were anxious for some " guarantee " that their manufacturing interests should not be injured by a sudden reversal of their Protectionist policy ; whilst the Free Trade majority of New South Wales were equally afraid that their fiscal faith would not be shared by the Federal Parliament. Sir Henry Parkes had always taken the high federal ground that the fiscal question must be left unreservedly and un-conditionally to the Australian people to decide for themselves. He placed Federation above any fiscal policy, and claimed that the other Colonies should do the same. This settlement, which was the only one possible, was embodied in the draft Bill.'

The Commonwealth was given exclusive power to impose duties by Customs and Excise, which were required to be uniform. Until uniform duties of Customs and Excise should be imposed, the State tariffs continued operative ; but the collection of duties passed to the Commonwealth immediately upon its establishment.

[1] *Annotated Constitution of the Commonwealth*, p. 132.

K

· 7 ·

It is curious that the problem of Finance, which the Convention of 1897–8 found almost insoluble, troubled so little the framers of the Bill of 1891. Sir Samuel Griffith, indeed, stated the elements of the problem with his accustomed lucidity :—

The great difficulty—and it is a difficulty peculiar to this Constitution, as far as I have any knowledge—is that the Customs revenue of the Colonies in all cases forms a very large share of the means of meeting the expenses of government ; and as we should only take over a very small part of its expenditure, the Commonwealth would start with an enormous annual surplus of many millions, which it could not retain or expend, but must return to the different States. That is a difficulty almost as great as the difficulty of making a levy upon the different States as States. . . . As long as we deal with the existing Customs duties there is no difficulty, because we know exactly what each State raises. But this must not be forgotten —that the circumstances of the various parts of Australia with regard to the consumption of dutiable articles are very different. The consumption in some Colonies is at least double what it is in other Colonies. For instance, one Colony may have a very large proportion of its population composed of persons who do not consume a large quantity of dutiable articles, whereas the case might be quite the reverse with another Colony of the group. Take a Colony with a specially sober, thrifty and frugal population, like, say, that of South Australia, where there is a large proportion of non-consumers of dutiable articles. They would receive very much more than they paid in Customs duties if the surplus were returned in proportion to population. In the case of other Colonies which did not possess the same class of population they would get back much less than they contributed to the Customs revenue.

Accepting this view, the Convention agreed that the surplus revenue, after meeting the needs of the Commonwealth, should be returned to the States according to their respective contributions. Customs and Excise duties were deemed to be contributed by the State where the dutiable articles were consumed.

The objection to this plan was the inconvenience of maintaining Customs officers and records, in order to ascertain in what State dutiable goods were consumed, which must become an irksome impediment to the freedom of inter-Colonial trade. Yet the alternative suggested by the Convention, which the drafting Committee had rejected, viz., the apportionment of revenue and expenditure between the States according to their respective populations, led to greater anomalies and inequalities. The proposals of the drafting Committee were agreed to after a long discussion, with an amendment empowering Parliament to alter the basis of contribution ; but, apparently, no Delegate suspected that, in the coming struggle, the attack would be concentrated on the financial proposals, or that these involved difficulties, which could not be dealt with adequately without experience of the new conditions which Federation would create.[1]

The control of the navigable rivers, which was a bone of contention later, was given to the Commonwealth in these terms : ' River navigation with respect to the common purposes of two or more States ;' and power was given also to the Commonwealth to grant bounties, ' but so that they shall be uniform throughout the Commonwealth.'

A power was given to amend the Constitution by a vote of the majority of the people and a majority of

[1] For a fuller discussion of the Financial Problem see *post*, p. 248.

the States. The site of the Capital was left to the determination of the Federal Parliament.

. 8 .

Elated by their success in overcoming difficulties, which had seemed, at an earlier stage, to be insuperable, the Delegates forgot that public opinion had not kept pace with their own progress. The report of their proceedings was accessible, it was true, to anyone who cared to read it ; and the discussions had been so full and frank that Mr. Deakin could say with accuracy that ' no enemies of Federation would be able to present arguments against the Bill which might not be found, in some form, already embodied in these debates.' Yet much had gone into the forming of the Bill which was not recorded in ' Hansard,' and which only the Delegates themselves could appreciate justly. To quote Mr. Deakin again :—

There is much that has operated upon the minds of members which is not stated in the record ; because the Delegates have practically lived together for six weeks in private as well as in public intercourse, and from the natural action and reaction of mind upon mind have been gradually shaping their thoughts upon this great question. The Bill which we present is the result of a far more intricate intellectual process than is exhibited in our debates. Unless the atmosphere in which we lived as well as worked is taken into consideration, the measure as it stands will not be fully understood.[1]

Under such circumstances it was surely a counsel of prudence to give the people time to catch up with the

---

[1] The Delegates to the Convention of 1897–8 experienced great difficulty in appreciating the doubts and misgivings of those who had not lived, like themselves, for twelve months in an atmosphere of Federation.

Convention :—' To take them into confidence,' as Mr.
Wrixon urged, ' and ask them to consider the points
the Delegates had been considering, and deal again,
if need were, with the questions with which the Convention had dealt.'

Simply to submit the Constitution [Mr. Wrixon continued]
for the approval or disapproval, Aye or No, of the people of
the Colonies was very likely to cause the whole thing to mis-
carry.   For the people were dealing with a subject which was
somewhat new to them and with a Constitution which they
had had no opportunity of fully considering.

Mr. John Bray (S.A.) and Mr. Playford spoke to the
same effect.   To Sir Samuel Griffith, however, such a
course appeared to be an abandonment of all they
had already done :—

We have laboured here [he said] for weeks, endeavouring
to frame a Constitution ; we have met conflicting views ; we
have endeavoured to arrive at compromises ; each Colony has
had strong views of its own and its representatives have
surrendered those views for the purpose of arriving at agreement.   The honourable member proposes that all that work
should go for naught and that the Constitution should be sent
back to each Colony. . . . In that case South Australia might
insist on re-opening the financial compromise ; Tasmania
might revive other demands ; Queensland might refuse to
join unless some other compromise were re-opened. . . . All
our labours in the way of conciliation and compromise will be
thrown to the winds if we submit to the people of the different
Colonies a draft for their consideration in which they can make
thousands of amendments if they think fit.

If logic governed human actions, such reasoning was
unanswerable.   Yet it was the insertion of the one word
' approval ' in the Resolution, which prescribed the

method of procuring the acceptance by the Colonies of the Bill of the Convention, in deference to these arguments, instead of the word ' consideration,' which, more than anything in the contents of the Bill, excited antagonism and prevented its acceptance. The Resolution, as carried by the Convention, was in these terms :—

That this Convention recommends that provision be made by the Parliaments of the several Colonies for submitting for the *approval* of the people of the Colonies respectively the Constitution of the Commonwealth of Australia as framed by this Convention.

That experienced politicians should have made this error is the more surprising, because Sir Henry Parkes, in reporting the Resolutions of the Committee, had warned the Convention that the Bill would meet with serious opposition. ' We know with what violence of feeling, with what violence of expression every great work at every period of history has been assailed by those who were opposed to it, and still more by those who assailed it for no reason at all, and under no guidance that could be intelligible. We know that at all times in the Mother Country when great constitutional changes have taken place—not less in America —the most violent and unscrupulous expressions of opinion and exhibitions of conduct were indulged in by persons who manifested them, not so much from their opposition to some particular constitutional change as from their disposition to do mischief. . . . The uninformed and reckless are always ready to denounce any work which they cannot comprehend.' That this warning should have gone unheeded proves that the Convention, representative as it was of both

political parties, was out of touch with popular sentiment.   In truth politics were in a state of transition ;
and new forces were coming into the field, under the
impulse of the Labour Party, with which the leaders of
the old school had little sympathy.   The Convention,
therefore,was not truly representative of public opinion ;
although no other body of men could have reflected it,
at that time, with greater accuracy.   Certainly it is
to be regretted that it was not less logical and more
conciliatory in the method which it proposed for the
adoption of the Constitution.   The Convention of
1891, however, had done its work.   In its six weeks'
Session Federation

had come down from the clouds to the earth ; it changed
from a dream into a tangible reality.   The idea was once for all
crystallised into a practical scheme, complete in all its details.
As to many of the details and even many of the principles,
there was still to be keen and protracted dispute ; but with
their definition the era of vague generalities ended and the
era of close criticism began.[1]

And although the Bill of 1891 did not pass, yet Sir
Henry Parkes prophesied truly, when he described it,
in the closing debate of the Convention, as ' a document
which will be remembered as long as Australia and the
English language endured,' and foretold that

whenever the time (for Union) comes—and it cannot be far
off—this admirably drawn Bill, so clear, so instinct with the
true spirit of well-ordered liberty, so instinct with a true
appreciation of stable and sober laws, so pervaded by the
spirit of Federation, must be in the foundation of the very

[1] Quick and Garran, *Annotated Constitution of the Commonwealth*,
p. 129.

edifice of federal liberty.   It can never be forgotten, it can never be depreciated, it can never be made less than it is to-day ; and supposing another Constitution should be framed by other men, to a very large extent the provisions of this Bill must be embodied in our Constitution.   So that this Convention has breathed into this Bill the breath of immortal life.

CHAPTER IX

PARLIAMENT AND THE CONVENTION BILL

PARLIAMENT, which was to take the next step—for the Colonies were waiting for the lead of New South Wales—met on May 19, 1891, forty days after the Convention had been dissolved. In that interval public opinion had ' hardened in favour of Federation. No enthusiasm was noticeable ; but the people were beginning to think on the question, and to recognise that, in this direction, the destiny of Australia lay.' [1] To Sir Henry Parkes [2] it seemed that 'interest in the question had not in any degree abated. The thinking portion of the population, in the churches, in official circles, in the public Press, had grown warmer in support from closer acquaintance with the project of Union.' Nevertheless, the Parliaments were still resentful of the action of the Convention in endeavouring to compel them to accept its work as final. Each wished to have a voice in the framing of the Constitution ; and none was content (to use a phrase of Mr. Reid's) ' to be a mere common carrier between the Convention and the people.' In the minds of many persons also, there was ' a vague feeling of distrust of the Constitution, as the work of a body somewhat

[1] Charles Lyne, *Life of Sir Henry Parkes*, p. 506.
[2] *Fifty Years in the Making of Australian History*, vol. ii. p. 370.

conservative in composition, only indirectly representative of the people, and entrusted with no very
definite or detailed mandate even by the parliaments
which created it.[1]   There was room, also, for much
difference of opinion as to the terms of the Constitution,
which was a compromise, with the faults as well as the
merits of a compromise.   Its federal principles were
new to Australia ; and it was not easy, even for well-
wishers, to foresee their working, when both Houses
had almost equal powers and there was no provision
for solving a possible deadlock.   Also, the old hostility
and misgivings, which have been described in earlier
chapters, continued in full force.   Yet, although every
indication pointed to the necessity for caution and
conciliation, it did not seem impossible to get the Bill
through the Parliament of New South Wales, and
thus advance it to the stage at which it could be referred back to the same or another Convention, charged
with the duty of harmonising the amendments which
might have been proposed by this and the other
Parliaments.   It became apparent, before the Session
was a week old, that this expectation would not
be fulfilled.

. I .

The Governor's Speech announced that ' no time
would be lost ' in laying before Parliament the Bill
of the Convention—' The result of much deliberation,
argumentative contention, and necessary compromise,'

---

[1] See Quick and Garran, p. 144. Compare the following passage from
Mr. Reid's speech in the Legislative Assembly on July 22, 1891 : ' A
national movement ?   No ! a movement confined to the great ambitious
statesmen of Australia ; in which there was no national heart, but
in which diplomacy and all sorts of contrivances were taking the place
of a great national, manly outburst of feeling ! '

—as a distinct part of the ministerial policy ; and on the second day of the Session Sir Henry Parkes gave notice of his intention to move ' that the House approved of the Constitution, while reserving to itself the right to propose omissions and amendments, to be fully set forth by the proposer in each case in a schedule, and to be finally considered, if deemed advisable by the House, by another Convention.' This Resolution, which was a departure from the procedure agreed to by the Convention, respected the susceptibilities of Parliament, and would have brought on a regular debate, which would have. given every opportunity for consideration and amendment of the Bill.   However, this procedure did not commend itself to Mr. G. H. Reid, who, immediately the Convention closed, had condemned its work at a public meeting in Sydney, presided over by Sir John Robertson.   He thought that Sir Henry Parkes might delay the submission of the Bill until it had been accepted by the other Colonies, and then use their agreement to bring pressure upon New South Wales, and he rose, therefore, directly after the seconder of the Address in reply, to propose a hostile amendment, pointing particularly at the Money Bill clauses, the omission to secure Responsible Government, and the clauses relating to the railways, rivers, and public debts.[1]   He calculated that, in taking this step to embarrass the Government, he would have the support of the Protectionist Opposition ; and that the defeat of the Ministry would destroy the Convention Bill.

[1] Since Federalists insisted always that the text of the Bill was the best answer to its critics, it will elucidate Mr. Reid's speech to print in full the clauses which he condemned.   See Appendix to this Chapter.

His own speech is the best commentary upon his action :—

In its very heart the Bill is vitally destructive of all the great rights and liberties of the large population of this country. It is a Bill which, deliberately, from the declared motives and design of the delegates, was intended to destroy the power of the people through their representatives in dealing with the revenues, expenditure and taxation of the country [1]. . . . The principle of Responsible Government was deliberately cut out, in order that; behind the backs of the people, the whole system of Responsible Government might be over-turned by any government that might happen to be in office.

Next, referring to the proposal to submit the Bill to a popular vote, he asked :—

Do we not see that the intention of that Resolution is that the Parliaments of these Colonies are to be mere transmitting machines for sending the Bill to the people ?. . . They are to act only as the medium of submitting the Bill and nothing else to the people of this country. . . . The Colony of Victoria, with its only chance of national pre-eminence under this Bill,

[1] Sir Samuel Griffith had anticipated this criticism during the Convention :—' I will mention a few of the subjects which are left to the States, for the benefit of those who think that this Convention has some sinister object, or desires to deprive in some sinister way the State legislatures of their autonomy. Their constitutions, the borrowing of money, the complete control of the government of the State, all the laws relating to property and civil rights, the whole subject of public lands and mines, registration of titles, education, criminal law and its enforcement, hospitals and such matters, all local works and under-takings, municipal institutions, imposition of licenses, the administra-tion of justice, both criminal and civil, and the establishment of courts, and an absolute power to dispose of their revenue as they may think fit—these are some of the subjects for a State to exercise its functions upon. Let any person, who thinks that by this scheme too much is taken from the State Legislatures, take up any volume of the Statutes of the State Legislatures and see how few of these deal with subjects with respect to which powers are taken from the States.'

will be allowed to push on and adopt it, and some other Colony will be allowed to push on and we will be told ' Oh ! you see that two of the Colonies have adopted it. If you do not come in now, you will be left out in the cold, and you must take it as it stands.'

Next, he denounced the Money clauses of the Bill, quoting from Sir John Downer's speech to show that ' the compromise ' about the powers of the Senate was understood differently by different members of the Convention :—

This [he exclaimed] is that wonderful compromise ; this is that triumph of harmony, which had avoided the rock upon which the project was to split, which had guaranteed the rights of the people and the people's House with the just rights of the Senate.

Up to this point Mr. Reid had been dealing with the proceedings of the Convention. Now he explained his attitude, as a Free Trader, towards Federation in what is perhaps the best remembered passage in his oratory. Referring to the willingness of Sir Henry Parkes to trust the fiscal question to the Federal Parliament he said :—

There is a recklessness about the Premier's position in this matter which reminds me of an anecdote which bears a very striking resemblance to it :—In a remote village there was once a teetotaller who had five drunken neighbours. The teetotaller, in his youth, had betrayed a slight trace of weakness in the same direction ; but he was reclaimed, and in the course of time he rose to be the head of the teetotal body. He had such ideas about the curse of drink that even moderate drinkers he called ' creatures ' and ' angels of darkness,' and every-body who was a total abstainer was an ' angel of light.' He often denounced the iniquities of those five drunken neighbours.

Suddenly, to the intense astonishment of everyone, he betrayed a rabid desire to live with them.   Some ascribed it to a rumoured Chinese attack on the village ; others thought that it was a remarkable development of missionary zeal ; others, again, thought that he had a recurrence of his old complaint. The five drunkards did not know what to make of him.   He was rich, and they were anxious to annex his money ; but they did not quite like the prospect of this nearer tie, so an arrangement was made that they should settle the question of liquids when they lived together.   A short time afterwards the whole six were found together in the village gloriously drunk. When the venerable teetotaller was reproached by his own teetotal associates, he explained that he much regretted his unhappy position ; but the very moment they took up house together, he submitted a motion that nothing but cold water should be allowed in the house, and, to his intense astonishment, it was defeated by five to one, and a motion carried that nothing but strong drink should be consumed on the premises. To that he attributed the unhappy condition in which he was found.   He explained that, of course, as a Christian patriot, he had to bow to the decision of the majority.   That is exactly the position of the Premier of this country with reference to the question of Free Trade. . . . I say that I will not put my principles of Free Trade in the power of the Victorian Protectionists.   I say, apart from theory, Victoria could not afford to give up Protection duties.   The thing is preposterous. Every man looking at the facts must see that the outcome must be Protection.

After this digression, Mr. Reid returned to a consideration of the Bill, claiming that, because the defects in it were such that the House ought to reject it on a second reading, it was idle to consider amendments in matters of detail.   Therefore, he preferred himself to consider it in general terms.   First, he reminded the House, a Federal Constitution was a partnership. We give to our five other partners, if they choose, power to dictate our policy as to trade ; to tax us to an unlimited extent ; to spend as much of our Customs revenue as they like, returning only what is left. . . . We must pay some regard to the business aspect of this transaction. The other Colonies did this. They all did make the best bargain for themselves, and the one Colony which was talking grand talk and which was full of generous sentiment was New South Wales.

Her representation had not even secured the Capital. They ' affected it was beyond their power ' to do so. Equal representation in the Senate was the next object of Mr. Reid's criticism. This he would only agree to if the Senate had no more powers than the House of Lords or the Legislative Council of New South Wales. He quoted at length from Mr. Bryce on the difficulty of regulating the relations between the two Houses of Congress, and dealt then with the legislative power :—

Another sub-section provides that, when a State law is inconsistent with the law of the Commonwealth, the law of the Commonwealth shall prevail over the law of the State to the extent of its inconsistency. But it ought to knock the law of the State on the head altogether. Honourable members will see the scope for confusion.

Passing from ' details ' Mr. Reid came to ' the vital part of the Bill,' which in his opinion was the power given to the Senate to ' suggest ' amendments in Money Bills :—

Every right the small States fought so zealously for is maintained. The Senate can send back, amended, nearly the whole of the Money Bills. Those which they cannot amend in the Bill itself they can amend by sending a sheet of foolscap along with it. Thus, in this matter, upon which there should be no risk of collision or deadlock, there is every opening for incessant quarrels between the different provinces represented in the Senate.

Another 'matter of vital importance' was the refusal to bind the Commonwealth Parliament to the system of Responsible Government. Mr. Reid would not admit that the words of the Constitution Bill affirmed, in effect, the continuance of the existing practice; but saw in it a dark design to enable the Crown to appoint Ministers who had not the confidence of Parliament, 'as in the days of the Stuarts!' The third point, which Mr. Reid considered 'vital,' was the power given to the Federal Parliament, under the Bill, of 'annulling the regulations of our great Department of Railways without compensation.' This, in effect, meant the 'abolition of differential rates,' and the result would be that 'Melbourne will become the commercial centre of Australia.' Without preferential rates, Mr. Reid thought the railways would be run at a loss :—

We had the burden of our railways upon our shoulders before we ever dreamt of Federal Union; and if the other Colonies are to make our railways a loss and reap the benefit of making them a loss, by taking the trade away from us, they ought at any rate to give us some compensation for them.

Next Mr. Reid called in aid of his argument the clause of the Bill, which forbade the Commonwealth Parliament to 'impose any tax on land or property belonging to a State.' These words, he said, absolutely prevent the Commonwealth from imposing a land tax and . . . if there is no power to impose a land tax they must raise revenue through the Customs House . . . Little did I think that Sir Henry Parkes would propose to sneak in Protection under the name of inter-Colonial Free Trade.

If the ' question of Free Trade were left open ' Mr. Reid was

prepared to join every honourable member in passing an Act that would enable troops to be sent from one Colony to another for Defence purposes—with a view to help any one Colony that might be in distress. I am prepared to do that now. We might do as is done in Berlin, where they have all the armies of the Triple Alliance mobilised on paper, so that they may be worked unitedly at a moment's notice. Do as was proposed at the inter-Colonial Conference in 1881, when we agreed to frame a uniform tariff. Frame a uniform tariff, and our freedom is still left. There may be eighty items upon the tariff we could agree to. You could pass a separate Act of legislation providing for a uniform tariff to-morrow. You can have a Council to frame uniform laws on a variety of subjects, which we can all adopt if suitable. All these things could be done to-morrow, and it is of no use for the Premier to say, as he did a year ago, that those who are not in favour of this Union breed disunion ; that those who will not vote for this Union have a terrible responsibility to face, as disunion may lead to civil war. It reminds me of the anecdote of the old gentleman who wanted his daughter to marry a man of dubious principles. The girl refused, whereupon the indignant parent exclaimed, ' Irreligious girl ! Do you not know that marriage is a sacrament of the Holy Church, and that by refusing to marry this man you are flying in the face of Providence and are a breeder of disunion ?' ' No, my father,' replied the girl ; ' if you send the proper sort of man along, you will find me most devout.' So I say to the Premier, if he will only send the proper sort of Bill along we will adopt it.

L

To say that 'because we cannot agree to a particular scheme of Union we are therefore set against all Union' seemed to Mr. Reid 'idle talk' and 'cheap rhetoric'; and he twitted Sir Henry Parkes with his slow conversion to the present scheme. To Mr. Reid there seemed danger in hurry. Local Government was of more pressing importance than Federation! At the same time he believed that 'in the future the scattered communities of Australia would form a great and united people. None the less he would oppose a measure like the Convention Bill, which was radically defective, because it contained principles which were dangerous to the public liberties and dangerous to the rights and interests of the people of New South Wales.'

. 2 .

It is impossible to miss the undertone of hostility to any form of Federation, which runs through this speech ; nor could Mr. Reid have been ignorant that the carrying of his amendment would give a fatal thrust at any scheme of Federation.[1] He had been associated on the platform with the declared opponents of Australian Union ; and it was idle to profess federal sympathies and insist, at the same time, that the other Colonies should guarantee the continuance of the fiscal policy of New South Wales. The speech of his ally Mr. Want was quite definite :—

I would sooner [he said] see chaos take the place of order in the Ministerial ranks. I would sooner see a Protectionist Government in power. I would rather see almost anything than see this hydra-headed monster called Federation basking in its constitutional beastliness—for that is what it is—in this

1 See *ante*, p. 108, footnote.

bright and sunny land. . . . I was the first public man to assert my intention of opposing to the bitter end any system of Federation, because there can be none which would not involve the surrender of our independence and liberty.

Despite the support of Mr. Want, Mr. Reid's amendment was lost by 67 votes to 35. He had miscalculated the temper of the House, and not anticipated that the Federalist Members of the Opposition would vote against him. Four Free Traders voted in the minority, but twenty-two Protectionists supported the Government. Nevertheless, Mr. Reid had achieved his object, and had prevented an open and unprejudiced discussion of the Convention Bill. Had he desired merely its amendment, he would have delayed until Sir Henry Parkes' Resolution was before the House, and not taken hostile action before the provisions of the Bill had been explained by its mover, who, as Premier and President of the Convention, was entitled to this simple courtesy. His conduct and speech on this occasion were the beginning of the breach with the Federalist party, which furnishes the key to many subsequent events.

· 3 ·

The victory of the Government on Mr. Reid's amendment seemed substantial and decisive, and the way was clear for the Convention Bill. Yet, on the next sitting day (May 22), Sir Henry Parkes announced, to the amazement of every section in the House, that a Local Government Bill and an Electoral Bill would take precedence of Federation in the order of Government business ! Mr. Dibbs at once gave notice of a

Vote of Censure, which was lost only on the Speaker's vote.[1] Next day the House was dissolved.

No incident in Sir Henry Parkes' leadership has been more canvassed than this change of front. His own explanation was the unfavourable temper of the House, and the state of public business in an expiring Parliament. He contended that the Government had been 'thrown into a new position by the irregular debate, which had been precipitated on the House, and the attempt to force a decision upon party lines upon a question to which the Government had studied to give no party colour'; and that, 'after this trial of strength, the Ministry was not justified in delaying the great measures, which the country wanted, by any second edition of this desultory debate.' One of his colleagues (Mr. McMillan) urged, further, that, since none of the other Parliaments was in Session, Federation could be as much advanced by dealing with it later as if it were decided at once; and Sir Henry Parkes confirmed this argument by a declaration that 'the time when the Federation proposals will be submitted to Parliament will not be behind the time at which they will be considered in the other Colonies . . . and, whatever takes place, we shall not be prepared to delay the consideration of this question beyond the end of July.' Yet none knew better than Sir Henry Parkes the truth of Mr. Bright's aphorism on the impossibility of driving six horses abreast through Temple Bar! He must have foreseen, also, that the postponement of the Convention Bill would remit the Federal Protectionists, on whose support he was

---

[1] Mr. Reid, Mr. Want, and two other Free Traders voted against the Government.

dependent, to their original party allegiance; so that a dissolution would become inevitable. Possibly, this was his desire! He may have thought that a new Parliament would discuss the Convention Bill with more sympathy and knowledge than one which had been elected in 1889, before Federation had taken shape; and that the cold douche of a general election would be beneficial to some of his colleagues! For, although he gave the conventional denial of Cabinet dissensions, it is known, now, that a majority of the Ministers did not share Sir Henry Parkes' view as to the paramount importance and urgency of Federation; and that the decision to postpone the Convention Bill was come to against his wish, although he accepted it without reluctance. The state of his health was another cause which indisposed him to continue the contest in a moribund and unfriendly Parliament.

Nevertheless, posterity will accept Mr. Barton's verdict on this unfortunate step that 'Sir Henry Parkes made an error of judgment, which does not, however, bring into question his sincerity in the cause of which he was the practical founder.' [1]

APPENDIX TO CHAPTER IX

Subjoined is the text of the Clauses in the Convention Bill specifically condemned by Mr. Reid.

MONEY BILLS

S. 54. Laws appropriating any part of the public revenue or imposing any tax or impost shall originate in the House of Representatives.

[1] Speech in Legislative Assembly, March 1, 1892.

S. 55. (1) The Senate shall have equal power with the House of Representatives in respect of all proposed Laws, except Laws imposing taxation and Laws appropriating the necessary supplies for the ordinary annual services of the Government, which the Senate may affirm or reject, but may not amend. But the Senate may not amend any proposed Law in such a manner as to increase any proposed charge or burden on the people.

(2) Laws imposing taxation shall deal with the imposition of taxation only.

(3) Laws imposing taxation, except Laws imposing duties of Customs on imports, shall deal with one subject of taxation only.

(4) The expenditure for services other than the ordinary annual services of the Government shall not be authorised by the same Law as that which appropriates the supplies for such ordinary annual services, but shall be authorised by a separate Law or Laws.

(5) In the case of a proposed Law which the Senate may not amend, the Senate may at any stage return it to the House of Representatives with a message requesting the omission or amendment of any items or provisions therein. And the House of Representatives may, if it thinks fit, make such omissions or amendments, or any of them, without or with modifications.

RESPONSIBLE GOVERNMENT

There shall be a Council to aid and advise the Governor-General in the Government of the Commonwealth, and such Council shall be styled the Federal Executive Council; . . . and the Members thereof shall be capable of being chosen and sitting as Members of either House of Parliament.

Railways and Rivers

The Parliament shall have, subject to this Constitution, full power and authority to make all such Laws as it thinks necessary for the peace, order, and good government of the Commonwealth with respect to :—

27. The control of railways with respect to transport for the purposes of the Commonwealth.
28. River navigation with respect to the common purposes of two or more States or ports of the Commonwealth.

The Parliament of the Commonwealth may make Laws prohibiting or annulling any Laws or regulation made by any State, or by any authority constituted by any State, having the effect of derogating from freedom of trade and commerce between the different parts of the Commonwealth.

Public Debts

The Parliament may, with the consent of the Parliaments of all the States, make Laws for taking over and consolidating the whole or any part of the Public Debt of any State.

CHAPTER X

CLOSE OF THE FIRST EPOCH

THE general election did not clear the situation, as Sir Henry Parkes had hoped it might, but, rather, made it more confused. Except in Sydney, where Messrs Reid and Want directed the attack, the issue of Federation was overshadowed by other issues arising out of the Maritime Strike.[1] For the first time in British history Labour had accepted the advice of its critics, to organise itself as a political party and seek redress of its grievances by legislation. Thirty members of this party were returned, and held the balance of power in the new Parliament. While not hostile to Federation, they regarded it as of secondary importance ; and were suspicious of the Convention Bill, and frightened by its unreal terrors.[2] In their view, the matters of first importance were electoral reform and social legislation.

[1] This was a sympathetic strike of the officers and seamen of the coastal vessels to assist the shearers in a dispute with the pastoralists. For a few weeks there was difficulty in transporting and shipping wool shorn by non-union shearers ; and the strike became a battle between organised labour and organised capital, in which the original pretext was overlooked. See the writer's *Commonwealth of Australia*, Chapter v.

[2] ' To the Labour Party and its constituents the draft Constitution bristled with imaginary dangers. It conferred " enormous powers " on the Governor-General : it was steeped in " Imperialism " : it meant the " crushing of the workers " by a military despotism ! ' (Quick and Garran, Introd. p. 144).

'The Labour Party,' writes Sir Henry Parkes,[1] ' behaved honourably enough.   They had been elected to obtain legislation for their fellow workers, and they would not have been honest men if they had not pressed for the introduction of the measures to which they were pledged. . . .   It was unreasonable to expect [that they would] agree to our setting aside all provincial matters—I use the term for the purpose of distinction—however important, for the great national question of Federation.'

Nevertheless, the issue of Federation was kept before the country ; and the Election, although it resulted unfavourably to the Ministry—(the numbers were Ministerialists 48 :   Opposition 56 :   Labour 30 : Independent 7)—gave no encouragement to the anti-Federalists.

. I .

The most interesting contest was in East Sydney, a constituency which had always treated Mr. Reid with special favour.   On this occasion, he barely retained his seat, being last instead of first of the four elected candidates, and ceding the pride of place to Mr. Barton. Mr. Want, also, had to be content with second place for his old constituency of Paddington, where his personal popularity was very great.   Mr. Dibbs, also, was defeated for South Sydney,—a defeat which was the more striking because two of his own party, Messrs. Traill and Toohey, were elected as Federalists, together with two Free Trade Federalists, Messrs. James Martin and Wise.   But this unwillingness to condone hostility to Federation did not evidence an active sympathy.   Rather, indifference was the prevailing

---

[1] *Fifty Years*, vol. ii. p. 377.

note ; as was natural, when the industrial issues of the late strike were being fought out at the polls. A time of social ferment cannot be favourable to the discussion of constitutional changes ; and the most that could be expected was that the leaders on either side should define clearly their attitude towards the Convention Bill.

Mr. Reid, in an interview published in the *Sydney Morning Herald* on June 4, stated his hostility unequivocally ; and declared that he would oppose any form of Federation, which would be destructive of Free Trade in New South Wales. He did not suggest, however, any alternative form of Union. He objected, also, to submitting the Bill to a popular vote until it had been discussed by Parliament. On this point, as has been observed before,[1] he was in accord with Sir Henry Parkes and Mr. Barton.

The latter, with equal definiteness, declared himself a supporter of the Convention Bill, while admitting that it was not perfect—'no Constitution, and particularly no Federal Constitution, can be so described'—and contended that, after it had been submitted for discussion and amendment to the several Parliaments, 'it would be such a Bill as might fairly be put before the people for acceptance or rejection.' His address to the electors of East Sydney continued in these terms :—

The more the Bill is read and understood the better it will be liked ; and, when people thoroughly grasp its meaning, they will know what to think of those who have endeavoured to delude them into the idea that it 'destroys our liberties' or 'barters away our birthrights,' or effects any of the numer-

[1] See *ante*, p. 39.

ous enormities attributed to it by the provincialists. So far from 'destroying Responsible Government,' it is only by that system of Government that it can operate. And as for 'destroying the independence and autonomy of the Colonies,' it guards and preserves these more completely than any Federal Constitution in existence.

He characterised Mr. Reid's amendment to the address as

designed, not to secure a perfected measure, but to get rid of the whole result of the labours of the Convention, and strike a deadly blow at the whole movement towards Australian Union.

On the fiscal question, he declared himself a Protectionist; but pledged himself not to alter the existing tariff, while there was an immediate prospect of obtaining Federation. But, if Federation were far enough from accomplishment to warrant the expectation that Protection would be beneficial to New South Wales and strengthen her position up to the achievement of Union, he reserved to himself the right, then, to give effect to his fiscal opinions. Both in his election address and in his speeches Mr. Barton made similar declarations. One other may be quoted from a speech on June 10 :—

'He would give no vote which would prevent the progress towards Union; but, if he saw that Federation was a few years in the future, he would support Protection as the best policy for the country. . . . If a Protectionist Government came into office and was desirous of playing true to Federation he should look upon it in a very different light; but so long as Protection meant a Ministry of enemies to Federation they would get no vote from him. . . . If Protection could be brought in by any friends of Federation, so that the two

might go hand-in-hand, he would fight for Protection ; but
his support would not be given to any enemy of Federation
merely because he called himself a Protectionist.'

These quotations must be kept in mind, if we would
understand Mr. Barton's action a few months later.

. 2 .

When Parliament met on July 14, 1891, Sir Henry
Parkes, sensitive always to the moods of public opinion,
decided to adhere to his programme of the preceding
Session, and placed Federation third, in the order of
Government business, after Electoral Reform and
Local Government.   Mr. Dibbs at once tested opinion
by a Motion of Censure, which, to the surprise and
regret of Sir Henry Parkes—' it might be well that
Mr. Dibbs and his friends try their hands with our
new masters '—was defeated by the vote of the Labour
Party.

It was significant that Federation was not made an
issue in the debate, and was not even referred to by
any speaker except Mr. Reid, who took an opportunity,
late in the debate, of protesting against ' the unjust
insinuation ' that he and Mr. Want were ' opposed to
Australian Union.'   He explained that he had endeavoured in the last Parliament to prevent the consideration of the Convention Bill, because Sir Henry
Parkes was proposing to ignore Parliament :—

I knew that he was going to take the Bill to the people for
that sort of answer which is a child's answer.   An infant
can lisp either ' Yes ' or No ' ; and the people were to be
cribb'd, cabin'd and confin'd to that miserable monosyllable
over this great national design !

He claimed—although the claim ignored the terms of the Resolution which it had been his object to prevent Sir Henry Parkes from moving [1]—that, as a result of his action, ' the Bill as it stood would never leave this House '; and he lent his support to the old complaint that it sprang from statesmen, not from the people :—

When you make your Constitution out of the brains only of statesmen, you may find that everything has been thought of for the statesmen—that everything has been thought of for the great ones of the earth, but that the great heart of the people, the great strength of the people has been neglected.

Nevertheless, he declared his intention to vote, upon this occasion, in support of the Government of Sir Henry Parkes ! Cynics affirmed that the lesson of the East Sydney election had not been lost upon him ! [2]

· 3 ·

Another trial of strength occurred on September 1, when Mr. Copeland moved a Resolution in favour of a Protective tariff, to which Mr. Barton moved, as an amendment, that

inasmuch as the anticipated Federal Union would bring about a common fiscal policy for all Australia, and as meanwhile the co-operation of all parties was necessary in securing urgent legislation, the financial requirements of the Colony rather than the rigid doctrine of any system of political economy should regulate the mode of raising any further revenue through the Customs.

The Labour Party again joined with the Government in supporting Mr. Barton's amendment and defeating Mr. Copeland's motion. Mr. Reid, who, on this occasion

---

[1] See *ante*, p. 139.   [2] See *ante*, p. 108, footnote.

also, voted with the Government, made only one reference in his speech to Federation. Professing his
inability to understand Mr. Barton's action he said :—

It is a curious position which he occupies ; but still it
satisfies me. When my honourable and learned friend puts the
date of his transmogrification from Free Trade to Protection
as the date on which Federation is accomplished, he puts
it at a date which also exactly suits me, because there is no
doubt that that question, however great, is one which is fraught
with so many difficulties that it may be a very long time indeed
before it is brought about. . . . I feel positively sure that
Federation cannot be early ; because the position taken up by
several of the smaller Colonies, on certain points, is so firm
that the inevitable amendments which will be effected in this
House, and which already to some extent have been effected
in Victoria, will put off any agreement on the subject for a long
time to come.

Mr. Barton, in his speech, explained again his attitude
upon the fiscal question, pending the accomplishment
of Federation. Starting from the postulate that,
under Federation, only the Central Government would
have power to impose duties of Customs, he made an
earnest appeal for a fiscal truce within the Colony,
during the 'few years' which would elapse before
the Commonwealth would be established :—

For over four and a half years this Colony has been torn
by dissensions between the factions of Free Trade and Protection, to an extent which even the most ardent advocate of
either faction must regret. It has been torn to such an extent
that a new party has come into the House [the Labour Party]
anxious not to have the progress of domestic legislation complicated by the fiscal issue. . . . I am tired of seeing this
constant struggle ; — not that I do not think there is a fiscal
policy which is the best this country can adopt, but because

I see that, whilst we are nearing year by year a consummation, the result of which will be that the fiscal policy of New South Wales must be determined by all the Colonies together, the more clamorous of our politicians seem to think that we should institute violent changes of one kind or another, the result of which can only be transient and will disappear as soon as Federation is accomplished. I cannot understand the common sense of a policy of that kind. . . . Nothing keeps the best of our public men apart but this question of Protection and Free Trade, and, in proportion as this becomes unimportant, in that very proportion they lose their justification for political dissension and faction. . . . Whatever we may do in this Colony must be re-opened the moment there is a Federal Union ; and what we shall have done and what other Colonies shall have done will be as nothing in the enlightened judgment and wider reaching grasp of a nation such as we shall be then. . . . For the future, there can be only one useful Protection, and that is a Federal Protection. I mean to fight for that Protection, and I expect to find my honourable friend [Mr. Copeland] and myself fighting on the same side. But, until that day comes, I do not want to see the Union of these Colonies delayed and hampered by expedients which will lead rather to dissension. . . . . I am not prepared to vote in favour of any proposition for carrying out the fiscal policy of Protection, if I see that the effect of voting for that proposition is to throw the policy of Federation one inch backward.

Mr. Barton's speech produced the effect which he contemplated. The sincere Federalists, on both sides, accepted his advice, to forgo the fiscal fight for the sake of Union ; while the Labour Party, applying his argument to their own case, were prepared to do the same for the sake of social legislation. Thus, the two new issues of Federation and Labour combined, for a time, to keep the fiscal issue in check ; and Mr. Barton's amendment was carried by a considerable majority. In one sense, therefore, this vote was an encouragement to the Ministry to proceed with the Federal Resolutions; but, in reality, it did not remove the difficulties.

· 4 ·

As parties were divided, the Labour Party, voting solidly together, could at any time incline the balance to either side; and the Government was powerless without its support. With this, it was humiliated. 'Support in return for concessions,' which was announced as the policy of the party by one of its ablest members, Mr. George Black, might have been the basis of an honourable bargain; but, with men who were unacquainted with parliamentary methods, it became a cloak for insults and dictation.

Indeed, it was so evident that the position must become intolerable that Sir Henry Parkes has been blamed for not anticipating the inevitable by an earlier resignation. But he had a difficult choice to make. If he pressed forward with the Convention Bill, defeat was certain. If, on the other hand, he delayed to do so, public feeling would cool and the opportunity might pass. If he need have considered only the tactical considerations, which so readily presented themselves to his critics at the time and have been urged against him since, his choice was easy. For the veriest tyro in politics could see that it was better to be beaten in a great fight upon an Australian question than to leave Office ignominiously, after a series of small defeats; and, doubtless, Sir Henry Parkes would have taken this course, had he been quite free to act upon his own judgment. It may be told, however, at this distance of time that,—(as Sir Henry Parkes informed his friends, although his sense of constitutional propriety restrained him from disclosing this to the public in his defence),—he was pressed by the then Governor, Lord Jersey, with an urgency which was almost a command, to remain at the head of affairs, in order to avoid a danger to the public credit. Rumblings of the coming financial crisis could be heard already by experts ; and loan negotiations were in progress, which depended for their success upon the confidence of London lenders in the Administration. Sir Henry Parkes was known and trusted by the money market ; while Sir George Dibbs, who would have been his successor, had not, at this time, made his mark as a financier. Lord Jersey, accordingly, who was a partner in Child's Bank, with a correct appreciation of the situation, urged Sir Henry Parkes to remain in Office until the loan was floated, and twice induced him to withdraw a proffered resignation.

· 5 ·

The Government fell at length upon a matter of trifling importance, before they had been able to submit the Federal Resolutions. On October 19, Mr. McMillan moved to re-commit a local Mines Regulation Bill in order to expunge an amendment limiting the hours of labour to eight. A motion of adjournment moved by Mr. Barton, with the Ministry's concurrence, was defeated by 51 to 49, twenty-two Labour members voting in the majority. Sir Henry Parkes seized the opportunity of casting the yoke from his neck. As he explained to the House :—

Motions which affect the existence of Ministries naturally divide themselves into two classes. One class are of a character

M

which necessarily compels the resignation of a Ministry,—unless circumstances justify an appeal to the people,—such, for example, as direct votes of want of confidence and direct votes of censure. Another class of motions, which may seriously affect the Government, do not partake of this character. They do not necessarily compel a resignation ; but they place the Ministers of the day in this position—that they are fully justified in determining their own course.[1]

In his political autobiography he puts the position thus :—

It did not appear that any serious thought was entertained of critical consequences of the division. Several members of the Opposition voted with the Government (including Mr. Dibbs, the leader) ; but the Labour members, capriciously voting with the small knot of mischief-brewers, gave a majority against us. . . . The result was that Ministers thought that they had had enough of this sort of treatment, and they resigned.[2]

. 6 .

With the resignation of Sir Henry Parkes the first epoch of the federal movement came to an end. In less than two years the courage and insight of a great leader had drawn Federation from the clouds, and made it the first issue of Australian politics. But, although much had been done in the way of education and construction, the impulse still was lacking to overcome the apathy and antagonism of the local Parliaments. In Victoria, the two Houses had differed over the powers of the Senate,—the Assembly having struck out the clause in the Convention Bill which gave that Chamber the right to suggest amendments in Money Bills, and the Council having restored it. Tasmania

1 *Fifty Years*, vol. ii. p. 318.   2 *Ibid.*, pp. 309, 317.

and South Australia also had proposed amendments to the Bill ; and it was apparent that drastic alterations would be carried by the Parliament of New South Wales. Parliaments, indeed, were hardly competent to deal with the Bill ; and, seeing that in Australia there were six independent Parliaments, each consisting of two Houses, the difficulties in the way of any agreement between them appeared the more formidable the more they were examined. As Sir Henry Parkes wrote a few months after his retirement [1] :—

To analyse, criticise, and synthesise (if I may use the term) a complex political organism seems beyond the functions of a body with many voices and conflicting wills, and in which the most competent and the most incompetent have equal weight in a general vote. It is almost like a skilful clockmaker being associated on equal terms with a sailor and a tailor, a shoemaker and a weaver, a blacksmith and a bricklayer, in the making or repairing of a chronometer.

The best that could be hoped was that ' if by moderate counsels and good fortune the Constitution should be approved by the New South Wales Parliament, with reasonable and relevant amendments, the example would have a powerful effect in the other Colonies.' Yet, if this could not be done, still ' the Australian people were masters of the situation.'
Then in noble words Sir Henry Parkes forecast the future, and advised the course, for which, later, others claimed the credit, which led to the final triumph of the federal cause :—

The Constitution framed by the Sydney Convention is before the world. If we take the ground of the extreme

[1] *Fifty Years*, vol. ii. p. 379.

objectors, very slight amendments, hardly touching its principles, would meet their pessimistic views.   The cavil which has been raised is more one of phraseology than of principle. Any Constitution that can possibly be embodied in language, if fit for a free people, must be largely—almost wholly—modelled on the Convention Bill.   Let the Australian people, from sea to sea—East and West, North and South—take heed of this, and if the question is too big for their Parliaments, let them take it into their own hands.   There is nothing to prevent the election of a Federal Congress representing all the Colonies and the whole people.   A council of founders might be chosen, to revise the draft Bill of the Convention, or to frame a new Bill, to be presented to the several Parliaments for acceptance or rejection.   Let it never be forgotten that it is not the approval of the few men who form the Parliament of the day, but the ratification by the people who constitute the nation, either through their representatives or by their direct voice, which is required.   It will never do to allow the destiny of Australia to be made the sport of paltering politicians, who are here to-day and gone to-morrow. If the people but once awaken to the full grandeur of the movement, the end of their labours will soon be in sight.[1]

1 *Fifty Years*, vol. ii. p. 380.

CHAPTER XI

MR. BARTON THE LEADER

WHEN he resigned office, Sir Henry Parkes resigned also his leadership of the federal movement. On the evening of the defeat of his Ministry he sent for Mr. Barton to his room, while suffering from extreme fatigue, and spoke to him very frankly of his physical and political troubles. ' Are you prepared,' he said, ' to take up the cause of Federation ? ' And he added, in reply to Mr. Barton's question ' Why this should be asked of him,' that ' He himself was unable to carry it through, because his health was so precarious that, whatever might be the result of that night's proceedings, it was absolutely necessary for him to retire from Office and probably from public life. He was living in dread of a paralytic stroke. It was his intention to retire at once ; and the conduct of the federal movement must devolve upon Mr. Barton.' [1]

The latter accepted the mantle of leadership, thus informally cast upon his shoulders.

[1] Sir Edmund Barton has given the writer the particulars of this conversation.

. I .

It will be remembered that, ever since the Tenterfield speech, Mr. Barton had championed the cause of
Federation against his own party; and that, so recently
as September 1, he had declared against an alteration
in the tariff, upon the ground that this would be an
obstacle to Union, and, by moving an amendment to
this effect, had defeated the attempt of his party to
oust the Ministry. It was known that, in consequence,
the political relations between himself and Mr. Dibbs
were very strained. Yet, on October 26, the public
learnt that Mr. Barton had become Attorney-General
in Mr. Dibbs' Ministry, the declared policy of which
was the immediate imposition of protective duties and
the postponement for a year of the Federal Resolutions!
Except Mr. O'Connor and Mr. Copeland, every other
member of the Cabinet had opposed the Convention
Bill. It seemed, at the time, a startling change of front;
but, with our fuller knowledge, while we may question
the expediency of Mr. Barton's conduct (and he himself, looking back, has often doubted whether he did
right), we cannot, like his contemporary critics,
question his good faith.

Every day for a week Mr. Barton had refused
Mr. Dibbs' request that he would join him in the
Ministry, although his personal regard for him was
very strong. Finally, he had yielded, upon Mr. Dibbs'
assurance—which was observed faithfully—that he
should have a free hand in the conduct of the federal
movement; and because he saw no other way out of
a tangled situation. Sir Henry Parkes was unable to
continue the fight for Union, and Mr. Reid as Federal
leader was, at that time, unthinkable. As a Minister,

Mr. Barton could give effective aid to Federation ; while, as a private member, he would be powerless in an indifferent House, with a hostile Premier and an Opposition led by 'the arch enemy.' To accept Office seemed to him, on the outlook of the time, to offer the best opportunity of furthering the cause he had at heart ; and every other course which suggested itself seemed to place Federation in a more difficult and dangerous position. Nor, when the financial position of the Colony at that time is considered without party feeling, can Mr. Barton be accused fairly of breach of faith towards the Free Trade Federalists, because he acquiesced in Mr. Dibbs' policy of postponing Federation to a protective tariff. Revenue was indispensable ; for there was a very real and large deficit, although this was not admitted, at the time, by the Treasurer of the late Ministry. Yet the money question was urgent ; and there was no way of obtaining immediate relief except through the Custom House. Nor did it appear that a year's delay would injure the prospects of the Convention Bill, which probably would have been defeated in the then temper of the House. True that Mr. Barton had been returned for East Sydney in the previous June, upon his assurance that he would put Federation before Protection ; but, in the clearest terms, he had reserved his freedom to give effect to his Protectionist views in just such a contingency as the present. Now, when the political crisis had destroyed all hope of dealing in the current Session with any subject except Finance, he could hardly refuse to support the only method of raising revenue which was consistent with his Protectionist belief. Moreover, Mr. Dibbs, as we know now, had promised Mr. Barton to keep the duties down to an average of 10 per cent., so that they should not create vested interests which would be hostile to a common federal tariff.[1]

On seeking re-election as Minister, Mr. Barton explained his arrangement with Mr. Dibbs :—(1) That the Ministers as a body should support a Resolution expressing general approval of the Convention Bill; (2) That, while it was not expected that every Minister would adhere to every provision of the Bill, yet none was to give support to any destructive amendment ; and (3) That the Government would bring forward the question early next Session.   This arrangement, Mr. Barton argued, would enable him to work steadily towards parliamentary approval of the Bill, with a view to submitting it, with any amendments, to another Convention, and ultimately to a popular vote.   His position, undoubtedly, was extremely delicate ; but it is difficult, if the immediate necessity for raising revenue be admitted, to question his conclusion that, in the then state of politics, he could give effect, quite consistently, to his fiscal opinions, without disloyalty to the federal cause ; and, certainly, his leadership would be more effective as a Minister of the Crown than as a private member.

The drama of life, however, unlike a stage-play, does not expose the motives of the actors ; and the rough judgment of the public, which does not refine upon extenuating circumstances, dealt very harshly with Mr. Barton upon this occasion.   To the *Sydney Morning Herald* (October 31) he appeared to have made

---

[1] Except in a few instances, when Mr. Dibbs and Mr. Barton were overborne by their colleagues, this limit was observed.   The maximum duty did not exceed fifteen per cent.

'a calamitous mistake,' and the *Daily Telegraph* upon
the same day described his association with Mr. Dibbs
as 'an unholy alliance.'   Mr. Reid and Mr. Wise expressed the same sentiments on behalf of the Parliamentary Opposition, 'Any Free Trader should be
supported for East Sydney in preference to Mr. Barton '
said the latter.   The former added, ' As Free Traders
we can give the Government no quarter.'   Even
The Bulletin refused to take seriously the arrangement between Mr. Dibbs and Mr. Barton about the
Convention Bill, and depicted the former inviting his
Attorney-General to sit upon a nest of addled eggs
which was labelled ' Federation ' !   Unfortunately for
Mr. Barton, he was unable, during his two years' tenure
of office, to advance the cause of Federation sufficiently
to give an answer to his critics.   The times, indeed,
were unfavourable to a discussion of constitutional
changes ;   and Mr. Barton was fully occupied in
dealing with the banking crisis of 1892 and its after-
math.   Probably, too, if the history of the time
were disclosed, it would be found that the anti-
federal sympathies of a majority of his colleagues
hampered Mr. Barton more than he anticipated when
he joined the Ministry.   ' ——,' he wrote to the
author in May 1912, ' was always strewing tacks in my
path.'   Nevertheless, as we shall see, he did carry a
Resolution through the Assembly (November 23, 1892)
approving of the principles of the Convention Bill ;
and Federation owes much, even during this period of
stagnation, to Mr. Barton's unceasing efforts to keep
alive interest in the question, by means of public
meetings.   Certainly, Sir Henry Parkes, who was
acquainted with all the facts, did not question

Mr. Barton's sincerity, and refused to associate himself with an attack upon the new Ministry. But this is to anticipate.

. 2 .

One unforeseen consequence of Mr. Barton's acceptance of office under Mr. Dibbs was that Mr. Reid became the leader of the Opposition. In the ordinary course, on the retirement of the Government, Sir Henry Parkes would but have crossed the floor to the Opposition benches, with his leadership un-questioned. But he had announced publicly [1] his wish to retire for a while from active work in Parliament, giving, as his reason, weakness and advancing years. If he remained in Parliament, he wished to do so, for the present at least, as a private member, with no responsibility other than that associated with private membership. It was suspected, too, that he was unwilling to associate himself again with those of his late colleagues with whom he had not worked har-moniously ; and it was known that he considered that Mr. Dibbs, having succeeded to Office constitutionally, was entitled to a fair trial.

An influential section of the party was willing to retain Sir Henry Parkes as leader upon his own terms ; but the younger members thirsted for a fight upon the fiscal issue, and were in no mood to accept Sir Henry Parkes' counsel of delay. The Federalists among them were incensed at what appeared to their partisan-ship to be Mr. Barton's breach of faith, and were

---

[1] See interview in *Sydney Morning Herald* of October 17 : ' I am glad to be rid of it all. I have never been the same man since my accident, and I have not the strength to endure the long sittings of the Assembly.' See also Charles Lyne, *Life of Sir Henry Parkes*, p. 518.

goaded almost to fury by the exultation of the anti-Federal Protectionists over their long-delayed triumph. Nor were they restrained by the higher duty of making provision for the financial needs of the Colony— which was Mr. Dibbs' justification for imposing Customs Duties—because the public accounts had been the subject of controversy for years, and they denied the existence of any deficit.[1] It may be questioned, however, whether any consideration would have operated as a restraining influence. For it is a characteristic of the doctrine of Free Trade that its adherents often lack the sense of political proportion, and, like fanatics, put their fiscal faith above all else. Their arguments pass so imperceptibly from the region of economics to that of morals that a political maxim soon gains a transcendental significance, which obscures its relevance to existing conditions. The mysterious harmony which appears to result from the interplay of selfish motives disposes them to regard ' free competition ' as an instrument of Providence ; so that they forget that competition can only be ' free ' when it is a competition between equal units, and that, in modern times, trusts and the organisation of land and sea transport by Governments have destroyed even the

[1] At this time the accounts were not closed at the end of each financial year—(this was Mr. Reid's reform in 1895),—but continued open until every vote had been expended. All expenditure was charged back to the year in which it had been voted, and the revenue for the current year was credited with any savings on the votes. Thus there was perpetual controversy between the financial experts as to whether any given year showed a surplus or a deficit. In this year (1892) the late Treasurer had shown a surplus, but had arrived at this by crediting the revenue with a large sum in respect of a prospective sale of Crown lands in the Centennial Park, which were not sold until 1904. He had also cut down the supplementary estimates very drastically.

appearance of such an equality. Free Trade appeals also to the cosmopolitan sympathies which are attractive to certain temperaments, and the influence of which is in inverse ratio to the strength of a national spirit. And in 1891 the national spirit was at a low ebb in New South Wales, as in the rest of the Empire.

Thus, conviction joined with party spirit to force a fight upon the fiscal issue, now that the ground was cleared by the postponement of Federation. To this end it was necessary to have a leader. Consequently a meeting of the party was summoned for November 17—two days before the date on which Parliament was to meet—to consider the situation.

· 3 ·

Two of the late Ministers, Mr. McMillan and Mr. Bruce-Smith, had legitimate reasons for expecting the reversion of the leadership ; but neither was acceptable to the Labour Party, on whose support the Opposition counted. An intimation to this effect was given to them both before the meeting opened. Mr. McMillan took the chair ; and Mr. Bruce-Smith, evidently by pre-arrangement with the chairman, proposed at once that Sir Henry Parkes should continue to lead the party and be asked to name a deputy to act in his absence. Mr. Wise objected to a divided leadership as fatal to energetic action, and because, under such an arrangement, the credit of success would go to Sir Henry Parkes and the blame of failure rest upon his deputy. This view prevailed ; but, on the suggestion of Mr. McMillan, it was agreed that no one else should be proposed as leader at that meeting.

It was decided, instead, after a long and heated discussion, that Messrs. Bruce-Smith, Wise, Inglis, and J. P. Cullen should wait upon Sir Henry Parkes and ascertain his intentions. The instructions to this Committee were quite definitely limited, and conferred no authority to ask Sir Henry Parkes to continue as leader. The latter, perceiving the narrow scope of this mission, merely repeated what he had already said in an interview about his unwillingness to resume responsibility. It is certain, however, that, if this deputation had made him an offer of leadership on behalf of the party, his reply would have been different. He wrote the same day to Mr. Bruce-Smith in the following terms :—

Balmain, November 17, 1891.

My Dear Mr. Bruce-Smith,

I gathered from what you said to me this afternoon that the object of yourself and the three gentlemen who accompanied you was not so much to request me to retain or assume the leadership of our side of the House, as to obtain from me some definite announcement of my intention in the matter. Though I should have preferred saying nothing at the present time, still I cannot, when thus appealed to, withhold a clear expression of my views of the situation, so far as I am myself concerned. The leader of the Opposition in the present Parliament should be not only a man of great political capability, but one prepared to remain at his post throughout the sittings. I fear that man would not be found in me at my time of life. But, irrespective of the state of my health and the personal inconvenience arising from my accident of last year, I am bound to say that there are other reasons which, in whatever light considered, would compel me to decline the honourable, but most responsible, office of leader, under existing circumstances. I do not say—and I do not think that I ought to be expected to say—that, whatever circumstances of difficulty may arise in the future, I would not accept the burdens of office.   But I wish to be understood as saying distinctly, now, that I am anxious to avoid any position that would cast upon me any responsibility other than that of a simple member of Parliament.   Probably, as a representative of the people, I may be able to render better services than in any other capacity.

Very faithfully yours,
HENRY PARKES.

This letter, which was read to the party at its next meeting on November 19, was taken as a refusal to continue leader ; and Mr. Wise proposed Mr. Reid for the position, pointing out that, although he had differed from Mr. Reid over Federation, yet he was the best man to fight the Government at this crisis.   Mr Varney Parkes seconded the motion. Mr. James Inglis then proposed Mr. Bruce-Smith, who, in a speech of sense and good taste, declined to be put in nomination.   Mr. Garrard, who became later one of Mr. Reid's colleagues, proposed Mr. Wise, and Mr. James Inglis seconded the nomination.   Mr. Wise,—although he had been informed by two members of the Labour Party that that section of the House would support a vote of censure on the Government, if it were moved either by himself or Mr. Reid—stood by Mr. Reid, in the belief that the latter was better fitted to deal with the emergency. However, the feeling against Mr. Reid was at this time so intense that, although he was the only candidate, it required all the efforts of his friends to compel a vote in his favour. At length, at 4 o'clock, just as the House was meeting, a vote was taken giving 14 for Reid, 8 against, and 18 not voting at all. The result showed that any other candidate would have had a majority.[1]

Thus inauspiciously began a leadership, which was to give Mr. Reid the control of the federal movement, and to cloud the remaining years of Sir Henry Parkes' political life. To the latter Mr. Reid's selection as leader was peculiarly disagreeable.

Promptly and publicly he intimated that he would not follow him, and scenes of considerable bitterness between them occurred in the course of debate . . . . Gradually Sir Henry Parkes fell away from the main body of the Free Trade party and assumed an attitude of independence.[2]

Henceforward the struggle for Union was to be complicated by personal rivalries ; and Federation became, during several years, a subordinate issue of local politics.

[1] It is a curious instance of the infirmity of human memory that when, in December 1897, a question arose as to the circumstances of Mr. Reid's election, no two persons who were present agreed upon what had happened. The version given above is taken from a letter written by the author to the Hon. A. H. Conroy on November 25, 1891. For the discussion of the question see *The Catholic Press*, December 26, 1897, and January 1, 1898, and *Daily Telegraph* of January 10, 1898.

[2] Charles Lyne, *Life of Sir Henry Parkes*, pp. 520–1.

CHAPTER XII

A LULL

As the great strike occupied public attention in 1890–1, so, in 1892–3, the banking crisis diverted interest from all other questions. Three events, however, mark the progress of the federal movement during this period : (1) a premature and futile attempt by Sir Henry Parkes to begin upon new lines by summoning an Elective Constituent Convention : (2) a recantation of anti-Federalism by Mr. Reid [1] : and (3) the fulfilment by Mr. Barton of his pledge, given upon taking Office, to secure the approval of Parliament to the principles of the Convention Bill.

. I .

On March 1, 1892, Sir Henry Parkes moved the adjournment of the House to discuss ' the most ex-pedient course to be pursued in bringing Federation to a successful issue.' He exhausted the hour, which was allotted by the Standing Orders to the mover of such a motion, by an elaborate review of the progress of the federal movement since 1889 ; and had just stated his conclusion, that Parliament was not a fit body to deal with this question, and that the only step which could be taken was for the people themselves

[1] See *post*, pp. 271-2 and pp. 319-20, for Mr. Reid's explanation of his position at this time.

to elect another Convention to revise the draft Constitution, or frame a new one if they pleased, when a point of order, which the Speaker was compelled to sustain, brought his speech to an end. Only in his reply, which was limited to twenty minutes, was he able to point out the reasons why local Parliaments were unsuitable bodies to deal with Federation, which he developed more fully in the passage from his political autobiography which has been quoted in an earlier Chapter.[1] His advice was that the 'Government should introduce a short Bill, negotiating with the other Colonies to take the same course, empowering the people to elect delegates to a Convention charged with the one object of framing a just Bill, which should be submitted then to the people for acceptance or rejection.'

Mr. Barton did not favour this suggestion, thinking it to be inexpedient, at that time, to take the control of the movement away from Parliament, and not having abandoned his belief that the Bill would be dealt with in the current Session. As to the proposal to submit the Bill to a popular vote, he thought it preferable that Parliament should decide as to the method of its adoption, after it had itself considered the proposed Constitution.

It is difficult to pass judgment upon these conflicting views. Sir Henry Parkes' proposal certainly would have been regarded by Parliament as an affront ; and it is doubtful whether the Bill for an Elective Convention, which he contemplated, could have been carried. Yet, as events proved, the local Parliaments were quite unfit to frame a Constitution ; and

[1] See *ante*, p. 163.

N

Federation never regained its vigour until it had been dipped in the waters of popular opinion. The Elective Convention, asked for by Sir Henry Parkes in 1892, was adopted by Mr. Reid in 1896; and the trivial or absurd suggestions, which were made later by the several Houses of Parliament in regard to the Bill of 1897, amply justify Sir Henry Parkes' opinion as to the capacity of those bodies to frame a Constitution.

. 2 .

The occasion of Mr. Reid's recantation of his anti-Federal views was a meeting of the Free Trade party held (November 14, 1892) to congratulate Mr. Cleveland upon his election as President of the United States, which, in the general ignorance of American affairs, was interpreted in Sydney, as elsewhere, to be the inauguration of a Free Trade policy. [It may be remarked that the message of congratulation was never acknowledged!] Mr. Reid's argument was that, if the Americans could be converted from Protection, Free Trade might be expected to prevail in the Federal Parliament :—

He was glad [he said] to say that the progress of recent events had removed from his mind many of the misgivings which he had felt with regard to Federation. He confessed, and he was not ashamed to confess it, that he had used any influence he possessed to put a drag upon the federal movement, because he felt that immediate Federation meant an evil beginning in that respect for the new Commonwealth. But he now hoped that a march of events would improve the prospects of Free Trade, and after the tremendous march of events of the last few days, which no one could have well foreseen in all its amplitude and decisiveness, he felt that, the great American Commonwealth having turned round to pursue the path of Free Trade, no Australian Federation would adopt Protection.

Although the progress of events in America proved this diagnosis of the situation to be erroneous, Mr. Reid did not weaken on his declaration, and never by any process of reasoning came back to the point from which he had started.

He repeated his contention in Parliament a few days later, during the debate on Mr. Barton's Federal Resolutions (November 23, 1892) :—

> Two and a half years ago I said 'I will not federate until I have a more rational and better idea that my principles will not be sacrificed.' I say now that I have a more rational and better idea that my principles will not be sacrificed.

And he gave as additional reasons, a single tax agitation in Victoria and the growing discontent in New South Wales with Mr. Dibbs' protective duties. The pretext was ridiculed : the recantation was remembered ![1]

· 3 ·

Mr. Barton's promise, to ask the House, as part of the Government policy, to approve of the principles of the Convention Bill, was fulfilled on November 23, 1892, when he proposed the following Resolutions :—

> 1. That this House re-affirms its opinion in favour of the Federation of the Australian Colonies, and having regard to the difficulties, as well as the necessity, of reconciling conflicting interests and coming to a common ground of agreement, it approves of the main principles of the Convention Bill.

[1] See *ante*, p. 108, footnote.

2. That the said Bill should be considered in Committee of the Whole, and such amendments as may be desired by the legislative bodies of this and the other Colonies should, together with the Draft Bill, be remitted for the consideration of a second Convention, similarly appointed and reporting to the several Parliaments ; and that the question of the final adoption by any Colony of any proposal for a Federal Constitution should be submitted to the people in their electoral capacity.

His speech, in support of these Resolutions, was both historical and argumentative. He recapitulated the events which had delayed the consideration of the Convention Bill, and explained again the conditions upon which he had taken Office. Then he entered upon an elaborate exposition of the nature of a Federal Constitution, as illustrated by the provisions of the Bill. He pointed out that Federation had two aspects from the point of view of a component State. It gave new powers, which the citizens of the State could not exercise previously, because the jurisdiction of a State is bounded by its territorial limits ; while it took away only such powers as could be exercised more effectively by the common action of all the States :—

That which the States are said to hand over in its largest sense is no handing over at all, because it is the constitution of a jurisdiction and a dealing which otherwise they would have no hand or part in . . . . And, as regards the rest of these things, they are not handed over. They are matters ceded to a general authority, because it is recognised that, if the citizens of the various States are willing to enter into partnership in matters of the kind, laws of general prevalence are not a diminution or a surrender of freedom but a true conservation of freedom.

Mr. Barton was followed by Mr. Reid, who, after explaining the change in his views which has been before referred to, set forth at length, and in temperate language, his objections to the Convention Bill.

First, he considered that the Senate's powers over Money Bills were excessive and dangerous. To allow that Chamber to amend Loan Bills and measures dealing with ' extraordinary expenditure,' as proposed by the Bill, seemed to him 'destructive of majority rule.' Nor could he admit that the power to 'suggest' amendments in the Appropriation Act was different, in substance, from a power to amend.

Secondly, he considered that the Bill did not give sufficient facilities for amending the Constitution. Without suggesting an alternative, he thought that the proposal to require an absolute majority, both of voters and of States, before any amendment could be made, would hamper the development of the country. Nor did he agree with the clause which required any amendment of the Constitution to be submitted for the Royal assent, because ' the day might come for a separation from the Mother Country.'

Thirdly, he considered that the clause permitting Ministers to sit in Parliament was not a sufficient guarantee of the continuance of Responsible Government ; but he did not point out under what other system the affairs of the Parliament were likely to be conducted, so long as Ministers remained in Parliament and Australian practice continued to be modelled upon that of England.

Fourthly, he objected to the power of the Commonwealth to abolish differential railway rates, although this was a corollary of inter-Colonial Free Trade. He desired that the Commonwealth should compensate the State for the loss of trade arising from their abolition.

Fifthly, he objected to the clause which gave the Governor-General 'such powers and functions as the Queen may think fit,' asking, 'What have we to do with Royal instructions in the Federal Constitution ? ' He forgot that every Colonial Governor had the same powers, and that the Federal Constitution limited the right of the Crown in conferring these powers and allowed it to be exercised only 'subject to the Constitution.'

Sixthly, he thought the clause prohibiting the Commonwealth from taxing 'the property of a State' damaging and ambiguous.

Seventhly, he would have preferred that the High Court should be made a part of the Constitution instead of being appointed by Parliament, as was proposed. This was done in the Bill of 1897.

Eighthly, he objected to Parliament giving the final voice as to the Bill to a popular vote, and

Ninthly, he thought that a time should be fixed within which a uniform tariff must be passed.

All these objections were worthy of consideration, although most of them were refuted by the text of the Bill ; and, if Mr. Reid had stated them on other occasions with the same moderation, no one could have questioned his desire to submit them to Parliament for an impartial consideration. Unfortunately, the evidence furnished by his own admissions [1] shows that his desire had been rather to confuse and mislead the judgment of the public than to argue out fairly the merits or demerits of the Convention Bill.

[1] See *ante*, p. 179, and *post*, p. 203.

The debate on Mr. Barton's Resolutions was interrupted by a Motion of Censure, moved by Mr. Reid, and was not completed until May 17, 1893, when both were carried. Neither side dared to oppose them; for Mr. Barton had let it be known that he would resign if they were rejected. This would have brought about a dissolution on the federal issue, which both parties feared,—the anti-Federalists because they thought the country favoured the Convention Bill, the Federalists because they feared the contrary. Immediately afterwards Mr. Barton became ill, and no further progress was made that Session. Mr. O'Connor, in the Legislative Council, carried the same Resolutions; and in his speech suggested, as a method of resolving deadlocks, the joint sitting of the two Houses, which, with modifications, was adopted by the second Convention in 1897–8. Parliament met again in September; and on October 12 Mr. Barton moved the House into Committee to consider the Convention Bill. A Free Trade Labour member, Mr. Arthur Rae, moved an amendment that Federation 'would do nothing to meet the social and industrial problems so urgently pressing for a solution,' and that the Convention Bill 'was of too rigid a character to suit the progressive character of Australian democracy.' Sir Henry Parkes moved the adjournment of the debate; and, before this was concluded, both Mr. Barton and Mr. O'Connor had resigne their offices 'as a matter of honour,' because of an unworthy attack which had been made upon them for being concerned, Mr. Barton as arbitrator, and Mr. O'Connor as counsel, in a dispute between a contractor and the Commissioner for Railways. The appointment had been made and the brief delivered before either of them had joined the Ministry. With these resignations all hope of Parliamentary action came to an end.   In short, the Parliamentary process, as Sir Henry Parkes had foreseen, had broken down hopelessly ; and it was plain that, if Federation were to be accomplished, it would be through the people, not the politicians.

CHAPTER XIII

' SCUFFLING ON THE STEPS OF THE TEMPLE '

UPON the resignation from the Ministry of Messrs. Barton and O'Connor (December 1892) it was recognised, even by the most sanguine, that no advance would be made by Parliamentary action ; and from this time, until the meeting of the second Convention, in April 1897, Federalists directed their energies to the instruction of the public in the principles of the Convention Bill. The very causes which had made Parliament indifferent to the question—the land boom, the banking crisis, the commercial depression,—were bringing home to the average citizen the solidarity of the interests of all the Colonies.[1]

Thus, attempts to create an educated public opinion upon federal problems, which had been premature in 1890 and 1891,[2] now became opportune and popular.

[1] 'A growing sense of the dangers of disunion was breaking down the isolation and mutual jealousy which prosperity had fostered. The bad times [to continue the quotation from Messrs. Quick and Garran's Introduction] set everyone inquiring for himself into the causes which clogged the wheels; and the folly of provincial tariffs became increasingly apparent. Federation began to appeal to the pocket as well as to the heart, and people began to wake up to the fact that the ' fad of Federation, ' with which the politicians and Parliaments had been dallying so long, meant the salvation of Australia.'

[2] See *ante*, pp. 100-2. Sir Henry Parkes, in his *Fifty Years*, prints a proposal for a ' Federal League of Australasia,' which he issued privately in the middle of 1891. A few meetings of sympathisers were held, but the League never had an effective existence.

. I .

It was natural that the border districts, where the irritation and absurdity of the provincial tariffs were most apparent, should take the lead in the popular movement.   A Federal League upon non-party lines had been formed already at Corowa through the efforts of Mr. Edward Wilson, a brother of Mr. H. F. Wilson of the Colonial Office, who became later secretary to Mr. Chamberlain.   In December 1892 Mr. Barton suggested that the scope of this League should be extended throughout the Murray valley; and, by the end of May 1893, fifteen branches had been formed in that district.   In March of the same year the Australian Natives' Association, which was very influential in Victoria, appointed a deputation to wait upon Mr. Barton, who was recognised already in the other Colonies as Sir Henry Parkes' successor, and urge upon him the formation of a Federal League in Sydney. Accordingly, in June 1893, Mr. Barton summoned a preliminary meeting of Federalists to consider the best means of uniting the local Leagues and concentrating public sentiment in favour of Federation.   No one could take this initiative more appropriately;   and no course would appear to have been more desirable. Unhappily it was the fate of every Federal leader, from which Mr. Barton did not escape, to be suspected of insincerity during some period of his leadership.   At this time his proposal was regarded by Free Traders as a party move;   and to those who would not recognise his difficulties the evidence appeared conclusive.

The charge was based upon the refusal of the Dibbs Government to entertain a proposal put forward by Sir Philip Fysh, the Premier of Tasmania, in 1892, for

tolerable if Federation had been imminent ; but the delays which had already occurred forbade this hope. As matters stood, the bargain appeared to be so one-sided that men were persuaded easily by party feeling that the Federal League was a mere Protectionist device for staving off defeat in the coming elections; and that the more prudent course was to hold aloof and draw tighter the old party lines. Certainly, when Mr. Barton, a year later, sought re-election for Rand-wick, the refusal of the Tasmanian proposals was used against him with fatal effect ; and Free Trade Federal-ists joined with the enemies of Union to put him out of Parliament. He was not returned again until 1898 ; and the echoes of the controversy which was raised by these proceedings were heard, as will be told, even in the final stage of the federal struggle.

· 3 ·

In spite of this inauspicious beginning, the Federal League did good service to the cause of Union. It did not advocate any particular form of Federation, but was pledged ' to advance the cause by an organisation of citizens owning no class distinction or party influence, and using its best energies to assist Parliamentary action, from whatever source proceeding, calculated to further the common aim of Australian patriotism.' Dissociated from politics it became a somewhat academic body ; but, as Mr. R. R. Garran, who was one of its most active members, has said truly enough,[1]

its history, if not sensational, shows a record of steady organising and educating work. It formed a nucleus for an active body

[1] Quick and Garran, *Constitution of the Australian Commonwealth*, p. 152.

of earnest Federalists in Sydney, and a connecting link between the country Leagues, which began to spring up in large numbers, especially in the border districts. The result was largely due to the indefatigable work of Mr. Edward Dowling, its principal honorary secretary.

The development of the popular movement, which this League inaugurated, will be the subject of the next chapter.

CHAPTER XIV

THE POPULAR MOVEMENT

THE formation of the Federal League immediately stimulated public interest. Not only were branches of it formed in every Colony, but Conferences were held between these, which resulted in the preparation of the scheme of action which brought the cause of Australian Union ultimately to a successful issue.[1]

. I .

The Border Leagues began at once to take an active part in the new movement ; and a Conference was held at Corowa on July 31 and August 1, 1893, to which representatives were invited from other Leagues, trading and commercial bodies, the Australian Natives' Association and kindred societies from both sides of the Murray. This Conference, which was well attended, is notable for the proposal, put forward there for the first time by Dr. John Quick, LL.D. (now the Hon. Sir John Quick), which marks an epoch in the federal movement, because it became the basis later of the Federal Enabling Acts. The new feature of the proposal

---

[1] The matter of this Chapter is taken from Quick and Garran's *Introduction to the Annotated Constitution,* who record the facts related in it—*quorum partes magnae fuerunt*—with such fulness and special knowledge that anyone covering the same ground must tread in their steps.

was that each Colony should pass an Act providing for an elective Convention and *in the same Act* make provision for the submission of the Constitution to a popular vote.   Dr. Quick elaborated the idea into a Bill which he submitted on January 1, 1894, to the Bendigo Federal League.   The procedure he suggested was as follows :—

That each Colony should pass an Act substantially in the same shape, providing :—

(1) For the election on its Parliamentary Franchise of ten representatives to a Federal Congress.

(2) That this Congress should frame a Federal Constitution.

(3) That, on a day to be agreed upon, this Constitution should be referred to the electors of each Colony, for acceptance or rejection.

(4) That, if the Constitution were accepted by majorities in two or more Colonies, it should be forwarded to the Imperial Government to be passed into law.

The novel and all-important element in this proposal [as is pointed out by Messrs. Quick & Garran] was the idea of mapping out the whole process in advance by Acts of Parliament,—of making statutory provision for the last step before the first step was taken.   Hitherto, each successive step in the framing of a Constitution had been left dependent on the concurrence of all the Parliaments or all the Governments for the time being ;   with the result that every hitch, every discouragement had led to delay ;   and all the zeal and labour expended on the Commonwealth Bill of 1891 seemed in danger of being lost.   But here was a scheme which, when once launched, would ensure the framing of a Constitution and its submission to the people.   Every step in the process would thus be invested, in the minds of the people, with a seriousness and importance otherwise unattainable. The people who had jested at the Convention of 1891 as a body of men engaged in the amiable and amusing task of drawing up a Constitution for the waste-paper basket, would have to admit that there was something serious about a Constitution which, when framed, the Government would be obliged by law to submit to the electors for their acceptance or rejection.

The other feature of the scheme—the direct popular initiative in the election of the Convention—was not new. It had been proposed, it will be remembered, by Sir Henry Parkes in 1892,[1] at a time when faith in Parliamentary action had not been lost entirely ; and had been opposed by Mr. Barton in that belief. Quite consistently, therefore, as President of the Federal League, to which Dr. Quick submitted his proposal, Mr. Barton suggested a modification, which, while it preserved to the people the power to protect themselves against mere political machinations, would give considerable influence to any Parliament, which chose to exercise its powers seriously, in the framing of a Federal Constitution. Mr. Barton feared, still, that the attempt to strike off a Federal Constitution at one sitting, without consulting the separate Colonies except for the final vote, might fail to secure adequate adjustment of conflicting interests, and thus lead to the rejection of the Constitution at the polls. The amendment, proposed by the Federal League, to Dr. Quick's scheme was to the effect that each Colony should first elect a provincial Convention to formulate its own ideas of a Federal Constitution ; that these should be submitted to a

[1] See *ante*, p. 177.

Federal Convention elected by the Parliaments, which should frame a Constitution in which the views of the several Colonies should be harmonised so far as possible; and that the Constitution to be submitted to the popular vote should be the one so framed.

At a later stage (February 6, 1895), at a Conference of Premiers, a modification of Dr. Quick's proposal was adopted upon these lines; and the Enabling Bill, as accepted by the Colonies, provided that the Elective Convention, after framing a draft Constitution, should adjourn for a period of not less than thirty nor more than sixty days; that the several Parliaments should consider the Bill during this adjournment, and submit their proposed amendments to the Convention, to be considered by this body, before the Bill was finally adopted. Thus the essential features of Dr. Quick's proposal were preserved, while the objections to it were removed.

. 2 .

In the meantime, Sir George Dibbs, in a letter to Sir James Paterson, Premier of Victoria (June 12, 1894), put forward, as an alternative scheme, the immediate unification of the two Colonies of New South Wales and Victoria, to be followed ' by the attraction of the neighbouring Colonies within the sphere of our extended influence.'

This scheme, impracticable as it was at the time, was supported by arguments which must carry greater weight with every year's experience of the inconvenience of a federal system, and every quickening of the spirit of Australian nationality. With great force Sir George Dibbs pointed out the ridiculous division of control over public debts, railways, and land revenues; the expense of a double system of government; the absurdity of equal representation in the Senate; and the immense advantage of

a complete pooling of our debts, our railways, our national establishments generally, with a view to extending our revenues and minimising our expenditure. We are none of us so badly off that we cannot be permitted to meet each other upon equal terms. In such a partnership, New South Wales would not be disposed to say to our neighbours ' Your debts are more burdensome, your railways and lands less productive than ours.' We would give to the United Government that prestige and supreme control, which is almost entirely denied under the Commonwealth scheme, wherein the Federal Legislature would be numerically and structurally wholly overshadowed by the provincial Governments; and, without haggling over the items, we would be prepared to hand over the Customs House, Post Office, and other necessary establishments for the common good, provided others did the same. I would confine the local governments, as in Canada, within subordinate limits and to strictly local purposes. Under such a scheme there would be no need for State Governors or for a separate State Representative in London.

Sir George Dibbs admitted that the Union which he contemplated must be limited, at first, to the Colonies of New South Wales and Victoria, and that the others could not be induced to join it in its early years.

' The division of Australia into two sections—the large States and the small States—and denying to the latter any voice in the form of the Union was ' (as Messrs. Quick and Garran point out) 'the serious blemish of the scheme.' For it is beyond doubt that the other Colonies would not have come into such a Federation—

which meant their practical annexation to New South Wales and Victoria ;—and the attempt to force them into it would have been an unfavourable auspice for Union.

Nevertheless, the practical advantages of a more unified Government are so great that, if present indications are a guide to the future, the arguments of Sir George Dibbs will receive greater consideration as the years go by. One essential preliminary to any large extension of the federal powers is the division of Australia into smaller States, which was contemplated by Sir Henry Parkes in 1891 ; because no federal system can work smoothly when the partners to the Union are few in number, and widely disproportionate in wealth and population.

Sir Henry Parkes and Mr. Macrossan, who had both perceived this difficulty, only abandoned their leaning [1] towards a more complete amalgamation of the Colonies when they perceived that closer Union was unattainable under the conditions of the time—a perception which was borne out fully by the indifference with which the public treated the proposals of Sir George Dibbs. ' Unification ' was never a serious political cry during the federal campaign ; although the opponents of Federation made occasional use of the phrase to belittle the Federalists as only ' half-and-half Unionists.'

· 3 ·

In the meantime, dissatisfaction with Parliamentary dallying was finding vent in steady propaganda work. The Federal Leagues expounded the Constitution in every Colony ; and Mr. Barton was delivering scholarly

[1] See *ante*, pp. 118, 119.

addresses on the characteristics of a federal system throughout New South Wales. He addressed nearly 300 meetings between January 1, 1893, and his election to the Convention in February 1897. Yet, to judge only from the sparse attendances, the question excited little public interest. But, if one regarded rather the composition of the audiences, it became plain that the young men whom he addressed would address others in their turn, and that Federation would owe its victory to their efforts. The younger generation of University men were specially active ; but perhaps the best service was done by others in a humbler rank, who had taken no part in politics before, but, from patriotism and without hope of reward or fame, now gave their services devotedly to the cause of Union. Thus, although the spread of the movement was slow, there grew up an organised body of federal sentiment, which proved strong enough, when the machinery of the Enabling Act was set in motion, to resist successfully all attempts to throw it out of gear. The control was passing from Parliaments to the people ; but some dangerous stages had yet to be gone through.

CHAPTER XV

' DRAWING OLD PARKES' TEETH '

As was expected, the Ministry was defeated at the General Election of 1894; but Sir George Dibbs decided to meet Parliament. On August 2, however, he resigned unexpectedly, in consequence of the refusal of the Governor, Sir Robert Duff, to accept some of his nominations to the Legislative Council. A meeting of the Free Trade party had been summoned for the next day to elect a leader; and a majority of members had declared their preference for Sir Henry Parkes. Sir Robert Duff, however, did not wait for an expression of opinion from the party, but sent at once for Mr. Reid, who thus acquired an unassailable position. It was one thing to elect a new leader of the Opposition, and another to displace a Premier; so that, when the party met, only three members, Messrs. James Martin, Brunker, and Wise adhered to Sir Henry Parkes. Mr. Brunker joined the Ministry of Mr. Reid two days later; Mr. Wise refused. The disappointment to Sir Henry Parkes was overwhelming. He had contributed more than Mr. Reid to the victory of his party, and he possessed the confidence of the Federalists, which was not given to Mr. Reid. True, he had withdrawn from the nominal direction of the Liberal Party; but he remained its natural leader and was the most powerful exponent of its principles. In short, he occupied towards Mr. Reid much the same position in the Councils of the party that Mr. Gladstone occupied towards Lord Hartington in 1880. No one could have foreseen that the impetuosity of a Premier, and the mistake of a Governor, would oust him from his place, and mar the crowning achievement of his long life. For the next three years Federation became the sport of faction.

Horace Walpole [1] has remarked that

Times of party have their great outlines which all can seize. But a season of faction is another guess-thing. It depends on personal characteristics, intrigues and minute circumstances, which make little noise, and escape the eyes of the generality. The details are numerous, and, when the moment has passed, they become too trifling and uninteresting for history. [All that can be done is] to endeavour to preserve the thread, but it is impossible to develop all its windings.

This is the right spirit in which to regard the Parliamentary manœuvres of the next three years.

. I .

When Mr. Reid came into Office, he was pledged to the hilt to an immediate abolition of the Dibbs duties, and the imposition of direct taxation. In a manifesto to the electors of East Sydney, after he had become Premier, he declared also ' that he would lose no time in restoring the subject of Australian Federation to its rightful position of importance and urgency '—a contemptuous reference to the labours of Sir Henry Parkes and Mr. Barton, which conveniently ignored his own persistent efforts to thwart their success. It will be remembered that the Convention Bill was still before Parliament, and that New South Wales was pledged

[1] Letter to Sir Horace Mann, June 26, 1765.

to the other Colonies to continue its consideration. Sir Henry Parkes, accordingly, gave notice, early in the Session, that he would move ' That it was desirable [for reasons which he set out] that Parliament, without loss of time, should resume the consideration of the Federation of the Colonies under one national Government.' Mr. Reid, at this time, was not seated firmly in the saddle. The responsibility of Office had convinced him of the danger of a premature abandonment of the revenue from the existing tariff ; and, because he was unwilling to make this confession, he had postponed the announcement of his financial policy until the following year, to the exasperation of those of his supporters who were not in the secret. Sir Henry Parkes, although aware of this dissatisfaction, was precluded by his election speeches from attacking the Government for delaying to alter the tariff or making other fiscal changes, which would further complicate the problem of federal finance by widening the difference between the system of New South Wales and that of the other Colonies. He perceived, however, that Mr. Reid was assailable upon his anti-Federal side ; but did not calculate that Mr. Reid's equally acute perception would turn him in a few months into a Federalist as ardent as himself ! Again circumstances conspired in Mr. Reid's favour ! [1]

On November 12, two days before Sir Henry Parkes' motion would come on, Mr. Reid was waited upon by a deputation from the Federation League, which placed before him Dr. Quick's scheme and the League's report upon it. He seized the opportunity in his reply to define his new attitude towards Federation.

[1] See *ante*, p. 108, footnote.

Those who recalled that in November 1892 [1] he had assigned the imminence of Free Trade in the United States as his reason for abandoning his opposition to Australian Federation, might have thought that, when events had proved that he had misinterpreted the meaning of Mr. Cleveland's election, the same reasoning would bring him back to his old position. But to argue thus was to misunderstand Mr. Reid. Without any reference to the United States, he expressed on this occasion a frank regret for his previous hostility to the Convention Bill :—

Looking back on the past I must confess that there are some passages in my opposition to the great national Convention which I reflect upon now with regret.

Now, he admitted that the Convention Bill ' would probably form the bulk of any future Federal Constitution.' His next sentence perhaps made it difficult to understand this praise of the Bill ; because he maintained still, and recapitulated, all his old objections to it, viz., that it did not provide for Responsible Government, nor give a power to resolve deadlocks, nor define clearly the relative powers of the two Houses over Money Bills. But his concluding comment was quite definite :—

That the Bill was the most admirably clear measure as a piece of draftsmanship which he had ever seen ; and, in that respect, was a monument for all time.

But, if there was some ambiguity as to his opinion of the Convention Bill, there was none as to his approval of the proposals of the League,—' a body of which, at

1 See *ante*, p. 178, and p. 108, footnote.

one time, he had been suspicious.' He concurred with the League's view that ' constitutional reforms ought to come from the people to the politicians, not from the politicians, however able they might be, to the people,' and was ' deeply impressed ' with the merits of their scheme. He could not commit himself, however, to any course without consulting the other Premiers, whom he would invite to meet him in Conference early next year, in the hope that they ' would evolve some scheme for united action at no distant date.' He repeated these sentiments on November 14, during the debate upon Sir Henry Parkes' Resolution, which was carried, but without enthusiasm, by 55 votes to 10.

Sir Henry's speech was one of his best—dignified, lightened by personal reminiscences, and full of sound advice. His tributes to Mr. Barton and Cardinal Moran have more than a passing interest. Of the former he said :—

At a time when the friends of Federation were very few, he rendered very important service indeed ; and there can be no ground for doubting his sincere efforts to bring about a Union of these Colonies.

Of Cardinal Moran he used these words :—

There is another person, who is an entire stranger to me, and, I should think, a gentleman who has no very high opinion of me, whose services I should acknowledge. Of all the voices on this question, no voice has been more distinct, more full of a worthy foreshadowing of the question's greatness and more fraught with a clear prescience of what is likely to come as the result of Federation, than the voice of this eminent prelate.

He made only a veiled reference to Mr. Reid, but deprecated throwing aside the Convention of 1891 and starting afresh with any less representative body. In words which excluded Sir George Dibbs' Unification scheme, he urged that

every step forward must be taken in concurrence with all the Colonies. We cannot dictate : We cannot make terms : We must realise that each Colony is as independent as we are.

Powerful as the speech was, all who heard it realised that the announcement of the new policy had spiked Sir Henry Parkes' guns, and that Mr. Reid was entitled to time to put this to the test.

. 2 .

The Conference of Premiers met, at Mr. Reid's instance, at Hobart, in February 1895. There was a difference of opinion as to the course to be pursued. Mr. Nelson, Premier of Queensland, objected to submitting the Constitution to a Referendum. Sir John Forrest favoured Parliamentary action and objected to a new start. Mr. Kingston preferred a more expeditious procedure, and would have asked for an Imperial Act, empowering the Colonies to adopt a Federal Constitution subject to the Royal assent. He would not vote, however, against Mr. Reid's proposals. Finally, a draft Bill was brought up by Messrs. Turner and Kingston, upon the lines of Dr. Quick's proposals, with the important modification that the Convention, after framing the Constitution, should adjourn for a stated period, in order to enable the several Parliaments to consider the Bill, and should meet a second time to reconsider its work, in the light of the amendments or suggestions made by the several Parliaments. Thus, while following in essentials the scheme of Dr. Quick, the measure agreed to by the Premiers obviated the objections made to this by the Federal League.

It gave time [write Messrs. Quick and Garran][1] for reflection and reconsideration: It gave an opportunity for the several Colonies, through their Legislatures or otherwise, to formulate their criticisms and objections, and it thus ensured a more thorough thrashing out of all questions of conflicting interest. The merits of the scheme were obvious and notable. It avoided all the great defects of the process of 1891. It secured popular interest by providing that Members of the Convention should be elected by the people themselves, and that the Constitution should be submitted to the people themselves for acceptance. It conciliated the Parliaments by giving them a voice in initiating the process, a voice in criticising the Constitution before its completion, and a voice in requesting the enactment of the Constitution after acceptance. In other words, whilst necessarily assigning to a single body, representative of all the Colonies, the task of framing the Constitution in the first instance and finally revising it, it ensured that both the peoples and the Parliaments of the several Colonies should be consulted at every stage—in initiation, in deliberation, and in adoption. And lastly, by making statutory provision in advance for every step of the process, it ensured that the matter once begun should be brought to an issue. No fuller security could have been given that the Constitution would be based upon the will of the people and of the people's representatives.

· 3 ·

The advantages of this new procedure to the cause of Federation seem, now, to be decisive in its favour ;

---

[1] *Introduction to the Annotated Constitution*, pp. 159–60.

but, at the time, these were not perceived so clearly as the advantage which it offered to a Premier who might possibly still be half-hearted in his Federalism. If Mr. Reid were striving to strengthen his own position by Parliamentary manœuvres, no suggestion could have been more attractive than that he should restart the federal movement from the beginning, and recommend the holding of a new Convention of elected representatives. He might rightly calculate that the passage of the necessary Acts by all the Parliaments, the election of delegates and other preliminaries, would enable him to stave off an embarrassing question for at least two years. The anti-Federal supporters of his Ministry, at any rate, did not hesitate to express their satisfaction that their leader had 'drawn old Parkes' teeth.' [1]

Certainly, the new policy did effect a very opportune disarmament of Mr. Reid's federal critics. A year elapsed, after the Premiers' Conference (February 1895), before New South Wales passed the necessary Act to authorise the election of delegates; and it was not until March 1897 (after Sir Henry Parkes' death) that the Convention met in Adelaide for the first Session. If Mr. Reid's later actions had not confirmed the impression that this delay was not displeasing to him, he, and not Mr. Barton, would have been the first Prime Minister of the Commonwealth. Rivalry with Mr. Barton for the leadership, by his own

[1] Mr. Tighe Ryan, the very able editor of *The Catholic Press*, often referred to this phrase. The *Sydney Morning Herald*, in a leading article, voiced the suspicions of the Federalists. 'The Hobart Enabling Bill may be described as a Bill to postpone Federation indefinitely. It breaks absolutely with the past and makes inadequate provision for the future.' See *ante*, p. 108, footnote.

admission, affected his conduct. During the election of 1894, when he was opposed by Sir Henry Parkes in the King Division of Sydney, he declared that the principle of his policy was ' always to be top-dog ' ; and, when reminded of this during the election of 1898 by an interjector, who suggested that his opposition to the Convention Bill was because Mr. Barton and not himself occupied that position, he replied with characteristic frankness, ' Well, there is a good deal in that ! There is a good deal of human nature in me ! '

· 4 ·

Mr. Reid's tardiness in submitting his financial policy has been already mentioned. On November 7, he announced in an interim financial statement that his fiscal measures would be postponed until March or April of the following year—(they were not in fact proposed until May 9)—and precedence given to a Land Bill and a Local Government Bill. This was the more galling to those of his supporters who had sunk their Federalism at the General Election, with extreme reluctance, for the sake of Free Trade and a land tax, because the postponement of a land tax, until after the passage of a Local Government Bill, had been the demand of the defeated Opposition.[1] It was not for this that Federalist land-taxers had broken with Sir Henry Parkes, their natural leader ; and it seemed to them, now, that in grasping at the shadow they had lost the substance.[2] Nor were their anxieties

[1] See *Daily Telegraph*, July 16 and 17, 1894, ' The Issues of the Election.'

[2] Students of local history will find a full statement of the case for and against Mr. Reid in the issues of the *Daily Telegraph* of October 10, 12 and 13, 1894, and the *Goulburn Penny Post* of November 12, 1894.

relieved when Mr. Reid brought down his Budget on May 9, 1895. Instead of an immediate abolition of the Dibbs' duties, this provided for a gradual repeal. The *ad valorem* duties were to cease on June 30, some other specific duties a year later, and other duties at different dates up to June 30, 1901. ' Free Trade on time payment ' as it was described by one critic, ' without adequate provision for the instalments.' A Land and Income Tax Bill was proposed to make up the deficiency.

It seemed to Sir Henry Parkes' sanguine friends that the dissatisfaction in the Ministerial ranks offered a favourable opportunity for a union of parties on the common ground of federal sympathies ; and, on May 16, Sir Henry Parkes, believing from the assurances he had received that a majority of the Assembly was favourable to a Coalition, moved a Resolution, with the assent of Sir George Dibbs, to the effect that ' The continuance of the Government in Office would retard the progress of much-needed legislation and seriously prejudice the cause of Australian Federation.' Such a motion, which might have been carried a few weeks later, was premature, so long as there remained a possibility, however remote, that the Land Tax would become law in the course of the Session.[1] The Ministerial ranks remained unbroken—only two Free Traders, Messrs. Martin and Ellis, voting with Sir Henry

[1] A pamphlet by the author, published in July 1895, entitled *A Year's Stewardship*, contains several documents relating to the dispute. Looking back and recognising that Mr. Reid had the knowledge, which his critics lacked, of the urgent needs of the Treasury, it would seem that the most that can be urged against him fairly is a certain deviousness in his methods of delay, owing to the impulsive particularity of his electioneering promises.

P

Parkes,—and the Resolution was defeated by 67 votes to 34.[1]

Nothing in Sir Henry Parkes' long career exposed him to more severe censure than this attempted Coalition with the Protectionists. Mr. Charles Lyne describes the effect upon public opinion with force and accuracy [2] :—

> That, in face of his life-long advocacy of Free Trade, Sir Henry Parkes could join the leader of the Protectionists in an attempt to overthrow a Free Trade Ministry, was what the newspapers, with one or two exceptions, from one end of the country to the other, professed their inability to understand, except upon the ground that Sir Henry was a deserter from the ranks of Free Trade and now a Protectionist.

Yet, in reality, he was but acting consistently with the course of action which he had followed for three years, and many times explained publicly. When Mr. Reid declared he was going ' to sail into the port of Federation with the flag of Free Trade flying,' it was mere loyalty to the cause which impelled Sir Henry to reply that, ' If Victoria were to make the similar assertion that she would enter the port of Federation with the flag of Protection flying, Federation would be impossible.' The situation became more dangerous when ' the flag ' was to be shown annually for six years to neighbours whom it irritated. ' How is it possible,' asked Sir Henry, ' to reconcile this policy of Free Trade by instalments with an honest endeavour to federate the Colonies ? ' Nor was common action for federal ends a new theme with Sir

[1] The writer endeavoured to dissuade Sir Henry Parkes from moving so soon. See *Parkes MS.* in the Mitchell Library, Sydney.

[2] *Life of Sir Henry Parkes*, p. 542.

Henry Parkes. In his first Tenterfield speech he had deprecated the intrusion of party spirit into the federal movement. In this, his last speech in Parliament upon the question, he renewed the appeal:—

Federation [he said] cannot be brought about by a fraction of the people of New South Wales. The whole people united —Free Traders and Protectionists alike—must join, before it will be morally possible to bring about the Union of the Colonies. The old local parties must be destroyed or this country can never join in creating a United Australia.

In a few words he explained his motive in taking this action:—

I am guided by three motives. The first is to hasten the advent of a United Australia; the next is to punish a Government of tricksters who never can be trusted by serious men; and the third is to try to consolidate in this country a party united for Federation, who, when the tariff struggle comes, will fight on the side of Free Trade with no surrender, but who know that the time is not yet come, leaving others to fight on the side of Protection.

There was nothing new in these sentiments. Even Mr. Reid expressed them, but in a different connection, when he was attacking Sir Henry Parkes in 1887 for removing the food duties before introducing Local Government:—

How [he had said then] can a Government which desires to despatch its business, to get through the Session, reconcile with any idea of common sense the bringing of this wretched tariff war before Parliament,—this wretched eternal debate between Free Trade and Protection, which is now becoming a substitute for useful legislation? We hear nothing now but Free Trade and Protection . . . . It is of infinitely more importance to this country that we should have a Local Government Bill, a Land Bill, and other useful legislation.

It marks the difference between the two men that, while Mr. Reid—the Free Trader of Free Traders—was ready to drop Free Trade for the sake of provincial objects, Sir Henry Parkes would put that policy upon one side only for larger objects of Australian concern. And if it were a crime in Sir Henry Parkes to vote with the Protectionists in 1895, had not Mr. Reid and his Attorney-General, Mr. Want, done the same in 1891,[1] with the difference that their votes had been given to stifle the federal movement, while Sir Henry's was to be given to advance it ?

None of these considerations, however, could prevail in May 1895 ; and Sir Henry Parkes' action was foredoomed to failure. It is tragic that circumstances should have made inevitable the rejection of his sound advice, which was never more worthy of attention than in the last months of his long life, when every cur was barking at his heels !

· 5 ·

But, although Sir Henry Parkes had failed on this occasion, Mr. Reid could see plainly that his own position was not yet secure ; and he prepared to strengthen it by a manœuvre which, by its *finesse* and audacity, has established his reputation as a party leader.

So far back as 1889 he had observed—what seems to be as true of England as of New South Wales—that there is no more effective election ' cry ' than

[1] See *ante*, pp. 139, 140.

' Reform of the Upper House,' because in such a contest
' the men who can talk best—who can kick up the
greatest amount of dust—are those who may come off
with flying colours ' ; [1] and he had lost no opportunity,
since he had become Premier, of stirring up antagonism
to the Legislative Council, the members of which he
had described as 'more reckless slaughterers than
any to be found at the abattoirs,' as 'mummies only
fit for a museum,' as 'men of sinister eyes and bull-
necks,' and as 'old fossils' whom the people should
'sweep away.'

A General Election upon the issue of Upper House
Reform was, in slang phrase, 'right into Mr. Reid's
hand.' Not only would it delay the financial dis-
location from the abolition of the Dibbs duties, but
it offered a rare opportunity of getting rid of his
Federal and Land Tax critics, who might be too
earnest or too academic to subordinate their views
to the issues of a fictitious constitutional struggle.
The occasion came from an unexpected ruling by the
President of the Council that any amendment to
reduce the limit of the exemptions in the Land and
Income Tax Machinery Bill would conflict with the
exclusive right of the Assembly to impose taxation,
and therefore could not be received.[2] Upon this
ruling many members, who might have supported
the second reading of this Bill, gave their votes against
it, so that it was thrown out (June 20, 1895).

The rejection of this Bill gave Mr. Reid the battle

---

[1] 'It is a grand thing to have a fight. The men who can talk best—
who can kick up the greatest amount of dust—are those who may
come off with flying colours in such a struggle. But what becomes of
the unfortunate country while these great battles are going on ? '

[2] See Hansard, vol. 78, pp. 7401–4.

ground which he desired ; and, on July 5, Parliament
was dissolved. The fact that Mr. Reid himself, as
recently as June 10, had asserted the right of the
Council to reduce the exemptions, and had explained
that the division of the Land Tax into two measures—
the one a taxing and the other a machinery Bill—had
been adopted expressly that the Council might be free
to exercise this power, was ignored or forgotten ; [1] or
else the allegation that the Council would have passed
the Bill if they could have dealt with the exemptions
was dismissed as ' bald hypocrisy.' [2] In the contest
which followed, everything—Free Trade, the Land
Tax, Federation—was subordinated to the issue of
Reform of the Upper House. ' The real issue,' wrote
the *Daily Telegraph* on June 27, ' is Upper House
Reform . . . and it has the advantage of a directness,
a simplicity, and an urgency which recent events have
thrown into a bold relief.' On polling day (July 24)
this view was expressed with even greater clearness.
' There is no question to-day as to how revenue shall
be raised. The question is whether the Legislative
Council shall continue to exist as a Conservative
sleeper on the rails of progress ; whether monopoly
shall continue to triumph over men. That is the
issue to-day—" Man *versus* Monopoly." ' Mr. Reid was
equally explicit : ' I have come to ask you to give this
Government power to reform the Constitution of the

[1] See Report of speech in the *Orange Leader* of June 15, 1905. ' The
Taxing Bill the Upper House must not touch, but the Machinery Bill
they may. . . . The exemptions will be in the Machinery Bill, which
they can do what they like with, so that they have no excuse for throwing out the Taxing Bill. The Taxing Bill was held back by the representative of the Government in the Council in order that the Machinery
Bill might be dealt with first.'

[2] *Daily Telegraph*, June 28, 1895.

Upper House . . . We are going to the country on that issue and we ask the people to assist us.'[1] 'Financial reform,' he declared on another occasion, 'and Constitutional reform were inseparable; and when he next sent the Land Tax to the Legislative Council not a letter or a comma of it should be altered.'

The elections resulted just as Mr. Reid desired. He came back with an increased majority; and both Sir Henry Parkes and the Independent members of his party lost their seats. For the next three years he was in a position of unquestioned authority.

It is hardly necessary to add that, after the General Election, nothing more was heard of Upper House Reform; and that, when the Legislative Council made 77 amendments in the Land Tax Bill, 71 of these were accepted by the Ministry!

. 6 .

Sir Henry Parkes made a pathetic attempt to stay the stream of Mr. Reid's popularity by standing against him for the King Division. The election is marked, even in our annals, for the venomous personalities on either side. An excuse may be found, perhaps, for Sir Henry Parkes, in his unnerving domestic sorrow. The illness of his wife, whose courage had urged him into the combat, interrupted the preliminary stages of his Committee work; and in the midst of his preparations she died. 'Let me,' he wrote to his Committee, 'bury the dear dead and I will return to my labours.' Immediately after the funeral he resumed the fight. 'Up to the last moments of consciousness'

Speeches, July 1 and July 11.

(writes Mr. Charles Lyne) ' the counsel of his wife had been "no surrender," and he followed the advice to the letter.' He was defeated by 140 votes. His pleading to ' cease trifling over a provincial fiscal battle which could have no result when Union should take place ' carried no weight against the clamour of the newspapers. He made one more effort—in February 1896—to obtain a seat at Waverley, but was beaten by a local alderman. On April 22 he died, embittered by poverty and disappointment, but with courage unshaken, and proudly conscious that his fame rested upon a surer foundation than popular caprice.

Honour to whom honour is due !

CHAPTER XVI

THE CHOICE OF DELEGATES

THE Australasian Federal Enabling Act, agreed to by the Premiers on February 6, 1895, was not introduced into the Parliament of New South Wales until October 1895. It became law on December 23 ; and by March 7 of the following year the four Colonies of South Australia, New South Wales, Tasmania, and Victoria had put everything in train for the meeting of the Convention, whenever Mr. Reid, to whom it had been agreed the decision should be left, should have selected a suitable date. Western Australia and Queensland, however, still stood out, and Mr. Reid preferred to wait another year for their concurrence ; although the prompt adhesion of Western Australia, when the date of meeting had been finally decided upon, was never in doubt, and the declared half-heartedness of Sir Hugh Nelson, the Premier of Queensland, made it equally certain that the northern Colony would hold aloof.[1]

[1] Western Australia from the first had declared in favour of choosing her representatives by Parliament and not, as in the other Colonies, by popular election. Sir Hugh Nelson's most encouraging utterance had been that ' it would do no harm to Queensland to have a voice in framing the Constitution ' ; but he threw away even this dubious advantage by proposing that the representatives should be elected by the Legislative Assembly alone, grouped according to the three divisions of the Colony—Northern, Central, and Southern. As the Legislative Council

Thus the election of delegates did not take place until March 4, 1897, two years and one month after Mr. Reid, to use his own expression, 'had lifted Federation from the gutter where Mr. Barton had left it,'—a delay which Sir Henry Parkes had foretold, and which was due to the subordination of the larger question of Australian Union to the minor issues of local politics, against which he had protested in vain.

. I .

Anyone who reads the tedious debates in the New South Wales 'Hansard' must be surprised that the opponents of Federation, who were numerous in both Houses, and, in the Legislative Council, a majority, regarded the passage of the Enabling Bill with such indifference. They appear not to have realised the importance of the step which was being taken.

They misjudged [as Messrs. Quick and Garran point out] the vitality of the movement and did not anticipate the stimulating effect of placing it on a popular basis. They expected that the new Convention, if it ever met, would be as futile as the last had apparently been. . . . and thought that Federation could be trifled with again, as it had been in the past.

They procured, however, an amendment in the Enabling Bill, requiring that the Constitution should not be deemed to be accepted, on the Referendum, unless a minimum of 50,000 votes should be recorded

claimed a voice in this election, an irreconcilable conflict ensued between the two Chambers; and Sir Hugh Nelson's Bill was laid aside in August 1896, so that Queensland was not represented at the Convention. Western Australia passed the Enabling Act on October 27; but, as has been said, this was a formal expression of a decision that was never in doubt.

in its favour ; and, doubtless, they deemed that this would be a sufficient security for its rejection. Later, when the movement had developed an unexpected momentum, they loaded the dice still more heavily against the Federalists by increasing the statutory minimum to 80,000, although this involved a breach of faith with Tasmania and Victoria, which had each fixed a minimum which represented the same proportion of its own votes as the minimum of 50,000 represented in New South Wales. This incident, however, belongs to a later period in the story.[1]

. 2 .

Forty-nine candidates in New South Wales contended for the ten seats. The Colony voted as one electorate ; and ' plumping ' was forbidden, i.e. each voter had to vote for ten candidates. The Labour Party, which at this time was strangely suspicious of Federation, ran a ' bunch ' of ten, upon an impracticable programme of one Chamber, elective Ministries, and the Initiative Referendum. 'Upon any other conditions ' they declared themselves ' opposed to Federation.' None of their candidates was returned, although the vote (41,516) given for Mr. McGowen, their leader, proved that he might have been successful if his party had not made this bold attempt to capture the Convention. Another ' bunch ' of five was nominated by ' the Patriotic League of New South Wales,' which represented the old Colonialism of Sir John Robertson. Their policy was pure provincialism. They wished each Colony to retain its own tariff, and objected to the Federal Government having any

[1] See *post*, p. 272, footnote.

power of taxation, except by way of a levy on the States. Their appellation of 'prudent Federalists,' which had been first assumed by their leader, Mr. L. F. Heydon,[1] provided much innocent merriment during the campaign. With these two exceptions, there was no grouping of candidates upon party lines, although Mr. Reid appealed to the electors to return his two colleagues, Mr. Carruthers and Mr. Brunker. The result proved that the electors voted for the best-known men. Mr. Barton, as the recognised leader of the federal movement, was returned by a majority of 15,000 above Mr. Reid, who was second on the poll. Mr. Barton's vote, 104,463 out of a total poll of 139,850, was a magnificent testimony of the public appreciation of his devoted services. The two other members of the Ministry, Mr. Carruthers and Mr. Brunker, were also returned. Mr. McMillan, an ex-Treasurer on the Free Trade side, although at the time not in political relations with Mr. Reid, also received the support which was due to a member of the 1891 Convention. The other successful candidates were Mr. Lyne, leader of the Protectionists, Sir Joseph Abbott (Speaker), Mr. J. T. Walker, and Mr. B. R. Wise. Mr. Walker was the only one of the ten who was new to politics. He was a Director, however, of the Bank of New South Wales and of the Australian Mutual Provident Society, and the banking and commercial interests had been organised effectively in his support.

In the four Colonies which had accepted the Enabling Bill on March 4, 1897, although the proportion of votes recorded was below the average except in

---

[1] See *ante*, p. 114.

New South Wales, the same wise discrimination was exercised by the electors, and the ten best known public men were chosen without regard to party. A notable instance was the return of Mr. Trenwith sixth on the poll in Victoria, although both *The Argus* and *The Age* newspapers had done their utmost to exclude him. Mr. Wise was the only other delegate from New South Wales and Victoria, whose name was not included in one or other of the ' bunches ' recommended by a daily newspaper. It is to the credit of the Press that they used with moderation the great power which an election of this nature gave them. The truce to party spirit was not long observed.

· 3 ·

Among the defeated candidates was Cardinal Moran, whose entry into the field of politics, while it stimulated public interest, evoked also an unpleasant outburst of that sectarian feeling, which is never far beneath the surface in the politics of New South Wales. Yet His Eminence's position was unambiguous. He stood for election, as he said, ' as an individual only ; not as Cardinal or as head of the Catholic Church, but as an Australian Colonist' ; and his services to Federation had been very great. On July 17, 1894 he had put forward, in an interview published in the *Daily Telegraph*, a terse and powerful appeal in favour of Australian unity, of which Sir Henry Parkes had remarked to the writer : ' We cannot overestimate the value of the Cardinal's utterances in favour of Federation. They reach thousands whom we can never hope to reach '[1] ; and he had attended the ' People's Federal

---

[1] See also *ante*, p. 204.

Convention' at Bathurst in November 1896, at which the Convention Bill of 1891 had been discussed in detail by some 200 representatives from Federal Leagues and other organisations.[1] It was probable, as he himself pointed out in the interview referred to above, 'that his influence might contribute to bringing Queensland into the Convention,' and it was undeniable that he had 'all along looked upon Federation as of vital importance to Australia.' His reason for this view is of interest to-day : 'I regard Federation as the only means of preventing one or other of the Colonies from going right over to extreme Socialism. I refer to the extreme communistic views which are in vogue among some of the Socialist organisations.'[2]

[1] The Secretary to this Conference was Mr. Jose, whose letters to *The Times* have furnished for several years past a most judicious and impartial commentary upon Australian affairs.

[2] Some extracts from the interview mentioned in the text may be read still with interest :— ' I am convinced that all our bishops and the great majority of our clergy, in a spirit of patriotism, look forward to the Federation of the Colonies as a matter of vital importance, which no political party can very long ignore. I don't think separation will be promoted by Federation. On the contrary, I think that, when the Colonies are federated, the connection will be strengthened ; for the full liberty which we shall then enjoy will satisfy all our aspirations. Separation from the Mother Country would deprive us of many material advantages. . . . But the present relations of the Colonies to one another are quite intolerable. The interests of the people are the same : their aspirations are the same. Very often members of the same family live in different Colonies, and still the frontiers between these Colonies are in many ways an impassable barrier to that union and mutual sympathy which should characterise the people, and which the people are determined to have. . . . I consider the question of Australian Federation not only a question of urgent political importance but a question also of patriotism. I wish to be associated with the people as an enthusiast in promoting it in every way in my power. . . . The example of Canada is one which should put this question in its true light. When the Canadian Colonies were distinct. . . Canada

· 4 ·

An election of this character, in which men were chosen on their public reputations, could not be expected to disclose any clear mandate as to constitutional principles ; and the addresses and speeches of the successful candidates show a wide divergence of opinion. On one point, however, progress had been made towards unanimity since 1891—thanks to the educational propaganda of the federalist party. All the successful candidates, except Mr. Lyne, whose consistent hostility to Federation rendered his opinion of little account, accepted the principle of equal State representation in the Senate, which had proved a stumbling-block for many years, and thus narrowed the dispute to a question as to the relative powers of the two Houses. Two of the ablest and best qualified of the candidates, Messrs. James Ashton and G. D. Millen, owed their defeat principally to their refusal to recognise that this concession to the smaller States was a practical necessity of any form of Union.

There was no agreement on any other point.

A crucial question was the taking over by the Commonwealth of the railways and public debts, which, admittedly, would have solved the otherwise insoluble financial problem. Only Messrs. Carruthers, Walker, and Wise supported this proposal. Mr. Barton and Mr. O'Connor opposed it ; and Mr. Reid, who in his address to the electors had recognised its advantages

exercised no influence whatever on other countries. Since the Federation of the Canadian Dominion her resources have wonderfully developed. . . . The same must happen in Australia. We need great trunk railways to open up the resources of the interior of the country ; and we need commercial alliances with all the countries that surround us. It is only a Federated Australia that can achieve this.'

without committing himself to its support, declared himself on their side, a week later, in a speech at the Protestant Hall :—

I don't think it is necessary to federalise our lines. I don't think that the requirements of the different parts of these vast Colonies could be properly attended to by a railway administration which has jurisdiction over such an enormous area. Besides this, I think we are much more likely to get a Federation if we do not include too much in it at one time.

Again, Mr. Reid and Mr. Carruthers were emphatic as to the necessity for providing for the supremacy of the House of Representatives, while Messrs. Barton, O'Connor, and Wise, while not opposing this suggestion, considered that the unlikelihood of a conflict between the two Houses deprived it of any importance. Mr. Reid's proposal for resolving a deadlock was a joint sitting of both Houses, at which the majority of votes should prevail. The significance of this proposal, which was developed in several speeches, will become apparent at a later stage of the narrative.

The difference of view between the State Righters and the Federalists was also very marked—Mr. Reid representing the former and Mr. Barton the latter. Mr. Reid, for instance, proposed in his address to the electors to ' limit the power of the Commonwealth to raise money by taxation, except by duties of Customs and Excise, to purposes of defence against foreign invasion,' and to limit its power of borrowing money to the same purpose, with the addition of a power to borrow ' for the cost of resuming land for federal purposes and erecting federal buildings.' His fear was lest the income of the Commonwealth should be so large that Treasurers would be tempted into extravagance and the finances of the States would be upset. Mr. Barton, on the other hand, was ready to give the Commonwealth Parliament the full taxing and borrowing powers which are an attribute of a supreme Government. He was in favour, too, of an unrestricted freedom of intercourse for goods and persons throughout the Commonwealth ; while Mr. Reid objected to the abolition of the preferential railway rates. As to the site of the Capital, Mr. Barton would leave the selection of this to the Parliament. Mr. Reid desired that it should be fixed by the Constitution, in federal territory, within New South Wales ; and, if this proved to be impossible, that Parliament should meet for two years in each of the existing Capitals in succession, ' with a strong doubt as to Hobart, because of the isolated position of Tasmania.' [1]

It is pleasant to note that, despite these differences of opinion, Mr. Reid was at this time no less enthusiastic than Mr. Barton in championing the cause of Federation :—

Much as we are prepared to fight for our own Colonies [he said at one meeting], much as we are prepared to look after the interests of our own Colonies, we must feel that the chief interest of each of the Colonies lies in compact of alliance between them all. It is absolutely impossible that Australia can fulfil her destiny if she is split up into hostile divisions, each trying to checkmate the other. But if this unneighbourly process is abandoned . . . . the generous sentiment of common Australian nationality will spring up in all parts of the Continent.

[1] Mr. Reid's address repeated the arguments against the Bill of 1891 which have been set out already in Chapter XII. See *ante*, pp. 180-2. An article of his in the Australian *Review of Reviews* for February 1897 may be referred to in this connection.

When the much-desired documented history of the federal movement comes to be prepared, the addresses of all the candidates for the Convention will be printed *in extenso*.   For the purpose of this work, it is sufficient to cite enough extracts to revive the feeling of the time, and explain the spirit in which the delegates entered the Convention.   Mr. Reid's address has been referred to sufficiently already.   Another was in these terms :—

The Government of Australia should not be a mere Constitutional Government, owing its existence to the sufferance of local bodies, but it must be a sovereign authority, which, while it leaves minor details of administration to local bodies, will command the respect and obedience of all Australians. To create such a body requires that the delegates whom you elect should enter the Convention, not as hucksterers who are seeking, each of them, to make the best bargain for his own province, but as Australians, who, realising that their main object is to merge our local citizenship into an Australian citizenship, will view every question as it arises in a national and not in a provincial spirit, and who will discuss all the grave issues of statesmanship, which the construction of a Federal Government involves, without temper and with full knowledge, at the same time keeping alive to that spirit of compromise which lies at the root of all stable representative institutions. We should recognise that every part of the Continent will be advantaged by increasing the power of the Federal Government, provided that these acquisitions of power do not injuriously affect the vitality of the States, from which alone the Federal Government can draw its sustenance.   In my view, the Federal Government will possess two distinct classes of attributes :—(1) Those which are created by the Act of Union, and (2) those which are surrendered by the various States. . . . As an Australian I put the Union of Australia before all other questions ; and I am prepared to trust the people of Australia with the decision of all matters, (such as the tariff, provision for Defence &c.) which affect Australia as a whole.

. . . I believe that each Colony must share in the general prosperity; and that each will progress, but in the degree in which it is bound up with the prosperity of all the others.

The same candidate, when developing the ideas of his address at a public meeting in Sydney, referred to the alarm of the ' Prudent Federalists ' lest the other Colonies should ' steal,'—(their own word),—the trade and territory of New South Wales :—

He was not disposed [he said] to ignore the possibility that Federation might bring about serious commercial changes, and that the course of trade might be altered throughout the Colonies. But it was difficult, if not impossible, for any to foretell the commercial result of Federation in any particular part of the Continent. Nobody could foresee exactly what the course of trade would be when it was left to its natural channels. But at least they could anticipate that the port which had the greatest natural advantages would get the greatest share of the trade . . . Mr. Heydon and his ' prudent ' friends endeavoured to show that Sydney was going to lose. Suppose there were to be some loss,—was it not a little grotesque that the ' Prudent Federalists ' in every other Colony were also arguing that their respective Colonies would lose by Federation, and all were agreed that New South Wales was the Colony which was going to gain ? Granting, merely for the sake of argument, that there might be some material loser, Federation was not to be regarded as a question of pounds, shillings, and pence . . . Australians meant that the Australians should be one people, and on a determination of that kind the maps and figures of the ' Prudent Federalists ' fell as the idle wind.

· 5 ·

The sentiments expressed in the addresses and speeches of the Free Traders who were standing for election excited the alarm of the more rigid members of the party, one of the most influential of whom, the late Mr. Frank Grimley, took them seriously to task in a manifesto, which was the first muttering of a coming storm. Appealing to Mr. Reid, Mr. McMillan, and Mr. Wise by name, he asked :—

How do you reconcile your former professions and teachings with your present advocacy of an arrangement that everyone knows must result in Protection in New South Wales, whether New South Wales wants it or not ?   All your political lives you have preached the gospel of freedom to produce and freedom to exchange.   You declared that policy was founded on ' truth, justice, and morality '—was, in fact, ' God's law.' You declared, with equal fervour, that the policy of Protection was ' economically false, unjust, demoralising, a drag on national progress—in effect a robbery of the many to benefit the few.' If Free Trade is all you said it was two years ago, it is the same to-day.   If you believed it was the blessing you described, how can you justify a course that will certainly deprive your country of its benefits for generations ?   If Free Trade was not what you said it was—if your teaching all these years has been false—what mischief you have wrought !   What a weary waste of time you have imposed on yourselves and your country !   What years of useless, bitter wrangling !   Either your teaching was true or it was false.   If true, you have no right to abandon the truth for a supposed national gain.   To do so will be to forfeit your right to be trusted.   If not true, what claim have you to public confidence in future ?

Similar remonstrances may be addressed again, and with equal sincerity, to those who, when Imperial relations become ripe for a better adjustment, may count it of more importance to unite the Free Dominions in one alliance, under the Crown, than to preserve free imports into the Mother Land.   Those who read aright the story of Australian Federation will not turn aside on that account.

CHAPTER XVII

THE CONVENTION OF 1897–8

THE Convention was summoned to meet, for its first Session, at Adelaide, on March 22, 1897. The journey of the delegates, after leaving New South Wales, was a triumphal progress. Cheering crowds met the special train at every stopping-place; and even signal-boxes were decorated with greenery and bunting. Only picked men could have survived the toasts and banqueting! All, however, was not ' cakes and ale ' !

. I .

On the day after their arrival in Adelaide, the delegates met in the library of Parliament to discuss, informally, the question of procedure. Such was the separation of provincial politics that probably seven out of every ten of those present made acquaintance with each other for the first time ; so that the protraction of the sittings of the Convention became of real advantage in developing that feeling of mutual confidence which is the condition of all fair compromise.

The change in *personnel*, since the Convention of 1891, was very striking. The lapse of six years had brought forward a new order of men, and a new generation of politicians. Sir Henry Parkes, President of the 1891 Convention and father of the federal movement, had died in 1895 ; Sir George Dibbs, the apostle

of Unification, had retired from politics to become
Manager of the Government Savings Bank ; Sir Samuel
Griffith, the draftsman of the Bill of 1891, had ex-
changed the uncertainties of political life for the
tranquil eminence of the Judicial Bench ; Mr. A.
Inglis Clark, his colleague in the work of draftsmanship, also had become a Judge ; Mr. Munro, the ex-
Premier of Victoria, had withdrawn into private life ;
and, of the leaders of the former Convention, Mr.
Kingston, Mr. Deakin, Mr. Barton, Sir John Downer,
Mr. J. H. Gordon, and Sir John Forrest alone remained.
Added to these, now, were Mr. Reid, the erstwhile
opponent of Federation, who, directly the late Convention had risen, had occupied himself in denunciation
of its labours, but who had become, in his own phrase,
' a proselyte crowding out the apostles ' ; Sir George
Turner, the Premier of Victoria ; Sir Graham Berry,
once the impassioned tribune of the people, now the
dignified and courteous Speaker of the Legislative
Assembly ; Mr. Isaacs and Mr. R. E. O'Connor, both
lawyers, but of opposite temperaments ; Mr. Higgins,
the urbane and cultured leader of the Equity Bar,
whose preference for being in a minority, to his own
disadvantage, was so pronounced and instinctive that,
the wits declared, he would record a solitary vote
even against his own proposals, if these found favour
with the rest of the Convention ; and Mr. Trenwith,
a former leader of the Victorian Labour Party, whose
constructive and political ability was very high.   Nor
must Mr. Glynn, Mr. Holder, and Sir Josiah Symon,
among the South Australians, nor Mr. Henry, the
Tasmanian, be passed by without recognition.

Opinions were divided as to the best method of

procedure. Some delegates preferred to start upon
the Bill of 1891 and consider it, clause by clause, in
Committee of the Whole ; others wished to begin
de novo, but were not agreed as to the best way of
making the new start. There was some deprecation
of ' speech-making,' because it was thought that the
time for generalities had passed. Others wanted an
opportunity to discuss the question in all its bearings.
Finally, it was agreed, upon the suggestion of Mr.
Trenwith, that the Bill of 1891, not having been
accepted by the people, should, for the time at least,
be laid upon one side, and a new one framed by the
Convention, in the same way as any other Parliamentary measure. This involved the submission of
Resolutions embodying the outlines of the Constitution, and a discussion of details later, in Committee of
the Whole.

Accordingly, upon March 23, after a preliminary
meeting of the Convention to elect Mr. Kingston,
President, and Mr. Blackmore, Clerk, Mr. Barton moved
for the appointment of a Committee to frame these
Resolutions. Objection was taken at once that the
business of the Convention ought to be directed by a
' leader ' and not by a Committee ; and Mr. Barton
was pressed to assume this position and himself bring
up the preliminary Resolutions.[1] No one opposed this
suggestion ; although both Mr. Carruthers and Mr. Reid,
in speeches which betrayed some of the jealousy excited
by Mr. Barton's position on the poll, disapproved
of proceeding by Resolutions. Mr. Reid was doubtful

[1] A preliminary affirmation was added to these Resolutions, on the
motion of the writer, declaring that their purpose was ' to enlarge
the powers of self-government of the people of Australia.'

also of the wisdom of being guided by an executive :
' if we must be guided by an executive I prefer to be
guided by a defunct one, because then no questions
would arise of want of confidence '!   He hoped that
Mr. Barton would not ' bring up a string of platitudes '
in the form of Resolutions, but would take the Bill
of 1891 ' openly and publicly as the basis of discussion
and amend it where desirable.'   Despite these protests,
the procedure which had been agreed upon was
followed ; and the Convention organised itself as a
Parliament to frame a new Constitution.

. 2 .

It lies outside the scope of a work, the purpose
of which is to revive the impressions of contemporaries upon passing events, to describe in detail the
shaping of the Constitution or to discuss constitutional
problems, except in so far as this is necessary for a com-
prehension of the issues of the struggle.   Besides, this
part of the history of the federal movement has been
told already, quite admirably, by Messrs. Quick and
Garran in their ' Introduction to the Annotated
Constitution of the Commonwealth '; so that whoever
would traverse the same ground must follow in their
footsteps.   Moreover, the solutions of federal problems
by the Adelaide Convention, except as to the powers
of the Senate over Money Bills, were admittedly
tentative ; and everyone recognised that they would
have to be revised in later Sessions.   The real importance of the Adelaide Session was that it brought
about a better understanding between the delegates
and encouraged the spirit of compromise, without
which Federation could not have been accomplished.

When the Convention opened, there was a general apprehension among the delegates lest there should be an irreconcilable difference between the representatives of the larger and the smaller States, and lest the latter would demand powers for the Senate which would be unacceptable to the two States of Victoria and New South Wales, which had the larger population. Nor were these fears diminished by the debate upon the Resolutions, in which the spokesmen of the smaller States yielded nothing of their pretensions. Confident of his majority—for West Australia, South Australia, and Tasmania could cast 30 votes against the 20 of New South Wales and Victoria—Sir John Forrest (W. A.) opened the proceedings in Committee with a motion to adjourn the consideration of all Clauses of the Bill up to Clause 52, in order to force an immediate decision on the powers of the Senate over Money Bills. The West Australian delegates had to leave Adelaide on April 14 to take part in their General Election. The motion was agreed to, despite the opposition of Mr. Lyne and two other delegates.

This was the first-fruits of that spirit of good will and conciliation which the meeting together in friendly intercourse had already engendered between political opponents. For the assent to Sir John Forrest's proposal was more than a simple courtesy : it was a frank recognition of the equality of the Federating Colonies. The burning question of the Convention, as all foresaw, was as to the power of the Senate to amend Money Bills,—upon which, as the Convention was then organised, the West Australian delegates could cast a decisive vote against the views of the larger Colonies. In their absence, the vote would be the other way. Every one recognised that the fate of the movement hung in the balance; and many voted to accede to the request of Sir John Forrest, with a heavy heart and much misgiving.

· 3 ·

On April 13 Mr. Reid brought the matter to a head by moving an amendment to deny the right of the Senate to *amend* Money Bills; and, for a time, it seemed as if the labours of the Convention would be in vain. Both Mr. Reid and Sir George Turner declared bluntly that the Colonies of New South Wales and Victoria would reject the Bill if such a power were given to the Second Chamber; and each considered its exercise to be incompatible with the practice of Responsible Government. Mr. Kingston was the first to declare himself impressed by these assurances; and he announced his intention to vote for the amendment, rather than imperil Federation. Mr. Glynn and Mr. Henry followed his example; but the other representatives of the smaller Colonies were equally dogged. 'If New South Wales and Victoria want Federation on these terms,' said Sir John Forrest, 'let them federate by themselves. West Australia would never consent to be handed over body and soul to the larger Colonies.' Mr. Adye Douglas and Sir Josiah Symon made similar declarations on behalf of Tasmania and South Australia. It was clear on the first day of the debate, as Sir John Forrest gleefully announced, that the smaller States would win the day: and Mr. J. H. Gordon (S. A.), confident of victory, moved that the Committee should divide.

Mr. Barton, however, had not spoken ; so, pleading a providential catarrh, he induced the Committee to adjourn its decision until the following day ! The contest was renewed in the delegates' hotels ; and it was late at night before Sir Joseph Abbott was able to announce to Mr. Barton that two Tasmanian representatives—Messrs. Lewis and Brown—had yielded to the representations of Mr. Deakin, Mr. O'Connor, Mr. Wise, Mr. Henry and himself, and, recognising that the rejection of Mr. Reid's amendment would be fatal to the cause, were disposed to vote in its favour, although they had not pledged themselves to do so. Next morning, Mr. Barton stated the case in a speech which is, perhaps, the highest of his efforts, and which completed the conversion of the waverers. The amendment was carried by 25 to 23, and in the majority were five representatives of the smaller States—Messrs. Henry, Lewis, and Brown of Tasmania, and Messrs. Kingston and Glynn of South Australia.

It was the most critical and exciting debate in the three Sessions of the Convention, and established once for all (as Messrs. Quick and Garran point out) that ' the Convention was a negotiating and not a legislative body ; and that the decision of a majority of representatives would go for nothing, unless it were acceptable to the people of all the Colonies.' Had the voting been the other way, Federation would have been wrecked ; and that this danger was evaded was due entirely to the ' federal spirit of compromise, which thenceforward grew, slowly but steadily, through all the sittings of the Convention, and spread from the Convention to the people.' The vote marked the turning-point in the federal movement. From that time forward there was no division in the Convention upon State lines ; so that Mr. Barton, speaking in Sydney upon March 24 in the following year, was able to

deny with all the authority of his leadership of the Convention the false suggestion that the three smaller States had ever combined for the purpose of injuring, depleting, or plundering New South Wales. There had been no single occasion upon which the three smaller States had voted solidly together. Their attitude, indeed, had not been one of aggression but purely one of self-defence, guarding against the possible danger that they might be swallowed up by New South Wales and Victoria and lose their individuality.

Nevertheless, as we shall see, the fable was propagated sedulously throughout the campaign that, owing to the equal representation of the States, the Convention had done injustice to New South Wales, and that there was risk, in consequence, of danger of further assaults by the smaller States upon the resources of their larger and wealthier neighbours.

· 4 ·

Some features of the Convention deserve special notice. The first was the immense superiority of the South Australian delegation over that from any other Colony, which was due, not so much to the individual ability of its members,—although that was great,—as to the cohesion and tenacity with which they fought for the interests of their Colony, a cohesion, which was the more remarkable, because several of the delegates were not on speaking terms. No other delegation showed the same suppression of personal and party feeling to a common duty. The Victorians, for instance, were divided into 'Liberals' and 'Conservatives,' while the New South Wales representatives met together only once for discussion during the whole three Sessions ; and it was a joke of the Convention that Mr. Lyne would cross the floor if he perceived that Mr. Reid was voting on the same side! [1]

Another point to be noted is the feeling of the Convention as to the site of the Federal Capital. As in the Convention of 1891, the opinion of the majority of the delegates was in favour of Sydney ; but it was not thought right to prejudge a matter which was the proper concern of the Commonwealth Parliament, and therefore no site was mentioned in the Bill. Mr. Lyne, however, who was consistent to the end in his opposition to Federation, moved at the Melbourne Session that the Capital should be in Sydney. The Committee determined to show its real attitude upon the question by treating the motion as a joke. Therefore, when Mr. Lyne's motion was defeated, Mr. Peacock proposed a motion in favour of Ballaarat, and a representative from each Colony was ready to propose in turn a site in his own Colony ! The Chairman, however, stopped this reduction to absurdity by refusing to put any more such frivolous motions. The jest was not understood outside the Convention ; and many people were persuaded, by the opponents of the Bill, that the rejection of Mr. Lyne's motion proved that Sydney was excluded from consideration as a possible Capital site.

[1] A *Bulletin* cartoon, entitled 'Watching the Cat Jump,' depicted Mr. Reid and Mr. Lyne astride a fence. Mr. Reid was a Siamese twin cat, and Mr. Lyne was saying 'I'm waiting until the cat jumps ; but this kind of animal seems liable to jump either way.'

· 5 ·

The Convention adjourned on April 23, in order
to enable the Premiers to attend the Imperial Conference. As it was impossible for them to be back
within the sixty days prescribed by the Enabling Act
as the period of adjournment, the device was adopted
of moving, on April 23, ' That the House adjourn until
May 5, and that at its rising on that day it do further
adjourn until September 2.'   On May 5, the delegates
having all departed, the acting President took the
chair, and, having solemnly but ineffectively rung for
a quorum, declared the Convention adjourned until
the later date ! All the questions of difficulty had
been discussed, but, except on the powers of the Senate
over Money Bills, no final decision had been arrived at.

The next step was the consideration of the Bill,
as drafted in Adelaide, by the several Parliaments.
The amendments which were proposed were submitted
to the Convention during its meeting at Sydney ; and
a final Session was held in Melbourne from January 20
to March 17, 1898, when the Bill, which was to be
submitted to a popular vote, was finally adopted.   It
was agreed that the Referendum should be taken
upon June 3.

CHAPTER XVIII

THE MATTERS IN CONTROVERSY

THE discussion of the problems of Federation in the Convention and the local Parliaments and the solution arrived at lie outside this narrative, and would furnish matter for a separate volume ; but some explanation must be given of the points which were most in dispute during the contest, which raged for the next year and a half, between the supporters and the opponents of the draft Constitution.

. I .

Equal Representation.—The most effective platform cry against the Bill of 1897–8 was that the composition of the Senate subverted the democratic principle of ' Majority Rule ' ; and the reasoning, by which this was supported, was exceedingly ingenious. The equal representation of the States in the Senate gave (so it was urged) ' to one man in Tasmania twelve times the voting power of one man in New South Wales ' ; because, although the one Colony had a population of 100,000 and the other of 1,200,000, each was represented by six Senators. This, as one orator declared, was to ' make New South Wales the bond-slave of Tasmania ! ' The calculation, however, ignored that every measure must be agreed to by both Houses, and that representation in the House of Representatives

was to be according to population.   The following table
shows the provision of the Bill in this connection :—

State	Population in 1897	Number of Representatives	Number of Senators
New South Wales . . .	1,277,870		6
Victoria	1,181,769	24	6
Queensland	360,550	9	6
South Australia	357,405	7	6
Western Australia . . .	101,225	5	6
Tasmania	100,834	5	6

From these figures it should have been clear that
no combination of the four smaller Colonies could
outvote the united representation of New South
Wales and Victoria, and that either of these States
could outvote any three of the others in the
House of Representatives. Nor, as Federalists
pointed out, was this the whole of the matter.
The Convention Bill, by adopting Responsible
Government, had given the controlling power to the
House of Representatives, where the larger States had
a numerical majority. And even this statement did
not display the full strength of the first Chamber!
Behind every political measure is the vitalising or
destructive force of public opinion, with the aid of
which any Legislative Chamber may go to the extreme
limits of its constitutional authority, but, unsupported
by which, neither Minister nor Chamber can exercise
the least of its powers. Now, it was beyond question
that the drift of public opinion would be manifested
more clearly in the larger than the smaller States ;
and that, therefore, the former would always derive
the greater power from expressions of the popular
will. The public opinion of the larger States would

always affect and modify the views of the representatives of the smaller States, as the public opinion of great nations affects and modifies the views of less important nations. Indeed, the analogy between the Federation of the Colonies and an International Conference was, in this respect, very close ; for, although all nations are equal at such a gathering and each has the same voting power, no one imagines that such countries as Belgium or Greece speak with the same authority as Germany or England.

But, underlying these arithmetical considerations, was the bald and decisive fact that, unless equality of State representation were conceded, there would be no Union. Dispute, theorise, criticise as critics might, human nature was above logic ; and the sentiment of national pride and love of one's own province, which is always most powerful in a small community, would most certainly have made Union impossible upon any terms which did not guarantee the preservation of the States as separate entities. The same feeling which led Tasmania, Victoria, and Queensland, successively, to break away from New South Wales, was active to keep these Colonies apart from any scheme which merged their separate existence in a unified form of government. Therefore those who spoke against equal State representation were speaking also, whether they intended it or not, against Federation.

Nor was the principle new. The matter, indeed, was a *chose jugée*. The historic independence of each Colony had been recognised in every attempt which had been made to secure united action. Each Colony had always sent an equal number of representatives

R

to an inter-Colonial Conference. The Federal Council Act gave each Colony an equal voting power. The Bill of 1891 had been based upon the same principle; and the Federal Enabling Act provided for the same equality. Each State, in fact, always had the power of giving or refusing its assent to joint action, and incurred no reproach, if it nullified the efforts of its neighbours to procure agreement. Surely it was a long step in advance to bring these separate powers into a Federal Union, by the terms of which each would be compelled to act in concert with the other Colonies, unless it could persuade two of them to join with it in thwarting the common design? For this was the utmost that the objection of the anti-Billites proved, viz., that, if three Colonies agreed, they could, by a vote in the Senate, block legislation for a time. Equal representation in the Senate gave the smaller States no more than a suspensive veto, in the improbable event that they should ever combine. As was pointed out, the more probable line of division was between New South Wales and Victoria; and certainly there was no sign of any combination between the smaller States against the larger. It was difficult, indeed, to see on what matters their interests would ever clash.

. 2 .

Deadlocks and the Powers of the Senate.—From the beginning of the federal movement there had had been two schools of thought—the one, represented by Sir Henry Parkes and Mr. Macrossan, urging a unification for limited purposes after the model of Canada, in which the States should have no longer any rights, as States, in respect of the matters transferred to the Federal Government ; the other insisting, on historic as well as theoretic grounds, that a Union of States implied a continued recognition of the States, as such. The latter view had prevailed both in 1891 and 1897 ; and, although at the Election of Delegates in 1897 a few candidates and the Labour Party advocated a limited consolidation, their views did not receive substantial support from any of the Colonies. Thus, from the outset of its deliberations, the Convention was pledged to a system of Federal Union, which meant in practical working that before any measure became law it should be approved by a majority of the Federating States as well as by a majority of the people. It followed logically from this conception of a Federal Union that each State,—the smallest with the biggest,—should be in a position of equality in the Senate or State House ; and it would seem to be a corollary of this principle of equal representation that the powers of the two Houses should be identical.

It has been told in a previous Chapter how insistence on logical consistency by the representatives of the smaller Colonies almost wrecked the federal movement at the Adelaide Session of the Convention ; and how wiser counsels in the first Convention had found a middle course in the 'Compromise of 1891.'[1] These provisions, however, intended as a recognition of the principle of Responsible Government, did not go far enough, because they did not enunciate with sufficient clearness that the responsibility of Ministers must be towards one House only—namely that which controlled

[1] See *ante*, Chapter XVII.

R 2

Supply. It is true that this practice is incompatible with the theory of a federal system; but the framers of the Constitution Bill were determined that, if they were compelled to make a choice, they would rather preserve the practice of Responsible Government than the logical cohesion of the federal idea. To this end, further provisions were introduced into the Bill to secure the ultimate supremacy of the House of Representatives in any conflict with the Senate.

Various proposals were debated at the Adelaide Session of the Convention,—a Joint Sitting, a simultaneous dissolution of both Houses, a consecutive dissolution, and the Referendum,—but none was adopted at that stage, and the question remained open for future consideration.

At the Sydney Session of the Convention it was decided, upon the motion of Mr. Wise, that, if the House of Representatives twice passed any Bill to which the Senate declined to agree, both Houses might be dissolved simultaneously; and that, if, after the dissolution, no agreement could be come to, a Joint Sitting of both Houses should be held, at which, if the Bill passed by a *three-fifths* majority of those present and voting, it was to become law. This provision for a Joint Sitting necessitated another provision for maintaining a balance between the numbers of the two Houses; and the Bill was altered, accordingly, to provide that the number of representatives should be, as near as might be, twice that of the Senate. Some delegates desired to go still further; and Sir George Turner found considerable support for a proposal, which he made during the Sydney

Session, that a bare majority should prevail at the Joint Sitting as at others. Since Mr. Reid, during the Referendum campaign, made the provision for a three-fifths majority a principal ground of his attack upon the Bill, it is of importance to observe that his vote was cast in Sydney *against* Sir George Turner's proposal. It is true that, during the last days of the Melbourne Session, he proposed to substitute a bare majority; but it was apparent then that it was too late to re-open such a tangled question.

It is difficult for us, who have had twelve years' experience of the working of Federation, to understand why so much stress was laid on these provisions for resolving deadlocks ; and why even those delegates who at Adelaide thought that conflicts between the two Houses would be infrequent, and that, if they did occur, a deadlock might not be disadvantageous, ultimately came round to the opinion that some provision, in the nature of a safety-valve, would be desirable. The explanation is that the perception of the true character of the Senate was obscured by the memories of traditional conflicts between the two Chambers of the local Legislatures. The ghosts of dead controversies still walked the political field ; and ' Liberals ' and ' Conservatives ' alike discussed the functions of a Federal Senate as though it were a local Upper House ! Thus, the strange spectacle was presented of ' Conservatives ' demanding the fullest authority for a body elected by the whole people of each State upon the widest possible franchise, and of ' Liberals ' insisting upon a limitation of its powers, in the name of democracy ! Only one delegate ventured to suggest that the question was of

antiquarian rather than practical interest,[1] and that
any disputes between the two Houses would be over
measures of social reform, and not over points of
constitutional etiquette ! Public opinion set steadily
against this view ; and the Bill was opposed, both in
New South Wales and Victoria, because the provision
requiring a three-fifths majority at the Joint Sitting
did not make the concession of equal representation
wholly illusory, but permitted the remote possibility
that a majority of the States might be able to protect
themselves against coercion by the representatives
of a larger population.

The Bill, said the manifesto of the anti-Convention
League,—(the opponents of the Bill became popularly
known as ' Antis ')—was ' The Death-Knell of Majority
Rule,' and ' The Deadlock Fraud ' was quite ' ineffective.' . . . ' In no case whatever (under the
three-fifths majority provision) could the majority have
its way unless it numbered forty-two out of sixty-four
votes in the representative Chamber ' ' whilst, if the
voting followed approximately on the lines of State
division, it would be possible for the representatives
of 860,000 people to outvote the representatives of
2,340,000 people.'

The best sedative for these alarms was furnished
by the text of the Bill, which provided that, if the
House of Representatives passed any Bill—it did
not require to be a Money Bill—and if the Senate
rejected this or shelved it, then, after an interval of
three months, the House of Representatives might
bring it up again, either with or without any amendments which the Senate might have made. If the

1 Hansard, ' Adelaide Session,' at pp. 106 and 487.

Senate rejected it a second time, the Governor-General (acting, of course, upon the advice of his Ministers) might dissolve both Houses of Parliament simultaneously. There was only one exception, viz. that this double dissolution might not take place within six months of the expiry of the House of Representatives by effluxion of time. In that case the matter waited until the General Election. After this double dissolution, if the House of Representatives again passed the Bill and the Senate again failed to pass it, or passed it with amendments unpalatable to the House of Representatives, the Governor-General was empowered to convoke a Joint Sitting of both Houses ; and, if the proposed Bill and any amendments were carried by a three-fifths majority of those present and voting, they became law, upon receiving the Governor's assent, whether the Senate approved or not. Since there were sixty-four members of the House of Representatives and only thirty Senators, it was not likely that the prescribed three-fifths majority would be difficult to get.[1] Certainly it was a misdescription, to use the mildest term, of these provisions to say that they gave the Senate the determining voice in legislation, when the three small Colonies would have only forty-eight votes in the Joint Sitting against the sixty votes of New South Wales and Victoria. If (say once in a century) it should prove impossible to secure a three-fifths majority, that must be on an occasion when the combination against the majority was overwhelming ; and, in such a case, public opinion would be overwhelming also, and the division would

---

[1] During the campaign for the Bill Queensland was standing out. The figures therefore imply that the Commonwealth would consist of only five States.

not be between the larger and smaller States, but
between parties. Deadlocks, after all, were not entirely
mischievous. They were the price paid for constitutional freedom, and could only be avoided under a
despotism !

Fortunately the danger was unreal. There never
has been, nor, so far as we can see, will there ever be, a
division of opinion upon State lines ; and the establishment of a Senate, in order to protect State interests,
appears now, as it appeared to Sir Henry Parkes,
to have been an unnecessary precaution.

· 3 ·

Finance.—The main strength of the attack upon
the Bill was directed against its financial clauses—
(which, it may be remarked, were the only ones not
framed by lawyers),—and the issue turned so much
on these that an attempt must be made to track the
dismal argument through the maze of figures. The
problem may be stated very shortly:—Each Colony,
by surrendering its power to levy duties of Customs
and Excise, deprived itself of its principal source of
income. *Per contra*, it was relieved of expenditure
upon the services which it transferred to the Commonwealth, e.g. Post Office, Defence, &c. ; but this was
less in amount than the revenue surrendered. Consequently, unless some arrangement could be made by
which the Commonwealth could make good the local
deficiencies, each State would be compelled to impose
fresh taxation or have its finances in disorder. New
South Wales, for example, by giving up Customs
and Excise, surrendered about £1,500,000 of revenue.
On the other hand, she was relieved of a net annual

loss on the transferred services of about £500,000,
making her deficiency £1,000,000.   Every other Colony
was in a similar position :—that is to say, none of them
was relieved of an expenditure equal in amount to
the revenue which it surrendered.   The problem was
to find some fair method of compensation ; and since
the duties of Customs and Excise, after deducting
the revenue derived from inter-Colonial duties, which
would cease after Federation, amounted in 1898 to
between £7,000,000 and £8,000,000, while the annual
requirements of the Commonwealth were not estimated
to exceed £1,750,000, it would seem to have been an
easy matter to meet the difficulty.   It was clear that
the Commonwealth would have a large annual surplus ;
and this could either be distributed among the States
to meet their requirements, or be absorbed in relieving
them of future expenditure.

The latter course was the simpler ; and the taking
over by the Commonwealth of the public debts and
State-owned railways,—which on the figures of that
time would have almost absorbed the surplus,—
presented an obvious means of making this adjustment, which was urged steadily upon the Convention
by a small party, who, although always in a minority,
had the satisfaction of seeing their numbers increase
on each division, and which was the solution advocated
by the *Daily Telegraph*.   It must be admitted, however, that this proposal would not have been carried
by the popular vote either in New South Wales or
Victoria ; so that escape from the financial complica-
tion had to be sought in a distribution of the surplus
among the States.   The task was to discover a basis
of distribution—whether *per capita* or *per* contribution

—which would not operate unfairly towards the richer States.

This, which seems so easy, was complicated by the fact that the proportion borne by the revenue surrendered to the total revenue collected differed in each Colony. Accordingly, any return of the Commonwealth surplus to each State according to its requirements would have cast an unfair burden upon those States which had the lowest tariffs. If, on the other hand, the surplus were returned *per capita*, then those States which consumed the greater quantities of heavily-taxed goods, such as alcohol and tobacco, would have to pay more than their fair share of the common tariff, in aid of taxpayers of such States as South Australia, where home-grown wine was the principal beverage. Further complications were introduced by the impossibility of determining beforehand what the yield of any item of the tariff would be in the several States, under the new conditions of inter-Colonial Free Trade.

The solution of these difficulties contained in the Bill was, in effect, the plan of 1891,—that is to say, ensuring each State a return on the basis of its contributions for five years, and leaving the ultimate mode of distribution to be determined by the Parliament at the end of that period. At least three-fourths of the revenue derived from Customs and Excise was to be returned to the States according to the amount contributed by each; and the expenditure of the Commonwealth was to be charged *per capita*. To give effect to these provisions a clause was inserted in Melbourne during the last sittings of the Convention, on the motion of Sir Edward Braddon, imposing an obligation on the Parliament to guarantee the necessities of the States, by compelling the return by the Commonwealth of 15s. out of every £1 collected from each State in Customs and Excise ; and another set of clauses provided for an elaborate system of bookkeeping, in order to ascertain the amount of the contributions of each State to the federal revenue by tracing the places of consumption of dutiable articles. It must be admitted that these proposals would not recommend themselves to unfriendly critics. Where they were precise they were clumsy, and alarming where they were indefinite. They gave a wide scope also for bold guess-work, in calculating both the probable expenditure of the Commonwealth and the share of each State's contribution towards it. On both these points there was much controversy.

The expenditure of the Commonwealth was of two kinds : (1) New expenditure for strictly federal purposes (e.g. on the High Court, the Parliament, &c.), and (2) expenditure on the services transferred by the States to the Commonwealth.

The highest estimate of the ' new ' expenditure was £300,000, made up as follows :—

Legislature	£103,000
Governor-General	15,000
Executive	14,000
High Commission	18,370
Treasury	12,500
High Court	23,715
Interest on Public Buildings and Maintenance	52,540
	£239,125
Add Contingencies	60,875
	£300,000

Divided among a population of 3,200,000, this, which Federalists claimed to be the total cost of Federation, worked out at 1s. 10d. per head,—'about a shilling less than it would cost to register a dog.' The 'Antis' made quite another calculation, and included in their estimate of the cost not only the 'new' expenditure, but the expenditure on the transferred services and the sum which the Commonwealth would require to raise in order to balance the finances of the States. Many estimates were made, which varied with the audacity of the calculator, from the £4 per head of the anti-Convention League to the 22s. 6d. which was finally adopted by the *Daily Telegraph*. This was the estimate accepted by Mr. Reid, from May to July 1898; until the result of the General Election, in August of that year, convinced him that the statisticians were in error, and that, for the sake of Union, New South Wales could accept safely the financial clauses, which, as Chairman of the Finance Committee, he had himself proposed to the Convention and denounced a few weeks later as 'intolerable'![1]

The expenditure of the Commonwealth upon the transferred services imposed no new burdens on the people, and did not add a penny to their taxes. The Postal and Telegraphic Services, Defence, Quarantine, Lighthouses, and the other sources of expenditure which the Commonwealth took over, were being paid for by the citizens of the several States, to whom it could make no difference whether they paid their share of the cost to the State or to the Commonwealth Treasurer. In most of the States the transferred services were being run at a loss; and a return presented to the Convention showed that the net loss in

---

[1] See *post*, p. 291, footnote.

the six Colonies was £862,631 per annum. Accordingly, the Commonwealth would have to raise this sum, in addition to the £300,000, the estimated cost of its new expenditure. There was a probability, however, that some savings would be effected by bringing these services under one control.

The third item of the Commonwealth Expenditure was the amount required to recoup the States for their surrenders of revenue ; and it was as to this that the most varying estimates were made. It was the element of uncertainty, which could not be eliminated, because it was impossible to foretell the amount which each Colony would contribute as its share of the common tariff.

Federalists insisted that there were not sufficient data for any useful calculation as to the incidence of federal taxation ; and that the elaborate calculations of experts on this question were pure guesswork, because there was no experience of a common tariff to guide to a conclusion. Even if the items of such a tariff could have been forecast, no one could say what each would bring in in the several States until inter-Colonial Free Trade had come into operation. All that could be predicted at the time with certainty was that, since the standard of living was much the same throughout Australia, the yield of a common tariff would tend to be the same, per head, throughout the Federation. But this tendency would not be effective until commerce and industry should have had time to adjust themselves to the new conditions of inter-Colonial Free Trade ; and even then there would be inequalities between the States, arising from the difference of habits and different pursuits. A mining State, for instance, consumes a greater quantity of dutiable goods than an agricultural, and a State which is developing rapidly generally has a preponderance of male population, and, consequently, a proportionately larger number of taxpayers than a more settled community. Therefore, Federalists contended, calculations as to the probable incidence of a federal tariff were 'attempts to resolve a problem, of uncertain factors, into terms of the unknown.'

One instance will be sufficient to illustrate the argument. A return submitted by Mr. Reid to the Adelaide Convention, 'with the special object of showing that New South Wales would contribute very largely to the Commonwealth revenue,' attempted to forecast the yield from New South Wales, if the common tariff were the same as the Victorian, 'upon the assumption that the goods would have been imported to the same extent no matter what tariff might be in operation,' which was (so Federalists said) 'as if one should assume that the same number of Chinamen would enter New South Wales if there were a poll-tax of £100 as if no such tax were levied.' The calculation proved that New South Wales would pay £2 13s. 7d. per head to the common tariff, while Victoria would pay only £1 9s. per head. Mr. Pulsford, who with Mr. Bruce-Smith conducted the controversy on the federal side, illustrated the fallacy of the assumption by one instance. The Victorian duty on soda crystals was £2 per ton. This, being a prohibitive duty, only produced £1 4s. 8d. in 1896. In the same year the imports of this article into New South Wales, where it paid no duty, were

700 tons.   Applying the federal tariff to both countries,
upon the same assumption, would prove that New
South Wales would pay £1,400 upon this line as
against Victoria's £1 4s. 8d.

Other calculations, on different bases, led to conclusions which were equally absurd.   All that could
be predicted was that the Commonwealth would
require a revenue of about £7,000,000 a year to meet
its own necessities and recoup the States ; and that
this would be raised, at first at any rate, by indirect
taxation.   It followed that the low tariff of New South
Wales could not continue ; and the certainty that the
Customs duties levied in that Colony would be in-
increased became, as Sir Henry Parkes had foreseen
when he protested against the abolition of the
Dibbs duties, one of the strongest arguments against
Union.

The object of bitterest attack was the unnecessary,
but practically harmless, proposal of Sir Edward
Braddon, before mentioned, which required the Federal
Treasurer to return to the States at least 15s. out
of every £1 collected from Customs and Excise.   This
clause, which became known as the ' Braddon Blot,'
and which, like a blot on a piece of paper, was an
excrescence, even although the writing might be
visible beneath it, was the cause of more misunderstanding and hostility than anything else in the Bill.
Intended as a rough but effective guarantee to the
smaller States, it was interpreted by the opponents of
the Bill as a direction, which compelled the Commonwealth to raise four times as much revenue as it needed.
If, however, it is remembered that the total Customs
and Excise revenue which was surrendered by the

States amounted to about four times the amount required by the Commonwealth for its own purposes, it will be seen that Sir Edward Braddon's clause only directed the Commonwealth Treasurer to do that which he would have been compelled to do, in any case, in order to enable the States to adjust their finances. Mr. Barton, accordingly, had objected to the clause as unnecessary; but Mr. Reid,—and this must be remembered in considering his speeches during the Referendum campaign,—had supported it for reasons which will be stated later.[1] It was hardly to be expected, however, that the harmless character of the clause,—which was manifestly out of place in a Constitution,—would be perceived except by that small portion of the community which kept before their minds the ratio between federal revenue and federal requirements.

· 4 ·

The Rivers Question.—Most of the rivers in Australia flow from the dividing coastal range towards the sea; but the Murray and its tributaries form a great system on the other side, which, having one source in the south-west of Queensland and another in the south-eastern mountains of New South Wales, carries the waters of the interior to its mouth in South Australia. The Murray itself forms a boundary between Victoria and New South Wales; but its principal tributaries, the Darling and the Murrumbidgee, run wholly through New South Wales. The Murray, the Darling, and the Murrumbidgee are all navigable, but, except in good seasons, only through part of their courses.

[1] See *post*, p. 267.

South Australia for many years has had a profitable carrying trade along these rivers, so that it is to her interest that their waters should not be diminished by being drawn off for irrigation. Victoria had made use of the Murray for this purpose for some years previously to 1897 ; and New South Wales had schemes prepared for utilising the Darling and the Murrumbidgee in the same way. Thus, the interests of South Australia came into sharp conflict with the interests of New South Wales and Victoria ; and a controversy arose, which was apparently insoluble, between those who advocated the use of the rivers for navigation and those who insisted that irrigation was the most profitable use to which the waters could be put. So much of the trade of South Australia depended upon the Murray being navigable that it was not until the last days of the Melbourne Session that any compromise could be reached. Finally, it was decided to add a new clause limiting the power of the Commonwealth over navigation, by prescribing that 'no law or regulation of trade or commerce should abridge the right of a State or of the residents therein to the reasonable use of the waters of rivers for conservation or irrigation.' Manifestly, this was only to defer the settlement of the question. But, while it was easy for critics to ridicule the use of such a vague term as 'reasonable,' at least it should have been remembered that no acute misunderstanding had arisen up to that time,—(nor indeed up to the present time),—and that, if the High Court or the people of Australia could not be trusted to settle difficulties as they arose, it was better to refuse to federate.

s

· 5 ·

Minor Issues.—Among the minor points in controversy were the omission to provide in the Constitution for the site of the Capital, and the provisions which prohibited differential railway rates. The reason for the omission has been already touched upon. The argument about the railway rates was the same as that which was used by the ' Prudent Federalists ' in 1890.[1] The Convention met the objection by providing for the appointment of an inter-State Commission, to be charged with ' such powers of adjudication and administration as the Parliament deems necessary for the execution and maintenance ' of the clause relating to Trade and Commerce, and that ' no preference or discrimination shall be taken to be unreasonable ' unless this body so adjudged. As a further concession to the States, the inter-State Commission was required, in coming to any decision, to pay ' due regard to the financial responsibilities incurred by any State in connection with the construction and maintenance of its railways.' As will be seen, not even these provisions prevented the opponents of the Bill from declaring that it would enable Victoria, South Australia, and Queensland to ' rob ' New South Wales of all its border trade.

The provision of the Bill that existing bounties should be paid by the Commonwealth, if they had been imposed before June 30, 1898, was another clause which excited alarm. It was remembered that Victoria had offered a bounty, before this date, upon the production of brown coal ; and it was argued, with an appearance of solemnity, that this would

1 See *ante*, p. 114.

have the effect of excluding Newcastle coal from the
Victorian market ! Mr. Reid made great play with
this ' argument ' in the speech which he delivered
at Newcastle on the eve of the first Referendum !

. 6 .

This brief summary of the principal points in
dispute will serve to show that, like all compromises,
the Bill was not entirely satisfactory to any section
of the public ; but, while the Federalists were willing
to accept it with its imperfections, the 'Antis,' being
essentially indifferent or hostile to Union, saw nothing
in its provisions but what was bad.   It is to no purpose
to recall that twelve years' experience of Federation
has shown that the bogies which haunted the
provincialists were of their own imaginations.   For,
in 1898, these seemed very substantial ; so that the
issue was in doubt until the end.

The opposition came from the two extremes—
the Labour Party and the wealthy classes,—the former
objecting to the constitutional provisions, the latter
taking alarm both at these and the financial.   A
Constitution which gave adult suffrage, an elective
second Chamber and Responsible Government, and
which empowered the Governor, on the advice of his
Ministers, to dissolve both Houses, was, it might be
thought, not one to be condemned as ' undemocratic ' !
But such was the power of the cry ' Majority Rule
in Danger ! ' that it was forgotten that the contingency
of a combination of the small Colonies against the
large, which was the bugbear of Labour speeches,
was most unlikely to occur, and could be met, if it
did occur, by the provisions against deadlocks.   The

wealthy classes,—the other party to this strange
alliance,—opposed the Bill on the opposite ground
'that it was too democratic.' They predicted, also,
that it would 'ruin Sydney,' by encouraging the
trade of other ports ; and they feared an increase
in taxation. The financial clauses, indeed, were
admittedly makeshifts, and left much to the good
sense of the Federal Parliament, which Federalists
were prepared to trust. Fortunately for the advocates of the Bill, while the statisticians and financial
experts in every Colony condemned these clauses,
their unanimity was the less terrifying, because each
foretold the exaltation of the other Colonies upon
the ruin of his own, and no two were agreed upon
the causes of the coming disaster or the methods
of escape ! The controversy soon became one of
arithmetic.

Controversial arithmetic, however, was not the
only weapon of the 'Antis,' who made their strongest
appeal to local prejudice. The position of New South
Wales was such that, from the extent and variety
of her resources, of all the Colonies, she could afford
best to stand alone. A majority of her people believed
in Free Trade ; and Federation meant a certain increase
in the tariff. But it was not generally perceived
that this increase was inevitable in any event, because
the revenue from loans and the sale of public lands,
which had made Free Trade possible, was coming
to an end. By ignoring the future, and looking only
to the present circumstances of the Colony, it was easy
for the 'Antis' to draw misleading comparisons between
the financial condition of New South Wales and that
of the other Colonies, which were swallowed the more

greedily because in no Colony was it easier for ignorance or malice to excite provincial jealousies.

Federation has wrought, already, such changes in the material conditions and the sentiments of Australians that the present generation can hardly remember what the difficulties were which Federalists had to overcome. The next generation will hardly believe that these existed, when they read of them in history!

CHAPTER XIX

' YES—NO ! '

WHILE Mr. Barton was gathering up his papers, at the close of the last sitting of the Convention, before the final revise (March 12, 1898), Mr. Reid, as he left the Chamber, had inquired of him, ' Are we going to be at loggerheads over this Bill ?   What are you going to do ? ' Mr. Barton answered that ' Mr. Reid knew well what he (Mr. Barton) would do ' ; to which Mr. Reid replied, ' There are a good many things in the Bill which I do not like ; but I think you will find that I shall not oppose it. I shall have difficulties with my own party ; but you will be glad to know that I do not intend to place any obstacles in the way of getting the Bill accepted at the Referendum.'[1]

This assurance was the more welcome, because it was feared that Mr. Reid's federal zeal had somewhat cooled. At Adelaide, when it was doubtful if a Bill would be agreed upon, he had spoken, in the true spirit of an Australian Federalist, of the necessity for compromise and breadth of view ; but, later, his dissatisfaction with the Bill had appeared to increase

---

[1] Both Mr. O'Connor and Mr. Barton referred to this conversation during the campaign ; and Mr. Barton repeated it to the writer a few moments after it had taken place. Mr. Reid disputed its accuracy. See particularly Mr. O'Connor's speech at Young, reported in the *Australian Federalist*.

as each obstacle to unanimity was overcome ! After
the close of the Convention, he preserved a studied
reticence about the Bill, which was the more marked
because all the other delegates,—except Mr. Lyne,
who, as usual, was waiting upon Mr. Reid,—had
defined their views. Mr. Barton gave an account of
his stewardship at a meeting in the Sydney Town
Hall on March 24. His speech was a worthy opening
of a great campaign,—a powerful, lucid, and dignified
explanation of the Bill and a trenchant exposure,
but without bitterness or partisanship, of the mis-
apprehensions of its critics. The public, however,
was thinking more of Mr. Reid than of Mr. Barton.
It was known that the Free Trade party had declared
against the Bill; and there was great curiosity as to
the sentiments of its leader.

. I .

Mr. Reid broke silence on March 28 at the Town
Hall, in a speech which, by the dramatic inconsequence
of its conclusion, has added the term ' Yes—No ' to
the political vocabulary of the English language.[1]
Still unconscious of his intentions, all the leading
Federalists took seats upon his platform ; and the
great hall was packed with an expectant and enthusiastic crowd. It was remembered afterwards that,
before the meeting opened, Mr. Reid showed signs
of nervousness, probably for the first time in his
public life.

He began with the assurance of his intention to
' deal with the Bill not as a partisan but as a judge,'
because there was ' a duty which he owed to the

[1] The word is included in the last two editions of *Webster's Dictionary*

people and to his colleagues at the Convention.' He would 'put the fairest construction on the words and motives' of the latter, because 'he could not help feeling that, if he had been a representative of one of the smaller Colonies, he might have acted very differently than as a representative of a larger Colony.'

He spoke next of the Convention, and reminded the audience that, because each State returned an equal number of delegates, this 'had been organised on the basis of minority rule.' He regretted, also, that some delegates from the larger States had been 'Conservatives who had a natural desire to make the Senate a very strong House.' The result, he said, had been that 'the representatives of the larger Colonies fought the battle of the larger population under considerable disadvantages ; and this was the reason why the Convention had not produced a better Bill.' Then, as the audience was beginning to wonder how the work of such a body could be good at all, he concluded this portion of his speech with an abrupt qualification : 'Still, the Convention was an enormous improvement upon the Convention of 1891 and had put the Bill in a vastly better shape.'

Next, 'in pursuance of his judicial duty' he noted in a few sentences three 'good features' of the Bill, viz.—

that the Union was to be under the Crown ; That it gave complete freedom of trade and intercourse ; and that, as the Commonwealth had unlimited power to tax, one of its first duties would be to spend money on Defence, so that by joining Federation they undertook to defend to their last shilling the integrity of the whole Union against a foreign invader.[1]

Having thus artfully called attention to a probable

---

1 All these provisions had been in the Bill of 1891.

increase in taxation, Mr. Reid explained the provisions
of the Bill in regard to the composition and powers of
the two Houses, in order to show that the burden
of the new taxes would fall unfairly upon New South
Wales :—

It is not true [he said] that the Senate is the trustee and
guardian of the States in matters of taxation.   If each of the
States paid an equal amount into the Federal Treasury to run
the Federation, then the claims of the States to have an equal
voice with the nation in matters of taxation and expenditure
would be absolutely just.   But since . . . . the taxation of
the Commonwealth is National, not State, the National House
ought to have more powers over it than it has.   And this is
not a trivial matter ;   and I am determined that if there is not
manhood and breadth of mind enough in the country—

[Surely the secret was coming out ! But no !
the sentence concluded thus :]

to vote for Federation in the full light of what it means, then
I say ' we ought not to have it.'   If there are sacrifices to be
made by New South Wales, it is infinitely better and nobler for
the future nation that it should make them with its eyes open.

Mr. Reid next reviewed the provisions of the Bill
relating to deadlocks, and found fault with the provision requiring a three-fifths majority at the Joint
Sitting :—

Mr. Wise very fairly put it that the united power of the
two larger Colonies at that Joint Sitting—[here he paused]—
if they all voted together (Voices ' Ah ! ') would be 59, and that
would carry the Bill for the House of Representatives.   But
if three happened to be away or voted with the other
side, 56 votes in the Joint Sitting would be powerless and 38
votes would win.   Now there is another way of putting this :—
Let us take this state of things, that the whole of the House of

Representatives were upon one side and the whole of the
Senate on the other—that would be 64 votes for the Lower
House and 30 for the Upper,[1] a flying majority for the Lower
House and the Bill carried.   But, if eight of the 64 went over
to the other side or were not present—[why all the renegades
or absentees should come from the larger States Mr. Reid did
not explain]—56 would lose and 38 would win.   That means
that, in the case of New South Wales, three-fourths of the
population, as represented perhaps by that majority, would
be powerless.

And this was the more dangerous because he thought
that

if ever a great appeal came about between the two Houses
it would be in matters in which the interests of the larger and
the smaller States came out sharply in conflict.   In such a
conflict the matter should be settled by the man who found
the money—the national taxpayer.

Dealing next with the financial clauses of the Bill,
he dwelt much upon the burden these would cast on
New South Wales :—

The Commonwealth will require, to carry on the services
with which it will be entrusted at present (and I don't think
the amount need seriously increase), £1,500,000 per annum, of
which New South Wales would contribute £640,000, Victoria
about £500,000 and the other Colonies the balance of about
£350,000.

But he pointed out that—'owing to the different
circumstances of the different Colonies'. . . West
Australia being ' taxed up to the eyes,' while the Customs taxation of New South Wales was 'ridiculously'
small—

[1] At this time Queensland was standing out, so that the Commonwealth consisted of five States.

New South Wales would require a cheque every year for £1,050,000 in return for surrendering her Customs Duties ; while Victoria would be reduced to a state of insolvency if she did not get back £1,668,000.   .. A uniform tariff which brought in £4,110,000 would give back to New South Wales all that she required (to balance her accounts), but, in order to compensate Victoria, the Commonwealth would have to raise a revenue of £6,030,000, while to make up to Tasmania (the revenue which she surrendered) the tariff would have to bring in £7,000,000 a year . . . On the Victorian basis, New South Wales would be taxed from £800,000 to £1,000,000 more than she wants ; while, on the Tasmanian basis, she would require a tax upon her of from £1,200,000 to £1,500,000 more than she needed to raise for herself.

He admitted that ' all the money paid over the fair average,' after deducting the Colony's share of the expenses, would be paid back, but

I must not say ' You get it back ' ; I never heard of a financial operation of that kind. The Treasury gets it back. (Laughter.)

He next spoke of the Braddon clause, which he declared to be ' the gravest blemish in the Bill,' ignoring that, less than six weeks earlier, he had spoken of this clause, in the Convention, as ' the most reasonable way in which the question has been put, and, from my point of view, the least objectionable form of guarantee (to the smaller States) that I have seen,' [1] and had voted in its favour against Mr. Barton. On this occasion, he described it as

an extraordinary provision that for every £1 raised through the Customs, 15s. must go back to the States . . . Thus if, in the vicissitudes of the Commonwealth, the Treasurer needed

[1] Hansard, p. 3424.

£200,000 he would have to raise £800,000 to get that amount.
The other £600,000 would go back to the States. But would
it go back to you ? (Laughter and cries of No !)

Mr. Reid emphasised the importance of dwelling
on the financial clauses, because under the Bill as it
stood 'it was certain' that the three small States
would block in the Senate any tariff which did not bring
in enough revenue to balance their finances, 'which
necessarily meant that New South Wales would be
taxed more than was necessary.' He guarded himself against the admission that such a tariff must be
protective, and declared his intention 'to continue
to fight for Free Trade.'

The compromise upon the rivers question, which
he regarded as a question 'of grave importance,'
seemed to him to be quite unsatisfactory, because no
one could say what was meant by 'a reasonable use
of the waters for irrigation purposes.'

Who is to say, when the rivers fall too low to be navigable,
what is a reasonable use of their waters for irrigation ? . . .
Until the High Court decides this I don't know where I am.

He commended the refusal of the Convention to
take over the railways and the public debt. 'It
would have been madness to put the policy of railway
construction into the hands of the Federal Parliament';
and he was pleased that he 'had always steadily
resisted this proposal.' He was glad that the Bill
established 'unequivocally' the practice of Responsible Government; and did not object to the
clauses limiting the right of appeal to the Privy
Council.

As to the Capital, he confessed his belief that this,

' which ought to be in New South Wales,' would be
fixed in Victoria, 'because human nature would be
too strong for New South Wales, and Victoria was the
most convenient situation.'

And then, just when all were looking for the 'judge'
to state the case for the prisoner, Mr. Reid—having
thus supported with the weight of his authority
the only four serious attacks which critics had made
upon the Bill, viz., on the constitutional provisions,
the financial provisions, the rivers compromise, and
the omission to fix the site of the Capital—began
his peroration :—

I feel myself under a peculiar and deep sense of responsibility. I, with my colleagues, brought the Governments of
Australia together in an effort, at last, upon democratic lines,
to bring this great work to a happy conclusion. . . . It is too
late to criticise the fact that in that Convention so many
people's representatives could outvote the representatives of so
many others. That was known beforehand, and so with equal
representation in the Senate. No man had a stronger re-
pugnance to such a provision than I had, but I looked upon it
as a thing without which Federation seemed to be an impossible
dream. Knowing these things, I knew also what would come
of them. I knew that, under a Convention so constituted,
under a Bill so framed, and under a Senate constituted as it must
be, there was only too much room for fear that in the great
crises the voice of the people might be strangled and the
voice of the minority, setting its resolute will in the citadel of
the Senate, might drive back the tide of progress.

A Voice.—So it will.

Mr. Reid.—I hope it will not be so, when we look on the
subjects which will be in the power of the Senate. I ask you
all in New South Wales, I implore of you that, when you fully
realise the absolute necessity of some day, and some day soon,
being one nation, I ask you, with that thought of brotherhood,

of Australian freedom,—to look at that Bill honestly and fearlessly, and decide on your conscience for yourselves. So far as I am concerned, I, with all the criticism I have levelled at this Bill, with all the fears I have for the future—I feel I cannot become a deserter from the cause. I cannot take up this Bill with enthusiasm. I see serious blots in it, which put a cruel strain upon me. I have not made up my mind about this Bill without a great deal of painful and anxious thought, because, after all, great as nationalisation is, great as Australian Union is—in these days of humanity, in a continent free as this is, we ought to have, I admit, a more democratic Constitution. And now I would say to you, having opened up my mind, having shown you the dark places as well as the light ones of this Constitution : I put it upon every man in this country, without coercion from me, without interference from me, to judge for himself, and therefore I may say that my duty to Australia demands me to record my vote in favour of this Bill.

. 2 .

It cannot be difficult even after a lapse of years to imagine the effect of such a speech upon the minds of men already tense for the struggle.

Federalists, reading Mr. Reid's unsparing condemnation of all the clauses in the Bill to which objections had been raised, and his half-hearted approbation of the few others, about which there was no difference of opinion, could conclude only that, under the specious guise of judicial fairness, he had marshalled nearly every argument which told against the Bill ; and that his faint praise was intended to be more damning than the most acute criticism. The 'Antis' on the other hand, while welcoming the support which the speech gave to their side, asked with amazement how it was possible for the Premier of the Colony

to vote in favour of a measure which his own arguments had ' torn to ribbons,' ' damned beyond re-
demption ' and shown to be ' rotten, weak, and unfair ' ! [1]
The puzzled public felt inclined to accept the cruel
suggestion of the *Daily Telegraph* ' that Mr. Reid
had taken two perorations with him to the meeting,
intending to use either as events suggested ; and
that, carried away by the temporary enthusiasm
of his audience, he had spoken the wrong one by
mistake ' ! His action, as one exasperated ' Anti '
wrote in the pungent paper warfare which followed
on the speech, was like that of a juryman who
should announce to his fellows after their retirement, ' Convention Bill is a sad rascal, and obviously
guilty ; but, as one of your number, I shall vote for
an acquittal ' !

Never, since Junius Brutus [wrote the *Daily Telegraph*,
which was the organ of the ' Antis '] condemned his
guilty offspring to be thrown from the Tarpeian rock, has
there been such an exhibition of flinty-hearted justice as that
furnished by Mr. Reid. He will vote for the Bill because
he is one of its authors ; but its provisions are foreign
to all his notions and every article of his political creed.

Yet Mr. Reid was the most astute of politicians,
and unlikely to expose himself wantonly to obvious
criticisms. His own explanation, given immediately
after the Referendum (Speech at Milton, June 12, 1898),
was as follows :—

When this Bill came before the public, I felt in a difficulty.
I had been so associated with the federal movement, which
brought forth the Bill, that I felt that, if I had said at the
meeting I addressed at the Sydney Town Hall ' I am going to

---

[1] Extract from interview with Mr. Want, March 30, 1898.

vote against it,' that Bill was doomed. I felt, under the circumstances, no matter what abuse I shall expose myself to, ' I will give the Bill a chance.' If I had voted against the Bill and killed it at the start, the whole course of Federation would have been shipwrecked. I preferred to stand up to be shot at from both sides of the hedge, in order to give the Bill a fair chance of being accepted.

There is weight, no doubt, in the contention that neither inclination nor prudence would have disposed Mr. Reid to bring to a summary end the movement which he had started himself in 1895. But a consideration of all the facts justifies the larger conclusion, that the speech was one of those daring strokes of leadership which is condemned when it fails, but easily might have had a different issue.

Mr. Reid's whole course of conduct shows that he both expected and desired the Bill to be defeated. It was at his instance that the 80,000 minimum had been inserted in the Act, by which the Parliament of New South Wales broke faith with the other Colonies ; [1] and, in March 1898, there seemed to be no prospect that this limit would be reached. Mr. Lyne, the leader of the Protectionists, was opposing the Bill, together with a majority of the Free Traders ; and, more powerful than either, the *Daily Telegraph*,

[1] The minimum of affirmative votes in the draft Bill agreed to by the Premiers at the Hobart Conference was, for New South Wales, 50,000. At the end of 1897 Mr. Neild, a supporter of Mr. Reid's Government and a strong opponent of Federation, introduced a Bill to raise this minimum to 120,000, which would have been a fatal impediment to the carrying of the Convention Bill. In Committee Mr. Reid suggested the figure 80,000, which Mr. Neild accepted, thus (as the *Sydney Morning Herald* wrote) ' loading the dice against the Federalists.' Mr. Reid voted against the third reading of this measure ; but it could not have been passed if he had made its rejection a Ministerial question.

under the direction of Mr. L. J. Brient, was fighting
the battle of provincialism, with an ability and vigour
without parallel in the history of Australian journalism.
Moreover, Mr. Reid, as Minister, had it in his power
to grant or refuse those legislative and administrative
facilities for recording votes on which the magnitude
of the poll depended. In fact, he made no provision
for an elector, who happened to be outside his electoral
precinct upon polling day, to record his vote ; and
due regard was not paid to the convenience of the
electors in the selection of polling places in the country
districts.

Expecting, then, that the Bill would be defeated,
and precluded from open hostility by his earlier action,
Mr. Reid boldly made a speech which should be
justified by the result of the voting, and, at the same
time, leave him free to direct the movement into a
new channel. Had this expectation been fulfilled,
the credit would have been given to his criticisms,
while his declaration that he would not be ' a deserter
from the cause ' would have permitted him to re-open
negotiations with the other Premiers. Also, his triumph
over Mr. Barton, who was pledged to the Bill, would
have been complete ; and that he was not insensible
to this gratification was admitted by himself about
this time.[1]

· 3 ·

Mr. Reid spoke again twice upon the Bill—at
Goulburn on May 12, and at Newcastle on May 26—

[1] When reminded by an interjector that, in 1895, he had declared
that ' his policy was always to be top-dog,' and that he might be
opposing the Convention Bill because ' Barton was now top-dog,' he
answered, ' Well ! that is quite possible. There is a good deal of
human nature in me ' !

T

but, except on these occasions, held aloof from the campaign. Each of these speeches was a *crescendo* of condemnation. The criticisms became more unsparing and the merits less conspicuous ; so the wonder grew that he could vote for such a measure ! The arguments in each were the same :—that ' equal representation had destroyed majority rule ' : that the settlement of the rivers question was ' not a broad recognition of the rights of New South Wales ' : that the financial clause imposed ' great sacrifices ' upon New South Wales : that the Commonwealth would be extravagant, and that a ' limit should be placed upon its expenditure ' : that the abstention of Queensland ' made the position of New South Wales so much worse ' that, ' if he had not been so deeply committed to the federal movement,' he would have brought it to an end : that the Braddon clause was ' an abominable blot upon the Bill ' : that the smaller Colonies would ' swamp New South Wales ' : and there would be ' a general scramble that would lead to log-rolling,' and ' a combination of the smaller States to get better terms out of the larger ones ' : that ' the Bill was so bad that he himself had often felt he would like to have left the Convention.'

Nevertheless, he would not advise that the Bill should be rejected :—

I tell you frankly [he said at Goulburn] that, under this Bill, you are called upon to make sacrifices which no other Colony is making. Make me a citizen of Victoria or Tasmania or South Australia, and I will stump the Colonies from end to end in favour of the Bill ; but it is on account of feeling that this Colony is called upon to make sacrifices much larger

CHAPTER XX

THE THIRD OF JUNE

THE fateful third of June broke dull and overcast, threatening the rain for which the ' Antis ' hoped, because it would reduce the poll ; but before eleven o'clock the sun had broken through the clouds,—an omen of success. All that was possible to win the necessary 80,000 votes had been done already by Mr. Barton and his friends, although few of us hoped for success. Therefore it was rather as a relief to nervous tension, than from any need to stir enthusiasm, that the day was spent in driving round the polling booths.

. I .

At seven o'clock we were to meet at the Empire Hotel, where some seventy of the more active workers in the campaign dined together in a room facing the office of the *Sydney Morning Herald*, outside of which the results of the poll were displayed as they arrived. Before half-past seven, the city and suburban returns showed 52,000 in favour of, and 51,000 against, the Bill. Those who feared that a small poll in Sydney would prevent the 80,000 being reached began to gain heart. Suddenly the totals jumped to 59,000 For and 58,000 Against ; and, when Mr. Barton rose to respond to the toast of his health, the board showed the Federalists to be 64,000 and 1100 ahead. Speeches were also made by Messrs. O'Connor, Wise, Walker, and See. The note of all was the same,—a warning against discouragement in the event of a defeat, and a determination, whatever the result, to sink all party difference until Union was accomplished.

Suddenly a roar, as of a multitude drawing breath together, rose from the streets below; and bursts of hysterical cheering drowned the speaker's voice. Some one at the window shouted 80,284; and, for twenty golden minutes, we believed that Union had been won. Emotion was too tense for speech. Men wept silently for joy. When Mr. Barton appeared at the window, the dense crowd, which filled Hunter Street so far as Castlereagh Street and stretched along Pitt Street for 200 yards, burst into fresh enthusiasm, and demanded speeches. In succession, Mr. Barton, Mr. O'Connor, and Mr. Wise spoke some broken sentences of gratitude and pride.

We had hardly retaken our seats, and were listening to Mr. Barton's final words, when Mr. Samuel Cook,— the aloof and imperturbable manager of the *Sydney Morning Herald*,—entered the room, and pressed towards the Chairman, with trouble and anxiety upon his face. Everyone knew, even before Mr. Barton could announce the fatal news, that some error had been made, and that the 80,000 limit had not been reached.

The disappointment was crushing; but it could not cancel the experience through which we had just lived. The thrill of exultation and pride in the birth of a new nation, and the sense of sudden gain in political stature, which thousands experienced in those happy, but mistaken, moments, had given a foretaste of what Federation, when it came, would mean, and was the impulse which carried us forward to the final victory. Yet the emotion was not one of partisan triumph, but the sense that a stage in our national growth had been reached, and passed.

. 2 .

The erroneous figures, posted by the *Sydney Morning Herald*, were copied on the board of the Hotel Australia, where Mr. Reid was watching the results. On reading them, he left the hotel, without a word to anyone, and was discovered later, after much searching, by a reporter of the *Daily Telegraph*, asleep in a box at the adjoining Theatre Royal![1] On learning the result, he joined the leaders of the anti-Bill party in a public demonstration outside the office of that newspaper ; and, after a dramatic reconciliation with Mr. Want in sight of the crowd below, offered his congratulations to New South Wales for rejecting his advice to vote for the Bill ! Mr. Want's speech on this occasion was characteristic. Going further than Mr. Reid, he looked to the future :—

You have been told [he said], by those people who supported this Bill, that you cannot have another Convention ; but I want you to watch these gentlemen. I say again, watch them. The very men who are now telling you there cannot be another Convention will be among the first to start out and boom another Bill. You will find that these men who have been booming this fraud and sham will be in the front ranks of those who will be starting to-morrow to try and run another monkey show.

[1] This apparently trivial circumstance is too characteristic to pass over. Mr. Reid, like Lord North, was of imperturbable temper, and neither failure nor success disturbed his serenity.

A fortnight later Mr. Reid restored Mr. Want to the office of Attorney-General, which he had kept open for him since his resignation !

It was evident that the fight would have to be renewed. The wishes of a majority had been thwarted by a trick, and provincialism had gained a new lease of life.

APPENDIX TO CHAPTER XX

The number of votes cast for and against the Bill at the Referendum of 1898 is shown in the subjoined table :

	N.S.W.	Victoria	S. Aust.	Tas.	Total
For	71,965	100,520	35,800	11,706	219,991
Against	66,228	22,099	17,320	2,716	108,363
Majority for the Bill . .	5,737	78,421	18,480	8,990	111,628

It has been said that the small number of votes recorded in New South Wales indicates indifference on the part of the people of that Colony with regard to the question of Federation. If due regard be paid, however, to the conditions under which the vote was taken, the polling was above the average of a general election. Owing to the intricate provisions of the Electoral Act and their stringent interpretation by the Government of the day, a large number of electors, who were absent from their divisions, were disfranchised. Also there was considerable delay and confusion in fixing the polling places in the country districts, which contributed to diminish the number of votes recorded. Taking these circumstances into consideration, a vote of 138,193 out of a total enrolment of about 270,000 cannot be considered evidence of apathy.

None of these administrative obstacles was placed in the

way of a large vote on the second Referendum in 1899 ; and it is probable that, if the same facilities had been given at the first as at the second Referendum, the 80,000 limit of affirmative votes could have been reached. A fact which had great significance for politicians, in view of the coming General Election, was that the Bill was carried in a majority of the constituencies.

CHAPTER XXI

'TRIMMING THE SAILS'

THE provisions of the Enabling Act were exhausted by the taking of the Referendum; and since, owing to the amendment made by the Parliament of New South Wales, the statutory minimum of 80,000 affirmative votes had not been reached, the movement came to a full stop. There was a majority for the Bill in every Colony; while the majority in its favour, taking Australia as a whole, was overwhelming. Yet the Federalists could take no action; because Mr. Reid held the reins of government, and the opponents of the Bill were well content to leave things as they were. Noisy advocates of 'Majority Rule,' when they were declaring that the Bill subverted this principle, now that the majority of the people of Australia had declared their views, the provincialists insisted that their own minority should prevail, and the wish of the majority be disregarded! During the lull which followed, both parties were manœuvring for position. The expiring Parliament, which had been prorogued during the Referendum campaign, was to meet on June 21; and there would be a general election in July. The policy of the Federalists was to sit still. They had a majority and no official responsibility. Of what use for them to propound a policy which Mr. Reid might both condemn and cap? Mr. Reid's position as Premier was more difficult. True, he had voted with the majority in favour of the Bill, but on the night of the Referendum he had praised the ' wisdom ' of the people in rejecting it,—applauding them for following, not his example, but his exhortations ! His party, too, was divided in opinion. A few of the more influential members (e.g. Messrs. Bruce-Smith, Pulsford, McMillan, and Walker) were whole-hearted Federalists ; but the majority still put Free Trade before Federation. The Labour Party, also, on whose support Mr. Reid had relied for four years, was antagonistic still to any form of Union which recognised the equality of the federating States. Nevertheless, the situation did not permit of inaction ; and, unless the expressed wish of Australia were to be thwarted, the federal movement had to be started afresh.

. I .

Mr. Reid, correctly appreciating the situation, so soon as the returns of the voting were complete, sent a Circular Despatch (June 7) to the Premiers of the other Colonies, inviting them to a Conference ' in order to consider certain changes in the Bill to make it more acceptable to New South Wales.' The Despatch continued : ' The Government sees no prospect of the acceptance in New South Wales of the Convention Bill at any stage ' (although a majority of 5000 votes had just been cast in its favour !). No indication was given of the amendments Mr. Reid desired, nor of the procedure by which these might be made ; and the large majorities for the Bill in the other Colonies were ignored. The tone of the Despatch was so unconciliatory that it is difficult to avoid the suspicion that it was not intended seriously, which the *Sydney Morning Herald* expressed without reserve. The Premiers showed by their replies that this was their view also.

Mr. Kingston answered first (June 8) for South Australia with characteristic directness :—

Hitherto we have most loyally co-operated with you, despite discouraging alterations in the Hobart agreement and of the Federal Enabling Act, to which alterations we were no party ; but we must decline to participate in an attempt to reject the Constitution which has been accepted by the direct votes of the majorities of the people of all the Federal States, and to substitute another more favourable to one State, and in respect to which it is not even suggested that the people shall be offered an opportunity of voting.

Sir Edward Braddon's reply for Tasmania was equally uncompromising :—

Holding that the Premiers have neither the right nor the power to amend the Constitution passed by the people at the Referendum in any way, I necessarily resent most strongly the proposal to alter the Bill in matters of substance.

Sir George Turner's answer, although more conciliatory in form, was, perhaps, of all the answers Mr. Reid received, the most embarrassing.   He simply inquired ' What amendments Mr. Reid proposed ? '—He received no reply !

Mr. Byrnes, who had succeeded Sir Hugh Nelson as Premier of Queensland, and whose early death was a great loss to Australia, having seen copies of these answers, replied on behalf of the northern Colony that ' A Conference would be sheer waste of

time, when the other Premiers did not admit the
necessity of making alterations in substance in the
Convention Bill.'

. 2 .

On receipt of these replies Mr. Reid broke off
negotiations, and fulfilled an engagement to speak
in the South Coast districts, which had been postponed while they were pending. During this tour,
Mr. Reid, while insisting upon his claim to be regarded
as 'as good a Federalist as Mr. Barton,' re-affirmed
his determination to obtain amendments in the Bill ;
but accompanied this demand with studied insults
to the other Premiers and truculent declarations that
discussion would be fruitless, unless things went all
one way :—

I am not surprised [he said at Milton on June 11] that
the other Colonies voted for the Bill. They have never had
such a good thing offered them in all their history. If these
Premiers think it will be well to wait and see whether the
coming New South Wales election will return a number of
members who will put that Bill through in its present shape,
I don't see that anyone can blame them for it ; because, you
see, they got so very near it. (Laughter.) When they get near
a good thing, it is terribly cruel, you know, if you do not give
it them. (Laughter.)

For his part, 'now that he was relieved from
giving the Bill a show'[1] he 'would insist upon substantial alterations in it ; and the other Premiers
would find that he was just the same old George
Houston Reid again, who would be just as frank and
just as blunt as anyone else ! ' Later in the speech,

[1] See *ante*, pp. 271–2, and p. 108, footnote.

he proposed, as a solution of all difficulties, that the Eastern Colonies of New South Wales, Queensland, and Victoria should form a Federation without the smaller Colonies, who should only be admitted as members upon special terms !

If these were the sentiments of a ' true Federalist,' the language was extremely infelicitous ; while their repetition at Moruya, next day, precluded the excuse of hasty utterance. Nor could they be explained as a mere error of judgment, arising out of a mis-understanding of the situation.   For no one had shown a clearer appreciation of the practical necessi-ties of the situation than Mr. Reid himself, when he described, in his first speech at the Adelaide Conven-tion, the spirit in which the problems of Federation ought to be approached and dealt with :—

When we deal with the broad constitutional principles which are to be placed in the Federal Constitution we must absolutely lay aside any thought of our local politics, or our varying degrees of development, the numbers of our population or the extent of our influence. We must absolutely forget our boundaries, bringing a common judgment and conscience to bear upon these matters ; because what is expected of us is not that we shall make a good bargain, but that we shall bring into existence a system of government which will prove equal to the varying conditions of the future, whether of adversity or prosperity, whether of peace or war.   I bring my own mind into this matter absolutely upon these lines (March 30, 1897).

On his return from the South Coast Mr. Reid took another step, which confirmed the misgivings of the Federalists.   At a banquet given him by his consti-tuents (June 16) he renewed his expressions of good-will towards Mr. Want ; and the next day Mr. Want resumed his Office of Attorney-General in Mr. Reid's Ministry, not having modified any of his anti-federal sentiments. Even the *Daily Telegraph*, knowing, as all men knew, the strength of Mr. Want's character, felt constrained to say that 'The Ministry had re-joined Mr. Want, not Mr. Want the Ministry.' When even Mr. Reid's own organ wrote in these terms, Federalists may be excused for having seen more significance in this one act than in all the professions of the Milton and Moruya speeches!

Thus 'Federalists' and 'Reidites' drew further apart ; and it became apparent that no progress could be made until it was known whether the General Election would confirm the voting on the Referendum.

· 3 ·

Mr. Reid's surmise that the other Premiers were holding back until it was determined whether he or Mr. Barton should be Premier is known now to have been correct. Immediately after the vote, Mr. Barton had written confidentially to Mr. Deakin and Mr. Kingston to suggest that the Bill might be amended, in order to remove the stumbling-blocks in the way of its acceptance by the minority in New South Wales ; and it soon became known, although this correspond-ence was kept secret, that the other Colonies would prefer to negotiate with Mr. Barton. This was made the ground of an attack upon the Federalists for in-consistency :—'Having,' it was said, 'told the people that unless the Bill were accepted there could be no Union, they were ready now to recommend a different Bill!' To comprehend this reproach one needed, as Mr. Barton said, ' to look at the facts of the

U

situation through goggles, which turned majorities into minorities.' Support of the Convention Bill did not involve a belief in the perfection of every clause ; and surely it was the part of statesmanship to reconcile the measure to a large minority of dissentients, if this could be done without destroying its substance ? It was not, however, any part of Mr. Barton's policy to disclose his proposals until Mr. Reid had formulated his. This was done in the Governor's speech at the opening of Parliament (June 21), which set out the amendments which the Ministry desired, as follows :—

(1) The substitution of an absolute for the three-fifths majority at the Joint Sitting of the two Houses.

(2) A re-casting of the financial provisions and the omission of the Braddon clause.

(3) A prohibition to the Senate to amend Money Bills.

(4) The insertion of a provision that the boundaries of a State should not be altered without its consent.

(5) That the seat of Government should be selected by the Queen, 'as in the Canadian Constitution.'

(6) That the appellate jurisdiction should be re-modelled.

In his Address to the Electors, Mr. Reid added that the Capital should be in New South Wales, and that the clauses as to granting Bounties, as to the use of rivers for irrigation, and as to the method of amending the Constitution, should be modified.

Well might Mr. Barton describe this programme as ' a placard of impossible demands ' ; because it meant, in effect, the reopening of all the questions which had been the subject of greatest controversy in the Convention, and the substitution of the particular views of a minority in New South Wales in place of the compromises which had been agreed upon by the representatives of all the Colonies, after protracted discussion. This throwing of the apple of discord did not appear to Federalists to be a direct method of promoting Union ; and the remembrance that Mr. Reid had supported at the Convention most of the clauses which he was now attacking did not inspire them with greater confidence ! [1]

Yet, ostensibly, there was no material difference between the policy of Mr. Reid and Mr. Barton. Both were prepared to amend the Constitution, and were

[1] At the Adelaide Convention Mr. Reid had expressed his views on equal representation in the following terms :

' I make no difficulty about equal representation in the Senate. . . . We cannot do business without equal representation. Therefore I vote for it. . . . I admit that equal State Rights is, as far as we have gone, one of the first principles of the federal enterprise, and therefore without any grumbling I have accepted it and have never sought to question it ' (Hansard, pp. 270, 666, 760).

It is right to add that Mr. Reid contended in the same speech that with equal representation the Senate should have no power over Money Bills.

His support of the Braddon clause at the Melbourne Session has been referred to already, see *ante*, p. 267.

In the Sydney Session Mr. Reid had voted against Sir George Turner's proposal for an absolute majority, and supported Mr. Wise's proposal of a three-fifths majority of those present and voting. At Melbourne he had voted the other way, but at a stage of the proceedings at which it was plainly impossible to reopen the matter.

In his speech at the Town Hall on March 28, 1898, Mr. Reid had said he had no objection to the judiciary clauses.

The financial clauses, which he desired to reconsider, had been proposed to the Convention by himself, as Chairman of the Finance Committee.

agreed upon the most important alterations. For Mr. Barton had let it be known that he also would recommend (1) That the Capital should be in New South Wales, which to most electors meant Sydney ; (2) That the Braddon clause should be eliminated ; and (3) That the absolute should be substituted for the three-fifths majority at the Joint Sitting. Yet, in reality, the difference between them was fundamental, because it was a difference of standpoint and method. Mr. Barton and the Federalists sought their amendments by 'negotiation,' Mr. Reid by 'insistence.' The latter would defy the other Colonies : the former recognised that, without their concurrence, no progress could be made. The General Election was to prove decisive of these differences ; for the drama was now, day by day, although through much confusion and bewilderment, approaching its climax.

CHAPTER XXII

THE CRITICAL ELECTION OF 1898

IT is easy to recognise now that the failure to attain the statutory minimum at the first Referendum was not altogether disadvantageous to the federal cause. In any event, Federation would have been the issue of the General Election ; because the Bill, had it passed, must have gone back to Parliament, in order to be forwarded to London for Imperial confirmation ; and, had the 80,000 votes been obtained in New South Wales, disguised enemies of Union might have won seats by professing a vague respect for the will of the majority, who, after their election, would have found a hundred plausible reasons for delaying the Address to the Crown. As matters stood, there was a clear issue, which no candidate could shirk,—that, at any future Referendum, the votes of the majority should prevail. Other matters for decision were the nature of the amendments to be made in the Bill before it was re-submitted, and whether Mr. Reid or Mr. Barton should have the future conduct of the movement. The contest was fierce and exciting beyond all precedent ; and, although political controversies, like the excesses of last night, should be blotted out of recollection when reason has resumed her sway, yet the importance and intensity of the General Election of 1898—the interest of which centred in the King Division, where Mr. Barton was opposing Mr. Reid—deserve to be remembered by a later generation which enjoys the fruits of the success, because it was the final triumph in the long fight for Australian Unity.

. I .

In all the speeches made by Mr. Reid since June 3, he had contrasted his own vigilant watchfulness over the interests of New South Wales with the alleged subservience of Mr. Barton to the other Colonies.   This he claimed to be the difference between them ; because, while he 'was as good a Federalist as Mr. Barton,' he did not agree with the latter as to the best method of obtaining Union. While Mr. Barton would 'negotiate' with the other Colonies, he would 'demand from them the just rights of New South Wales,' and listen to no compromise. 'There must be no more compromises, no more Conferences and no more concessions,' he had said in June, after the failure of his own attempt to get a Conference.[1] The *Daily Telegraph* expressed the same idea more crudely in its election edition (July 25) : 'The issue is whether Mr. Barton shall be given a brief for the other Colonies, or Mr. Reid shall be given one for New South Wales.'   Mr. Reid's Committee improved even upon this in their election posters.   'Barton' these said,

[1] In taking this stand Mr. Reid furnished another of the many parallels between the federal movements in the United States and Australia, which must strike every student of the history of the two countries.   Just as Patrick Henry, in his loyalty to Virginia, would have forced the views of his State upon the Union, declaring that ' the other States cannot do without Virginia, but Virginia can do without the other States, so that we can dictate to them what terms we please,'—so Mr. Reid, with unconscious plagiarism, insisted that New South Wales was in a position to demand her own conditions of accepting Union.

' is bought by Victorian gold, therefore vote for G. H. Reid ' ; and much play was made during the campaign with a donation of £20, which was sent to Mr. Barton's Committee by Mr. King O'Malley from Western Australia.

This difference of standpoint and method was apparent even in the matters on which Mr. Reid and Mr. Barton were agreed. While Mr. Barton would only excise the Braddon clause ' if some alternative proposal could be found,' Mr. Reid was emphatic for its omission in any case—' that of course must go ' ;[1] and, while the substitution of the absolute for the three-fifths majority at the Joint Sitting was a matter of abstract right to Mr. Reid, Mr. Barton regarded this as ' a concession to the minority in New South Wales which voted against the Bill.'

But a more potent influence in keeping Mr. Barton and Mr. Reid apart was the ineradicable mistrust of the latter's federal sincerity.

It was not until after this General Election had destroyed his majority that Mr. Reid appeared to ' bring his mind into the subject ' on the lines of his speech at Adelaide which has been already quoted.[2] Up to the hour of his defeat he seemed to be still balancing between two opposites—as a Federalist, talking of a Conference ; as a Provincialist, denouncing the rapacity of his invited guests and stirring up ill-will by appeals to prejudice. That course (so the motive of it was interpreted by Federalists at the time) might enable Mr. Reid to control the federal

---

[1] Address to the electors of the King Division. In the event, as will be seen, Mr. Reid agreed to retain this clause for ten years.

[2] See *ante*, p. 288. See also p. 108, footnote.

movement in any eventuality ; but it did not incline men, to whom Federation was the supreme object of their lives, to ally themselves with one who appeared to have regarded it always as a subordinate issue of local politics. This mistrust may have been unfounded ; and the verdict of history may be that, if patriotism had prevailed over personal considerations, there would have been no contest as to leadership, but that Mr. Barton and Mr. Reid would have worked together for the common end. Indeed, some plain citizens thought, even at this time, that an armistice should have been proclaimed between them ; and the *Daily Telegraph*, perhaps not quite disinterestedly, formulated this opinion in a striking leader (June 28) headed, in reminiscence of the phrase which Mr. Barton had once used with such effect,[1] ' Scuffling on the Steps of the Temple ' :—

It would seem that Mr. Barton is afraid of being superseded in the federal leadership by Mr. Reid ; that Mr. Reid is afraid of being overshadowed by Mr. Barton's federal supremacy, and Mr. Lyne afraid of his leadership being extinguished by either or both.

But to argue thus was to ignore facts. Rightly or wrongly,—and this is the key to the political situation,—mistrust of Mr. Reid made co-operation between himself and Mr. Barton impossible. And this mistrust was so great that it appeared to Federalists that the future of Federation depended on the contest as to leadership. If Mr. Reid won, the future was remote and unknown. If Mr. Barton won, it was immediate and on the lines of the Convention Bill.

[1] See *ante*, p. 188.

The *Sydney Morning Herald* expressed these views in a leading article (June 27, 1898) :—

Two conditions are absolutely essential to the success of a Conference.   One is that the work should be in the hands, not of the enemies of Union, but of its friends.   The aim is that those to whom it is confided should have the confidence of true Federalists, not only in this Colony, but in the other Colonies also.   How far these conditions are met by the party led by Mr. Barton, Mr. O'Connor, and Mr. Wise, and how far by that led by Mr. Reid, Mr. Want, and an outside organisation led by Sir George Dibbs, will be one of the questions submitted to the people for decision at the General Election.

Extracts from the election addresses of the rival candidates give forcible expression to these differences.
Mr. Reid wrote :—

We claim that the Convention Bill ought to be altered in certain important particulars, not only because it would make the Bill more popular in New South Wales, but because, in the interest of the future Commonwealth as well as in the interest of New South Wales, it is necessary that these alterations should be made ; and we point out what these alterations should be.   Those on the other side take an easier course and commit themselves to nothing.   But the electors of New South Wales are not likely to give their confidence to those who leave them in the dark as to their real opinions.

Mr. Barton's reply was vigorous and effective :—

It is essential that progress should be on such lines that it will be possible for the Federalists of the Colonies to assist. . . . This is the key to the policy which must be adopted if the great cause is to succeed.   Mere placards of impossible demands, coupled with objurgations of our neighbours, sneers at their importance, and innuendoes against their honesty, can be no part of a federal policy. . . . Least of all can we hope for

success by such methods when they have agreed, by overwhelming majorities, to a Constitution which the authors of
such a placard and the utterers of such insults have combined
to denounce and deride. When it is remembered that the
work so treated is work which the leader of these anti-Federalist
methods has himself helped to fashion, when it is remembered
that he has himself supported, and in some cases suggested,
provisions which he now turns round to condemn, you have a
measure by which to gauge at once the sincerity of himself
and that of his associates in office. When again their tactics
immediately precede, and for the rest immediately follow, a
reunion with a former colleague [Mr. Want] who has not only
been the ringleader of denunciation and derision, but whose
entire conduct from the beginning shows him to be the dire
implacable enemy of every form of Union, you can have no
doubt but that such alliance is for the destruction, not for the
furtherance, of the national cause. . . . The real contest is not
a conflict between two sets of amendments, but a question
whether a thinly-disguised hostility to Federation is the pass-
port to Federation, and whether the leadership of enemies will
guide you into the ranks of your friends or your foes.

In a word, the issue of the election was the rival
claims to confidence of Mr. Reid and Mr. Barton.

. 2 .

That there should have been any serious controversy as to the claim of Mr. Barton or Mr. Reid
to the federal leadership seems even now, as then,
to be a manifestation of the comic spirit which hovers
over human affairs to their confusion !

Mr. Barton had been a member of the Convention
of 1891 : he was the designated leader in succession
to Sir Henry Parkes : almost unaided, he had sustained
the flagging interest in the cause amid the pre-occupa-
tions of the financial crisis by numerous and scholarly

addresses to scanty audiences : above all, his direction of the last Convention, which displayed his powers and judgment at their highest, had given him an undisputed pre-eminence among the federal leaders. Mr. Reid, upon the contrary, by his own confession, had at one time been opposed to Federation ; while his later ' Yes–No ' attitude towards the Referendum had been pleasing to neither side. And yet the competition was more equal than it seemed.

Mr. Reid, relying upon the proverbial shortness of the Australian political memory, could claim with confidence to have given a new life to Federation by passing the Enabling Act, thus ' lifting Federation ' (as he said) ' out of the gutter where Mr. Barton had left it.' True he might be reminded of his former objections to a Referendum [1] and other incidents which put this conduct in a different light ; but the public at election time is not attentive to inconsistencies, and Mr. Reid already had too many to his score to be affected by another. It was more to the point that, in asserting thus his own claim to confidence, Mr. Reid, with extreme adroitness, transferred the charge of insincerity from himself to Mr. Barton. The charge is stated best in Mr. Reid's own words :—

Mr. Barton was returned for East Sydney, before the electorate was split up, as a Federalist who sank Protection. Well, he sank Federation instead, and put in Protection. Mr. Barton said on the East Sydney hustings, the last time he addressed the electors, that he had pledged himself to go into Parliament to support Sir Henry Parkes, the leader of the federal cause, and to oppose to the death the arch-enemy of Federation, Sir George Dibbs. After making these solemn

[1] See *ante*, p. 156.

pledges to the assembled electors of East Sydney, who put him in on the faith of his promises that he would not interfere with the Free Trade policy of the country, within four months he deserted the old man and joined Sir George Dibbs, becoming Attorney-General ; and before the year was out he had brought into the Assembly the most obnoxious and irritating system of protective duties that had ever been known in this part of the world.[1]

Thus was revived the old attack[2] of the Free Trade Federalists which had cost Mr. Barton his seat in the local Parliament at the election of 1894. His subsequent services to the cause were too well known for any doubt to be cast in 1898 upon his federal sincerity. But, if the charge failed of its direct object, yet it served as an easy transition for the introduction of the fiscal issue, which Mr. Reid was too shrewd a tactician to neglect. Skilfully recognising that party cries retain influence long after they have lost significance, he charged Mr. Barton with making use of federal sentiment for an assault upon Free Trade ; and, as Mr. Barton's defence admitted too much to be effective with the crowd,—(who found it easier to remember that, elected as a Federalist, he had introduced Protection than to recall the justifying circumstances),—there was not much difficulty, with the aid of the *Daily Telegraph*, in representing his present policy as more fiscal than federal. A factitious support was given to this innuendo by the action of Mr. Lyne, who, as leader of the Protectionist Opposition, had issued a list of candidates which included

[1] Speech in the King Division, reprinted in the *Daily Telegraph* Election issue (July 25, 1898).

[2] See *ante*, pp. 167–9.

several well-known anti-Federalists. Mr. Lyne himself had opposed the Convention Bill as vigorously as
Mr. Reid, and with more consistency. His provincial
outlook obscured his faith in any speedy accomplishment of Union ; while his political ambitions prompted
him to keep Protection in the front, because, as he
said, ' he might be leader himself ' when the time for
action came.

Mr. Reid drove home his argument in an exceedingly effective election address which betrays the hand
of Mr. Brient in many passages :—

You are asked by our opponents to take the federal cause
out of the hands of men who have fought for your rights and
for the sound principles of government in order to place the
cause at the mercy of those whose course of action has suited
every Colony but their own. The present combination to
defeat the Government and the cause of Liberalism in Australia
is one of the most sinister and unscrupulous on record. The
federal leader and the parliamentary leader (Mr. Lyne) are
so much at variance about principle and policy that they
cannot even decide who is to be the leader until the battle is
won. If that happen, it is easy to see that the Protectionists
will outwit the Federalists, and that Mr. Lyne, not Mr. Barton,
will be Commander-in-Chief. Ranged behind the Government
are a vast majority of the strongest candidates—men who
have shown their power to combine loyally and unselfishly
for the accomplishment of important reforms, and who stand
to-day before you with unbroken ranks, harmonious principles,
and definite aims.

Upon the other side you see two parties as uncertain in their
politics as they are in the choice of a leader, united by no
single tie of principle, bound together only by the hope of
sharing or fighting over a division of political spoils. On
one side of their flag you see ' Federation,' but on the other
you see ' Tariff Restriction. Border Warfare.'

That Mr. Lyne and his followers should fight under such a contradictory flag was to be expected ; but that Mr. Barton, Mr. Bruce-Smith, Mr. O'Connor, and Mr. Wise should do so is one of those things which no one can understand who has not gauged the force of their dislike to be ' left out in the cold,' and the strength of their desire to take leading parts in the more confined sphere of ' federal politics,' which is in their estimation so much above ' the petty concerns of provincial politics ' !

· 3 ·

Mr. Barton was no match for Mr. Reid in this style of controversy. His address and speeches were logical, but somewhat dull, historico-legal arguments, illumined here and there by a happy phrase—(such as, ' the Bill was carried by vote but not by law ' : ' Placards of impossible demands ' : ' defeated in negotiation, distrusted by Australia from sea to sea, he is destitute of resource or suggestion ' : ' Friendly negotiation is of the very essence of the situation ')—and not in the style which impresses a mob. Except to point contrasts between Mr. Reid's present and past attitudes towards Federation, which was legitimate criticism in such a contest, he refrained from personal reference to his opponent.

His answer to the charge of duplicity was definite and emphatic :—

The fiscal question should be sternly left in abeyance during the struggle to obtain Federation. It would be unjust, as well as impolitic, to endeavour to revise the fiscal system in this Colony in the meanwhile. Not only do I hold that opinion strongly ; but *I shall resist any attempt at such revisal during the present Parliament.'* [1]

Yet this assurance did not dissipate the suspicions

[1] Address to electors of the King Division, July 1898.

which had been fostered so artfully. 'Was it not' (so it was said by the 'Reidites') 'a mere repetition of Mr. Barton's assurance in 1891? And was not the following of Mr. Lyne numerically stronger than the Federalists?' Mr. Wise and Mr. Bruce-Smith tried to stem the tide of prejudice by issuing a manifesto to their fellow Free Traders, in which they pledged themselves to oppose any attempt to alter the tariff; but Mr. Reid countered this by a reminder that Mr. Bruce-Smith had been of Counsel in the McSharry Arbitration,[1] and that Mr. Wise was actuated by the sole desire 'to down Mr. Reid'! Both of them were 'traitors to Free Trade' and 'engaged in a conspiracy against New South Wales.' Mr. Barton, of course, was 'a nominee of the other Colonies. They are not afraid of him; but they are afraid of George Houston Reid.'[2]

Mr. Reid spoke so often in this style that even the *Sydney Morning Herald* felt constrained to write

that his speeches were apparently directed to asperse and vilify opponents by bitter and malignant charges, and by invective, innuendo, and all the arts of the speaker to present the leaders of the federal party as a set of dangerous if not disgraceful persons.

Yet Mr. Reid knew better than his critics what the public wanted, and with what it was to his advantage to supply them. Long experience had given him a great contempt for popular opinion, and the conviction that it could be won by flattery; so that no speaker ever had greater success with a Sydney

[1] This was the case in which Mr. Barton and Mr. O'Connor had been engaged (see *ante*, p. 183). Mr. Bruce-Smith was of Counsel for the plaintiff.

[2] Address to electors of the King Division, July 1898.

audience. He was at his best upon a hotel balcony,
where he was not bound by rule or custom. His
method was to play upon the simplest emotions of
his audience; and he was never afraid of a descent
into sentimentality or melodrama. Yet—such is the
force of personality—he could at times be very impressive. Usually, however, he preferred that people
should laugh at him than that they should not laugh
at all. At one great meeting in 1899, when he was re-
pelling the charge of being duped in his negotiations with the Premier of Victoria, he ran a red
bandanna handkerchief round himself, remarking
in his high-pitched drawl: 'You see it takes a
great deal to get round me!' He was at his best in
answering interjections; and indeed, if there were
no interjections, his speeches became dull. For one
Session of the Federal Parliament he had to give
up speaking, because the Ministerialists, under Mr.
Deakin's instructions, refrained from all interrup-
tions! Perhaps his happiest sally was when a meeting
of miners at Zeehan greeted his rising to speak with
organised bellowing. Waiting until they paused to
take breath, he piped out with an inimitable look of
innocence: 'Well! I only called you "Gentlemen!"'
During this election he was struck by a bag of flour
at Newtown, which smothered his face in white.
' He made no attempt to wipe it off [the report is from
the *Daily Telegraph*], but bowing and kissing his hand
towards the crowd, which laughed heartily at the
grotesque spectacle, he seized a moment of silence to
drawl out : "You see even my opponents make me
look a white man. The more they attack me the
whiter man they make me!"'

He was not so successful with the more serious country audiences or in the other Colonies ; but his *flair* for every current of Sydney opinion used to be infallible, so that, even when his audiences became restless at these personal attacks—' Leave Barton alone ' was a cry often heard after July 21—he humoured their wish without losing popularity. Nor was he injured by Mr. Barton's references to the inconsistencies between his speeches then and his votes at the Convention. A Sydney audience, which always got from him exactly what they wanted, readily forgave these political eccentricities. ' After all, it was only George Reid,' to whose meetings they went as to a public entertainment and whom nobody took seriously !

Mr. Barton was no match for such a master of platform arts. Nevertheless, the tide of federal opinion ran so high that, as polling day approached, electioneering experts had already given him the victory. Two days before the poll, however, the Orange Lodge—(the division between the Orange and the Green is never far beneath the surface in the politics of New South Wales)—scenting the Scarlet Woman either in the Constitution Bill or in the support of it by Cardinal Moran, decided to support Mr. Reid, who was returned by a majority of less than two hundred. But it was a Pyrrhic victory. The Federalists carried the country ; and Mr. Reid's majority, counting the Labour Party on his side, fell from 37 to 2 ; while three of his Ministers lost their seats. The effect of the contest is described in the following letter written by Mr. Deakin to Mr. Barton immediately after the result was known :—

MY DEAR BARTON,—I have this moment read the returns for the King Division, and, as I anticipated, have found them adverse to our hopes. At such a moment, I write to say how strong the conviction is in me and many others that you have achieved a real and permanent success, in spite of this apparent overthrow. There are but two or three other returns posted as yet, so that I am looking merely at your own gallant fight and its result. There is, first, the success which you have achieved for the cause by driving your antagonist into the federal camp, for lip service at all events. Then there is the success of encouragement and increased energy, which your example inspirited among your followers. Finally, there is the success of having fought like a gentleman, descending to nothing that you could wish unsaid or undone. It will always remain a political duel, probably the most famous that Australia will see for decades, and certainly more notable than any yet seen. The issue has been so much higher and wider than those which belong to the provincial arena, and it has concentrated upon itself so close and eager an attention from all the Colonies, that it must live as the great election contest of our day. To have fought in that as chief of the National party, to have fought so chivalrously and so devotedly, is of itself more than a distinction and an honour, and must be one of the most prized recollections of a lifetime where successes have been many and great. For the event you are in no way responsible. For the fight for principle you are responsible, and your children and your children's children will be proud of it for generations to come. Accept my warmest congratulations and heartiest assurance of the feeling that prevails everywhere of admiration for your splendid loyalty to the great cause we are all proud to serve—but only you have been able to serve so royally.

Yours very truly,

ALFRED DEAKIN.

CHAPTER XXIII

' THE SECOND REFERENDUM '

THE new Parliament, which met on August 16, if not in sympathy with Federation, at least had learnt from the election that Federation was not unpopular.

Mr. Reid, accordingly, announced in the Governor's speech that the first business of the Session would be 'the submission of a series of Resolutions specifying the amendments (in the Convention Bill) which (the Government) deemed of urgent importance,' and explained, in a conciliatory speech during the debate upon the Address, that it was 'more convenient' not to bring down any specific proposals until after this had been agreed to.[1] He pointed out too that 'the matter concerned every other Colony in the federal movement, and New South Wales could not come forward and dictate to them the mode by which its proposals should be considered.' Also, in answer to an interjection, he declared that at any second Referendum no statutory minimum should be required, but the votes of a majority should prevail. These were two great points gained as a result of the election.

---

[1] In 1890, when Sir Henry Parkes had urged the same plea, Mr. Reid, it will be remembered, had insisted upon moving an amendment to the Address (see *ante*, p. 139). Thus once more he seemed to be the sport of circumstances which put either his past or his present conduct in the wrong.

Nevertheless, the Federalists were still suspicious, although they refrained from moving a motion of censure until 'the terms of the Resolutions had disclosed the Ministerial policy.'

.. I ..

These were submitted without delay on August 31 in terms which would conciliate both sides. For, while the preamble affirmed that ' the Bill was not acceptable to the Colonies in its present shape,' the first Resolution affirmed that ' steps should be taken *in conjunction with the other Colonies* to bring about the completion of Federal Union.' Seven matters were mentioned as ' being most generally objected to in New South Wales ' : viz. (1) the three-fifths majority ; (2) the Braddon clause ; (3) the omission to fix the Capital in New South Wales ; (4) the inadequate protection to the States against an alteration of their boundaries ; (5) the Rivers compromise ; (6) the power of the Senate over Money Bills ; and (7) the alternative appeal to the Privy Council.

A third Resolution supplemented the suggestion for the removal of the ' Braddon blot.'

(3) Although prepared for the sake of Union—if it be placed in other respects upon a fair and just footing—to accept the financial system embodied in the Bill, with the one exception mentioned, this House earnestly invites further inquiry into, and a more thorough consideration of, the financial clauses, regarding as evils to be avoided if possible excessive burdens of taxation, a prolonged system of book-keeping, uncertainty as to the amount of the surplus to be divided, and uncertainty as to the method of distributing it among the States.

In the admirable speech in which he moved the adoption of these Resolutions, Mr. Reid made a lengthy and elaborate defence of his conduct during the preceding eight years, claiming that the differences between the present Bill and that of 1891 had 'abundantly' justified his opposition to the latter ; and that 'the wonderful change in the temper of the people from the keen feeling of separation, of hostile tariffs, of provincial ideas, to a general idea and ambition for Union' was due in a large degree to his action in popularising the movement. Coming to the events of the preceding two months, he admitted that the Premiers were justified in waiting for the verdict of the people, before they agreed to his proposal for a Conference. At the same time he recognised that not he, but the House, must speak, and that he must 'carry with him (to any Conference) the judgment and support of a majority in Parliament.' Therefore he asked the Opposition, 'unless they were prepared for a clear-out issue of "the Bill and nothing but the Bill," to lend to him the patriotism of their efforts in carrying this great movement through.' 'Suppose,' said an interjector on that side, 'we all say "Yes—No!"' Mr. Reid then explained at length the reasons for the proposed amendments. He declined to express any opinion as to the method of obtaining these 'until he had consulted the other Premiers and discussed the procedure with them freely and fairly.'

It indicates the temper of the time—or, it may be, the bitterness of party spirit—that an amendment was moved to these Resolutions by Mr. Lyne, who was acting, in Mr. Barton's absence, as leader of the Opposition, which, whatever the protests of the mover, could not be regarded by the Government as other than a motion of censure. The preamble was the first object of attack, and it was proposed to amend this by omitting the statement ' The Bill was not acceptable to the electors of the Colony,' and inserting what Federalists regarded as the more correct description of events, viz. that

in view of the clearly expressed determination, as shown at the recent General Election, of the people of New South Wales, it is inadvisable to hamper future negotiations for procuring Federation by laying down any preliminary conditions, fully believing that such amendments and modifications of (the Bill) will be agreed to as will render it acceptable to the people of this Colony at the next necessary Referendum.

It was proposed also to omit any reference to specific amendments, and, instead,

authorise the Government to open up negotiations with the other Colonies . . . with a view of procuring a joint considera- tion of the present position, the question of Federation, and of the methods and particulars in which the Bill may be dealt with.

The amendment also expressed the hope that Queensland would be invited to take part in these deliberations.

Mr. Reid had an easy and congenial task in opposing this amendment, moved by one whose antagonism to the Bill and rivalry with Mr. Barton as to leadership were both notorious. He could twit the Federalists also with having condemned him a few weeks earlier for inviting the Premiers to a Conference without disclosing his proposals.[1]   Yet, although events proved

[1] See *ante*, p. 285.

that the Opposition were misjudging Mr. Reid, it was not at the time improper to have a trial of strength. The new Parliament was divided into at least four sections—Ministerialist, Labour, Federalist, and direct Opposition ; and, after a general election, which appeared to have returned an equality of parties, it was natural and proper that the Opposition should take an opportunity of presenting their policy, as an alternative to that which was proposed by the Government. The Ministerial Resolutions were open also to severe animadversion,—if the sincerity of the Government were in doubt,—because of the opportunities for delay which the procedure offered,—if delay were desired. The time seemed to have arrived now when it was necessary to make Federation a party question, on which a Government should stand or fall. To leave it, as these Resolutions proposed, to Parliament, while this might be flattering to the vanity of members, ' deprived it,' as one speaker said, ' of its legitimate protector.' What was everybody's business would be nobody's business,

and if the question were left alone outside of party it might fade away in general indifference or be destroyed by one of its enemies. . . . The responsibility for the ultimate result ought to rest on the proper shoulders, and it was the business of a Government to govern and of leaders to lead. . . . Nothing was easier than to be a Federationist when the profession involved nothing definite ; or to declare oneself zealous for Union, if one's zeal imposed no personal responsibility. On the other hand the amendment, if it were carried, would compel Ministers, after the Conference, to submit definite amendments to the House for acceptance or rejection. The original Resolutions, too, left in doubt the most important question : Whether the proposed alterations were mandatory or directory, which, it was contended, was essential to be known by Ministers proposing to 'negotiate.' The House was entitled to know whether these were the proposals 'for which' Mr. Reid 'would fight to the last,' or was it intended to waste months in futile discussion and then come back to the House for a general authority to negotiate freely ? Again, was the Legislative Council to propose separate or additional amendments, and, if so, would the Parliaments of the other Colonies do the same ? In that case the delays would be interminable.

These somewhat academic arguments carried no weight with the House ; and Mr. Lyne's amendment was rejected on September 15 by 58 votes to 54. The defeat discredited the Opposition, because it seemed a check to an unseemly eagerness to snatch at Office. Mr. Reid gained another success by defeating on October 6, by a majority of 8, another motion of censure, moved by Mr. Lyne in consequence of alleged improper promises by the Minister for Works to spend public money in the Hastings-Macleay Electorate, if Mr. Barton, who was being opposed by one of Mr. Reid's defeated colleagues, were not returned ! The debate, however, disclosed a desire on the part of the Ministry to keep Mr. Barton out of Parliament, which seemed to be more consistent with the opinion of the Attorney-General, Mr. Want, than with the federal professions of the Premier.[1] The debate on the Resolutions was resumed on October 12, and continued as the principal Government business until September 21. In the interval Mr. Barton had returned to Parliament, and replaced Mr. Lyne as leader of the Opposition.

[1] Mr. Want left for England in December 1898, and resigned his office on April 18, 1899.

In addition to the Resolutions proposed by the Government another was carried, at the instance of the Labour Party, proposing that the Constitution might be amended by a mass vote of the citizens, without requiring the assent of a majority of the States ; and Mr. Reid undertook to submit this, with the others, to the Conference of Premiers. The Legislative Council also modified the Resolutions by omitting the one last mentioned, by fixing Sydney as the site of the Capital, and by striking out the declaration of ' readiness to accept the financial clauses for the sake of Union.' No attempt was made to harmonise the amendments of the two Houses.

The passage of these Resolutions, even in their amended form, was a notable triumph for the Federalists. No alteration was proposed in the clause relating to Bounties, with which many people had been scared in the late campaign ; and the ' acceptance of the financial clauses of the Bill for the sake of Union,' which was agreed to without discussion or explanation, was a striking proof of the little confidence felt in their own figures by the ante-Referendum prophets of financial ruin. In four essential points Federalists, although out of office, had carried the day :— ' Negotiations ' were to be opened with the other Colonies, and the policy of ' insistence ' and ' demands ' abandoned ; the Bounty bogey had been laid for ever : the financial clauses were admitted, in effect, to be the best which were then procurable : and —most important of all—no legislative trick would stultify the votes of the majority at the next Referendum.

. 2 .

On November 2 Mr. Reid made his financial statement, which, as though he had been the sport of some malign fate, involved him again in gratuitous self-contradictions, and lost him the growing confidence of Federalists, just as he was gathering all the threads of the movement into his own hands.

The clear understanding between all parties at the General Election had been that the fiscal question should not be raised until Federation were disposed of ; and Mr. Barton, Mr. Lyne, and Mr. Wise had pledged themselves in definite terms not to alter the tariff during the life of the Parliament. It will be remembered that Mr. Reid had expressed an insulting scepticism as to the sincerity of these assurances. It was natural, therefore, that feeling should run high, when he himself proposed to reimpose duties on tea, rice, coffee and cocoa, and retain the duty on sugar, which would have expired by instalments under the provisions of the Act which he had passed in 1895.[1]

Mr. Barton, who waited until the Federal Resolutions had been passed (Nov. 3), on November 15 moved a resolution of censure to the effect :—

That, in view of the fact that at the recent General Election the Members supporting the Government pledged themselves to maintain the existing Free Trade policy, while Opposition Members were as distinctly pledged that, so far as they were concerned, the fiscal question should not be raised until this Parliament had decided the question of Federation, this House is of opinion that to vote for the fiscal proposals now submitted

[1] See *ante*, p. 209.

by the Treasurer would be unconstitutional and a direct breach of faith with the constituencies.

The motion was lost on a strict party vote by 63 to 40 ; for, although several Free Traders expressed their concurrence with its terms, they were unwilling to replace Mr. Reid by Mr. Barton. The debate, indeed, made clear that no motion moved by Mr. Barton would receive the support either of Labour Members or of the extreme section of anti-federal Free Traders ; and that, if it were desired to put out Mr. Reid, another leader must be found. The shade of Sir Henry Parkes must have smiled with grim amusement to see the same duties reimposed in 1898, in the alleged interests of Federation, which had been taken off for the same alleged purpose in 1894, against his earnest protest !

· 3 ·

The Conference of Premiers, which met at Melbourne on January 29, 1899, at the instance of Mr. Reid, did not open its deliberations to the public. Queensland, which up to this time had stood aloof, was represented by its Premier, Mr. J. R. Dickson. The result of the deliberations was announced on February 2. The Premiers had agreed to five out of the six amendments proposed by Mr. Reid, and to another allowing Queensland, if that Colony came into the Federation, to be divided into three for the purpose of electing Senators.

The requirement of a three-fifths majority of those present and voting at the Joint Session of the two Houses was replaced by a provision that ' an absolute majority of the total number of the members of both Houses ' should carry the day.

The financial clauses were left as they stood, except that Parliament was empowered to repeal the Braddon clause after ten years, and that a new clause was inserted empowering Parliament to grant financial assistance to any State.

The Federal Capital was fixed in New South Wales, subject to two conditions : viz., that it should not be within 100 miles of Sydney, and that the Parliament should sit in Melbourne until it met at the capital.

It was agreed also that no alteration should be made in the boundaries of a State without the assent of a majority of the electors voting in the State affected.

The proposal of the Labour Party to amend the Constitution by a mass vote was rejected ; but it was provided, instead, that either House of Parliament, by approving of a proposed amendment in two successive Sessions, could secure that it be submitted to a Referendum, at which it would be carried, if it were supported by a majority of voters and a majority of States.

No alteration was made in the clause relating to Rivers, Money Bills, and Judicial Appeals.

It was not for Federalists to scrutinise too closely the nature of these proposed amendments. Enough for them that they promoted agreement ; and if they also furnished an excuse for a departure from untenable positions, no friend of Union would depreciate them upon that account.

If I say [said Mr. Barton in the Legislative Assembly on February 21] that I do not think that these amendments are exceedingly substantial, I am still bound to qualify the statement by adding that the Premier was in a position of

extreme difficulty in dealing with the other Premiers, three of
whom stood on the ground that their Colonies had accepted
the Commonwealth Bill on June 3 by enormous majorities;
and it would not be fair to underrate the difficulties of
the Premier's position in the work he had to encounter
arising out of that consideration. I do not think that the Bill
has been altered so materially as some honourable Members
appear to think; but that is no reason why I should refuse
to support the Bill as proposed to be amended.

. 4 .

Mr. Reid's prompt action showed that he, at any
rate, had no misgivings as to the improvements which
had been made in the Bill by the Premiers' amendments.
He called Parliament together on February 21, 1899,
and announced in the Governor's speech that he
made the acceptance of these a Government question.
' Federation is now narrowed to an issue between those
who really desire Federal Union and those who do not.'
He defined his position at once in a speech upon the
Address : repudiated with indignation ' the mean
insinuations which have been of late levelled at
the honesty and honour of the leaders of the other
Colonies : '[1] ridiculed ' the owners of Sydney property
and Sydney shopkeepers who wanted the Capital
at their door on the magnificent heights of St.
Leonards or in the Centennial Park ' : denied that
the Braddon clause ' made necessary an enormous
tariff,'[2] and protested against ' theoretical tariffs,
built up of figures showing the necessity of raising

[1] See *ante*, p. 287.

[2] Compare this extract from Mr. Reid's election address in July
1898 : ' The Braddon clause, of course, must come out. . . . In the
opinion of the Finance Committee and the statistical experts it entails
upon us the prospect of an enormous customs tariff.'

an £8,000,000 or £9,000,000 tariff.' 'All these were
"useless" because it was impossible for any set of
men or any financial experts to define what will be
the precise financial policy of a Government and
Parliament not yet in existence.' 'Besides,' he added,
'there would be considerable savings on the transferred services to set against 'these alarming estimates of a Customs tariff.'[1] No mention was made
of the 'sacrifices' New South Wales would have to
make! As to the Enabling Bill, he announced his
intention to provide in this that 'any voter should
record his vote at any polling booth in any electoral
district which might be most convenient to him.'

Parliament responded to Mr. Reid's appeal, and
the Bill to enable a Referendum to be held on the
amended Constitution was sent to the Legislative
Council on March 1. There its reception was very
different. Three vital amendments were passed by
large majorities: one to defer the Referendum for
three months : another to require that the Bill should
be supported by at least one-third of the total number
of electors on the roll; and a third making the inclusion of Queensland a condition of the acceptance
of the Bill by New South Wales. Mr. Reid refused
to agree to these amendments ; and, after the failure
of a free Conference, advised the Governor to pro-
rogue Parliament (March 30) and appoint twelve
new members to the Council. Parliament was called
together again on April 11, and the Enabling Bill was
sent again to the Council. The new appointments
were a sufficient hint, and the Bill became law on
April 22. Parliament was prorogued again until

1 Compare *ante*, pp. 266-7.

after the Referendum, which was to be taken upon June 20.

· 5 ·

The adhesion of Mr. Reid ensured the carrying of the Bill at the second Referendum; but the Federalists did not on that account relax their efforts. A 'United Federal Executive' was formed to conduct the campaign, consisting of members of the old Federal League and of the Opposition and the Ministerial parties; and public meetings were held every night until the eve of the poll in all parts of the Colony. Mr. Reid was one of the most frequent speakers for the Bill; while the case against it was presented, as before, by Dr. Maclaurin, the *Daily Telegraph*, Mr. Lyne and Mr. W. M. Hughes. The arguments on either side were for the most part a repetition of those which had been used the year before, although those of the 'Antis' gained fresh point from the contrast between Mr. Reid's speeches and those which he had made during the preceding year. Every argument which he advanced in favour of the Bill was matched by another which he had used against it; and 'Reid on Reid' became the standing heading of a column in every issue of the *Daily Telegraph*. He turned the point of this criticism by a frank admission that he had 'changed his opinion in the light of great public events' (speech at the Masonic Hall); and at Adelong (May 17, 1899) he was even more frank. 'I must acknowledge that I have fought in the past, perhaps wickedly, against Federation.'[1] And on June 18,

---

[1] Compare the extract from a speech he made at Mittagong on April 27, 1897: 'Most persons will agree that I and persons like me have blocked the federal movement long enough.'

1899, during a speech at Wellington, he explained the reason for his change of views in answer to an interjection that he was becoming a Protectionist :—

He did not know about becoming a Protectionist, but he had got broad enough in his mind now not to have only one idea. It had taken him years to get broad enough for that. Seven years ago he used to walk into Sir Henry Parkes like a tiger because he was still a fanatical Free Trader ; but as a man grew older and got responsibilities he got more broad in his opinions and saw them in their true proportion. He had now room for more than one idea, where he used to have only room for the one idea of Free Trade. He never used to think of anything else. Now he thought of National Union.

In another speech he dismissed the calculations of the financial critics as being ' built upon a staircase of Ifs,' which, although true, was not consoling to those who had lived during the past year in the hypo-thetical edifice of his own construction !

His good-humour never deserted him. At one meeting an interjector called out ' Double-faced !' ' Look at him,' said Mr. Reid, screwing his eyeglass into his eye—' I am sure *he* has not got two faces ; for, if he had, he would have left that one at home ! ' Once, however, even his composure was temporarily upset, when a man in the Town Hall mounted on a chair and silently reversed his coat, repeating the proceeding at frequent intervals with irresistible solemnity, until he had drawn the attention of all the audience. Even when the *Daily Telegraph* crudely charged him with a personal ambition to be first Prime Minister, he admitted that this was true ' with

the frankness which experience had taught him that
his constituents liked.' It is a remarkable proof of
Mr. Reid's real power that he should have come out
of such a difficult campaign with increased reputation.
Yet it is impossible not also to extend sympathy
towards those simple folk who had voted against the
Bill on the first Referendum, because they accepted
his arguments against it. For, as the stalwart 'Antis'
urged throughout the second campaign, the amended
Constitution was in fact, in all essentials, 'the same
old Bill.' It still imposed 'excessive burdens' upon
New South Wales, and was not the less an instrument
for 'robbing' the Mother Colony, because a Premiers'
Conference had been unable to find an alternative
to the predatory financial clauses! The Bounty
clause, having been preserved unaltered, either still
threatened with ruin the inter-State trade in Newcastle coal, or else the former expounders of the Bill
must confess that their interpretation had been
erroneous. The same as to the Rivers compromise.
Those who had believed up to June 3 that this would
prevent the irrigation of the western plains were not
to be reassured by the assertion that 'a reasonable
use of the rivers for irrigation' was all that was necessary, unless they believed their neighbours to be
knaves and traitors. Rather, it seemed that they
must either eat their words or vote for an injustice.
Nor was the alteration of the deadlock clauses a
satisfactory equivalent. The 'absolute majority' was
little less destructive of 'majority rule' than the
original provision of the Bill ; and New South Wales
would still be defeated in the Joint Sitting—if a

majority of her representatives were absent![1] Indeed, the amendment might, under some conditions, make the Senate stronger ; because, under the first Bill, the three-fifths majority was a majority of those ' present and voting,' whereas the ' absolute majority ' of the amended Bill was a majority of all the members of the two Houses. Thus, if 48 members chose to absent themselves—to do what is known in American politics as ' filibuster,'—the other 46 members, not being an absolute majority of the total 94, could do nothing. The Senate also gained power by the amendment, which permitted it to submit a constitutional amendment to the people without the concurrence of the House of Representatives.

[1] Mr. Reid, speaking at Goulburn (May 1898), had put the argument thus :—

' If the whole of the members of the popular House—that is, sixty-four—were pitted against the thirty members of the Senate, if 8 of the 64 were, some of them with the Senate, or absent, or ill, or could not vote, the Lower House would not prevail. This is the rule of the minority.'

Mr. Holman, during the debate on the Enabling Bill (Feb. 28, 1899), made a similar calculation to illustrate the working of the ' absolute majority.'

' The Premier said : " If 8 members were away, what would happen ? " I will take 9 as a more convenient number. At a joint meeting there would be 94 members : 64 members of the House of Representatives and 30 members of the Senate. If 9 members were away that would leave a total voting strength of 85 persons : and under this Bill as it stood when it received this heavy condemnation from the Premier, out of this 85, 51 would be required to pass the measure, 51 being three-fifths of 85. If the Bill under this system was destructive of democracy, under the present system which the Premier lauds 48 would be required to carry a measure through—the difference between 51 and 48 being 3. Everyone who is away is counted against the measure, and an absolute majority out of 94 is 48. By this change, the majority necessary to carry a Bill against the opposition of the Senate has been reduced from 51 to 48, 3 votes being the difference between the suppression of democracy and the triumph of every democratic impulse ! '

The Bill, nevertheless, was carried on June 10 by a majority of 24,679 the vote being—Yes, 107,420 ; No, 82,741. In the other Colonies the majorities were even larger than before. Queensland came in on September 2, and Western Australia on July 31, 1900.

CHAPTER XXIV

IT has been told in earlier Chapters of this narrative how twice, in crises of the federal movement, its leader was sacrificed to faction, because he urged a too exalted wisdom on an unappreciative public. Mr. Barton lost his seat in 1894 for having dreamed that he could sway a hostile Cabinet to the support of Federation; and, in the next year, Sir Henry Parkes was driven out of public life, because he counselled a truce to party warfare in the interest of a higher patriotism. Each of these events had turned to Mr. Reid's advantage, at a time when he was still waiting upon Providence! Now, when he had done finally with doubt and indecision, ironic Fate was to deal him the same shrewd blow!

.. I ..

Upon the acceptance of the Constitution Bill at the second Referendum, it became apparent that, whoever was Premier of New South Wales at the date of the inauguration of the Commonwealth would be the first Prime Minister of Australia. Federalists and 'Antis' combined, but for different reasons, to thwart Mr. Reid in this legitimate ambition :—one party deeming that he had not earned the honour, the other desiring to punish him for his alleged desertion. For a time, however, it was impossible for these allies to act in concert, because the Constitution Bill was not even yet quite safe. The two Houses had still to agree upon an Address to the Crown, praying that the Imperial Parliament would pass the necessary legislation to bring it into operation ; and while the 'Antis' saw in this procedure another opportunity to block the Bill, Mr. Barton and his friends were unwilling to relieve Mr. Reid of the full responsibility for its successful passage :—'Having watched his career with a great deal of care, they had their doubts whether, if he were displaced from office, the cause of Federation would be safe in his hands as leader of the Opposition.'[1] Nothing in Mr. Reid's conduct, at this time, justified this misgiving. On the contrary, he made the Address to the Crown the first business of the new Session (July 18), and pushed it forward with such vigour that it was passed by the Assembly on August 9 and by the Legislative Council on August 12. There was only a majority of three in its favour in the latter Chamber ; the votes being Ayes 24 ; Noes 21. The next step was to be taken in London, and nothing that might be done in New South Wales could affect the passage of the Bill. The way was thus clear for a contest upon local party lines ; and, if Federalists and 'Antis' coalesced, the defeat of the Ministry was certain.

. 2 .

One discontented section of the Ministerialists consisted of extreme Free Traders, who regarded

[1] Extract from Mr. Barton's speech on the Address in Reply (July 18, 1899).

Mr. Reid's acceptance of the Constitution as a surrender of their policy, and suspected from his speech at Wellington [1] that he was already preparing to make terms with the Protectionist majority in the new Parliament. Another was the Labour Party, which was known to be seriously divided on the question of supporting Mr. Reid, although, in accordance with their rules, its members voted as a body on all critical divisions. Neither of these sections— whatever grievances they might have against Mr. Reid—was prepared to displace him in favour of Mr. Barton, who was obnoxious to the Free Traders for his Federalism and to the Labour Party for his supposed Conservatism. Mr. Lyne, however, who had opposed Federation consistently and was sympathetic towards the Labour programme, was able to unite both sections of the Ministerial malcontents. It was proposed, accordingly, that he should replace Mr. Barton as leader of the Opposition, without contesting the claim of the latter to continue to be Federal leader. Mr. Barton welcomed this arrangement as a relief from uncongenial labours, and accepted without suspicion the assurance of Mr. Lyne that he would not be a competitor for the distinction of first Prime Minister of the Australian Commonwealth.[2]

[1] See *ante*, p. 320.

[2] Lord Hopetoun was informed of this arrangement before he left London by a veteran Federalist, ex-Judge Casey, C.M.G., who so far back as 1870 had sat on a Royal Commission to report on the inconveniences arising from the separate legal systems of the Colonies. This may account for the Governor-General's action in asking Mr. Lyne to form the first Ministry, which was received in Australia with a gasp of astonishment, although now it is an open secret that His Excellency was advised to make this unfortunate choice by two gentlemen holding high official positions in Sydney. It was noticed at the time that the

· 3 ·

The occasion for a trial of strength came very soon, out of one of those fortuitous trifles, which often decide the fate of the strongest governments. Mr. Reid had entrusted one of his supporters, Mr. J. C. Neild, with the preparation of a report upon Old Age Pensions, but had promised Mr. McGowen, the leader of the Labour Party, that he would give no payment for this without the sanction of Parliament. Later, he had good-naturedly acceded to Mr. Neild's request to make him an advance in anticipation of a vote, on the ground that the work had occupied more time and was of greater value than had been contemplated either by himself or by the Government. On August 30 Mr. Lyne moved a vote of censure on account of this matter in general terms : ' That the present Government does not possess the confidence of this House.' Although it was certain that the Labour Party could not condone this payment, Mr. Reid had no anxiety as to the result, because he had arranged that a whitewashing amendment should be moved by a supporter, which, while condemning the Neild transaction, should express confidence in the Ministry on other grounds ; and this, he had reason to believe, would be supported by the Labour Party.

commission was in an unusual form. It only entrusted Mr. Lyne to form a Ministry ' acceptable to the Governor-General.' Mr. Lyne did not decline the commission in Mr. Barton's favour, as Lord Hopetoun probably expected ; but Mr. Barton's friends refused to serve under him, and after some delay the commission was withdrawn and entrusted to the latter. Unfortunately, Lord Hopetoun's error introduced into the first Federal Parliament much of the bitterness which had been the unenviable distinction of the Parliament of New South Wales, and gave a tone to Commonwealth politics from which they did not recover for several years.

This expectation was defeated by a device of greater ingenuity. An amendment was drafted with great secrecy in the following words :—

That there be *added* after the word ' House ': ' and deserves censure for having made payments of public money to Mr. J. C. Neild without asking Parliament and contrary to the assurance given by the Premier.'

and, in order that this might anticipate any amendment from the Ministerial side, a typewritten copy of it was given to each of the six or seven members who were most likely to be called upon by the Speaker to continue the debate after the speech of Mr. Reid, who would reply to Mr. Lyne. The choice fell upon a whilom member of Mr. Reid's party—Mr. Fegan— and when he sat down the Ministry was doomed. For one does not need to be a student of parliamentary procedure to perceive that the Labour Party could not vote against *the addition* of the proposed words without condoning the breach of the undertaking given to their leader, and that they could not *add* the words without joining in the Vote of Censure. The Ministry was defeated by 38 votes, and Mr. Lyne became Premier. The road to federal office was thus barred to Mr. Reid. Once more the tortoise had beaten the hare ; and consistency, even in hostility, had been preferred to inconsistent friendship.

· 4 ·

The time has not yet arrived for passing final judgment upon Mr. Reid's varying attitudes towards Federation. His first opposition in 1890 probably was the natural impulse of his temperament and surroundings ; while his adhesion to the movement

in 1893[1] certainly was a tactical move to secure his
position against Sir Henry Parkes. He loyally
carried out the arrangements for an elective and non-
party Convention, and showed himself in the first
Session of this body conciliatory and sympathetic ;
yet his attitude at the Sydney and Melbourne Sessions
became that of a man who neither expected nor desired
that the deliberations of the Convention should bear
fruit, and it was noted that his criticisms increased in
asperity and became more numerous with every approach towards agreement on the disputed questions.
It was at this time that he concurred in the breach of
faith towards the other Colonies, which, by raising the
statutory minimum of affirmative votes at the Referendum to 80,000, 'loaded the dice' against the supporters
of the Convention Bill. Yet it may be (as he and
his supporters asserted) that, had he opposed the Bill,
the majority would have been against it upon June 3 ;
but it is certain that he did not realise, before the vote
was taken, how strongly the tide of public opinion had
set in favour of the Bill.   After the General Election of 1898 he had shown great courage in defying
the prejudices of his party ; and the success of the
Federalists at the second Referendum was due beyond
question to his efforts. Thus, consistent only in in-
consistency, Mr. Reid had played in turn the part
of open enemy, candid friend, and enthusiastic supporter, contradicting himself in each character with
imperturbable serenity. It was difficult to understand him at the time. Posterity may find this
impossible. He is the enigma of the federal movement, who played a part which historians cannot

[1] See *ante*, Chapter XV.

ignore, but the explanation of which may prove a formidable difficulty.

Mr. Barton did not take office in Mr. Lyne's Administration, but with Mr. Deakin, Mr. Dickson (Queensland), Mr. Kingston (South Australia) and Sir Philip Fysh (Tasmania) went to London, on the invitation of Mr. Chamberlain, to watch the passage of the Bill through the Imperial Parliament. The difficulties, the details of which are told fully by Messrs. Quick and Garran, were chiefly over the clauses relating to appeals to the Privy Council. The Imperial Act enacting the Constitution was assented to on July 9, and a week later it was announced the Earl of Hopetoun would be the first Governor-General. The inauguration of the Commonwealth and the swearing in of the first Ministry took place in Sydney on January 1, 1901, and His Majesty the King, then Duke of York, opened the first Federal Parliament in Melbourne on May 9.

· 5 ·

The long contest was at an end, and Australia entered upon a new era of political and material progress. It is too early yet fully to appraise the greatness of the change. The breaking down of provincial barriers and the establishment of a protective policy have stimulated every industry, and a cycle of good seasons and high prices has diffused and increased a general prosperity. Provincialism, however, died hard, and is struggling still in its death throes ; but the wider horizon of a national life will never contract, and the responsibilities of nationhood are being accepted with courage and cheerfulness.

If Parliament has not fulfilled all expectations, it is nevertheless superior to the legislative bodies of the States ; and it must be remembered that its usefulness has been impaired by unexpected decisions of the High Court against the validity of many of its most important measures. No reflecting person would return willingly to the old provincial divisions. The remedy for the defects of the Constitution is to be found rather in the extension of federal powers, with an extension of local government by subdivisions of the larger States. Only by this means will be secured that ' enlargement of the powers of self-government of the people of Australia ' which was the declared object of the Constitution.[1]

1 See Preamble to the Resolution at the Adelaide Convention.

APPENDICES

APPENDIX I

THE STRUGGLE IN VICTORIA

ALTHOUGH the battle for Union in Victoria lacked the dramatic intensity of the struggle in New South Wales, yet in the southern Colony also there was a difference of opinion, based on local interests, which, but for the influence of Mr. David Syme, the editor and proprietor of the Melbourne *Age*, might have become a serious menace to the federal cause. The position cannot be understood without a glance backward towards the origins of Victorian politics.

This Colony was peculiarly fortunate in the character of its first settlers. Capable and adventurous young men, attracted from Europe by the discovery of gold, they resembled rather the picked colonists who founded Christchurch and Dunedin in New Zealand than the immigrants who settled independently and by haphazard in the back country of the larger Colonies. Such men, concentrated in a small territory, could not be blinded by local patriotism to the advantages of Union, but sought very soon a wider outlet for their energies and in 1857, a year after the grant of Responsible Government, that Select Committee was appointed to consider the question of Australian Federation, from whose report Sir Henry Parkes quoted with telling effect at the Melbourne Conference of 1890.[1]

A Royal Commission was appointed in 1870 to consider the inconveniences arising from the independence of the courts of the several Colonies, and to report upon the best

---

[1] See *ante*, p. 55.

method of assimilating procedure and providing for the execution of judgments of the courts of another Colony outside its territory. Of this Commission the sole survivor is ex-Judge Casey, beloved of many friends and the hospitable entertainer of the stranger within the gates.[1]

The times, however, were unpropitious to the acceptance of a new form of government on the initiative of Victoria. Her separation from New South Wales had left a feeling of bitterness in the Mother Colony, which a series of disputes over boundaries, border duties, and mail services hardened into a deep resentment; and after 1865, when Protection became the national policy of the younger Colony and the expenditure of loan moneys and the revenue from land sales produced a rapid and unparalleled prosperity, it seemed even to friendly observers that the Victorian advocacy of Federation was prompted rather by a desire to establish the hegemony of that Colony than from a fraternal wish to share the burden of her neighbours in developing a common heritage. Thus grew up that mistrust of Victoria which became the fixed idea of the Robertson-Want school of New South Wales politicians, and proved to the last to be the chief obstacle to a closer Union. Partly as a consequence of this ill-feeling, and partly because, as the Colony developed, its sentiment became more concentrated on Victorian interests, the desire for Federation perceptibly cooled. The pressure of economic causes, however, soon brought back public opinion into the old channels. Until the bursting of the land-boom in 1890, Melbourne was the money centre of Australia, and Queensland, the western districts of New South Wales, and portions of Western Australia were all developed by Victorian capital, the return from which was reduced by the existence of the local tariffs. During the same period, under the fostering influence of Protection, numerous manufacturing industries were established on a sound footing in the southern Colony. The time was approaching, however, when, unless there were a large influx of immigrants, the local market would be over-supplied, and

---

[1] Since this was written, Judge Casey, too, has died.

it would become imperative to seek new outlets for the surplus. The collapse of the land-boom and the Banking Crisis (1893) postponed the urgency of this demand, which again became insistent in the later 'nineties,' when the losses had been repaired. Thus, by the time the vote was taken on the Convention Bill, the interest both of capitalists and manufacturers in Victoria demanded inter-Colonial Free Trade—the one in order to reap the full benefit of their enterprises beyond the Colony, the other to escape the danger of over-production. And without Federation inter-Colonial Free Trade was impossible.

More potent, however, than any economic pressure in forming Victorian opinion on the question of Federation, was the influence of the proprietor and editor of *The Age*—Mr. David Syme—who was one of the most remarkable among the men who have aided in the development of the Empire. His life has been admirably told by Mr. Ambrose Pratt, and is a fascinating record of a great career.[1] Born at North Berwick in 1827, he joined his brother Ebenezer in the purchase of *The Age* for £2000 in 1856. After 1860 he became its sole owner, and from this time forward devoted himself to forming and directing public opinion through its columns. His independence and courage marked him as a leader in the struggle against privilege and plutocracy, which is nowhere more fierce than in a young community ; and by the middle 'eighties,' after many vicissitudes, he had won the confidence of the democracy—and a democracy is slow to withdraw a confidence once given—and become the uncrowned king of Victoria, who made and unmade Ministries at will. Governors, Prime Ministers, Leaders of the Opposition, all looked to him for guidance ; and to each he gave his counsel without loss of dignity or suspicion of self-interest. He would never be the first to make overtures ; and whoever wished to see him, even the King's representative, must attend at the office of *The Age*, or be content with a visit from the proprietor's subordinate. Few men could have gained such power without losing their

[1] *David Syme* : Ward, Lock & Co., 1908.

directness or simplicity. Syme's secret was his devotion to a cause ! He was Father of Protection in Australia ; which he regarded, not as an end in itself, but as an instrument of national greatness. Other measures of the day were also important in so far as they furthered an advance towards the same goal ; but none, in Syme's opinion, was of equal importance to Protection. Yet, with regard to each question as it arose, the attitude of *The Age* was definite ; and no politician could hope for its support who did not adopt loyally its explicit programme. Always the electors were taken into confidence ! *The Age* left no one in doubt as to its opinions, so that none could misjudge its attitude towards a public man !

Mr. Syme was not sympathetic with Sir Henry Parkes, although he respected his powers. Syme's enthusiasm and imagination were held in check by his intellectual precision and Scotch sense of order, the very qualities in which Parkes was lacking ; and both men were too masterful to make the allowances which would have been required by friendship. This want of sympathy coloured the comments by *The Age* upon Sir Henry Parkes' proposal in 1889 to make a fresh start in the federal movement ; and its articles, which expressed without reserve suspicion of Sir Henry Parkes' motives, were the influence behind Mr. Gillies' alternative proposal to proceed through an enlargement of the Federal Council. The courage with which the New South Wales leader adhered to his larger view could not fail to impress such a man as Syme ; and *The Age* became more friendly as time revealed both Sir Henry Parkes' sincerity and the greatness of his conceptions. It is within the writer's knowledge that the misunderstandings between these two men—each in his way a zealot and a patriot —were removed entirely before Sir Henry Parkes' death, and that afterwards no one spoke more generously than Mr. Syme of the latter's services to the cause of Union.

When the Premiers agreed, in 1895, to pass Enabling Acts to constitute the Federal Convention, it was largely due to the strenuous advocacy of Mr. Syme that the Victorian Parliament gave effect to this agreement ; and the ten delegates who represented the southern Colony were all the recommendations of *The Age*. The issues of local politics, however, could not be ignored entirely even in the federal struggle ; and *The Age*, in opposition to *The Argus*, advocated what was called ' the Liberal ' side in the Federation controversy—that is to say, the supremacy of the nation over any combination of States ; while the ' Conservatives,' adhering more logically to the federal idea, desired to give the Senate or State House an equal power in matters of taxation with the House of Representatives. The fortunes of this struggle, and the compromise which was arrived at finally, have been related in previous Chapters. It is sufficient to note, in this connection, that the concessions, which the Convention Bill made to the smaller States were opposed consistently by *The Age*, and that it was doubtful for a long time whether the support of the paper would be given to the Bill. This uncertainty was reflected in the policy of the Victorian Ministry ; and Mr. Isaacs, the Attorney-General, to whom fell the duty of submitting the Convention Bill to the Victorian Parliament during the absence of the Premier, Sir George Turner, at the Jubilee celebrations, performed his task without enthusiasm, and expressly reserved for the Government the right to determine, later, whether they should support or oppose the measure at the Referendum. The decisive event was the annual meeting of the Australian Natives' Association, which in 1898 was held at Bendigo on March 15.

This body, which had been a school for politics for many Victorians, was very powerful in that Colony ; and its annual meetings, like the Lord Mayor's Banquet on November 9 in London, was a recognised occasion for important speeches. Mr. Isaacs again spoke on behalf of the Ministry, and was again carefully non-committal. Indeed, he pleaded that the Government ought not to be required, at present, to make up their minds about the Convention Bill, because they could not consider it in all its bearings upon Victorian interests until the draft was complete—(the final revise of the Bill yet had to be presented to the Convention by the drafting committee)—or until the Railway Commissioner and the officers of the Treasury and Customs had reported upon its provisions.   Finally, Sir George Turner was ill, and he (Mr. Isaacs) had had no opportunity of consulting with him.   This did not satisfy Mr. J. L. Purves, K.C., the able and impetuous leader of the Victorian Bar, who baldly interjected an inquiry whether Mr. Isaacs was for or against the Bill.   In answer, the latter claimed that his actions during the Convention were a sufficient index of his attitude, because he would not have made so many concessions had he not desired Union.   ' Yet,' he repeated, ' it was the duty of the Government not blindly to reject or accept the Bill ; but they should rather obtain all possible information as to its practical working, and submit this to the people, so that votes might be given with knowledge.'   The occasion was singularly inopportune for such a speech.   For years the Australian Natives' Association had worked for Federation, and success was within their grasp.   Victories are not won by cold criticism on the eve of a battle, but by the stimulus of unwavering conviction and exalted hope.   Fortunately Mr. Deakin, who also was a guest of the Association, spoke after Mr. Isaacs, in a manner worthy of his powers and the occasion. Not ignoring ' the surrounding gloom ' from the Minister's speech, he called his hearers to a yet more energetic and strenuous campaign.   ' The friends of Federation,' he said, ' had been microscopic : now was the time to be telescopic.' In this tone he summarised the contents of the Bill, and, speaking with a luminous enthusiasm, dislodged the doubts which had overclouded temporarily the hopes of Federalists, and struck the keynote of the popular campaign which followed. This meeting of the Australian Natives' Association at Bendigo became thus the turning-point in the Victorian campaign, and the success of the Bill in that Colony was assured when Mr. Deakin sat down.

Still *The Age* was unconvinced, and expressed the view that, at Bendigo, enthusiasm had usurped the place of judgment. Two days later, however, it withdrew its opposition to the constitutional clauses, and maintained that the Bill, notwith-standing its imperfections, was a signal triumph for ' Liberal-ism,' because it gave ' one man one vote,' secured the ultimate supremacy of the House of Representatives over the Senate, and assured a protective policy. Again, on March 21, while regretting that the Referendum was not a provision of the Bill, it pointed out that the double dissolution was a more ' liberal ' provision than any in the Constitution of the State. Never-theless, it laid stress upon the sacrifices which Victoria would be called upon to make for the sake of Union. It considered that the Riverina trade would go to Sydney, and thus be lost to the Victorian railways ; and that the duty-free imports into New South Wales would, in the first year of the Common-wealth, compete unfairly with Victorian products. The writer has been informed by one in the confidence of Mr. Syme that another alarm, which was never publicly expressed, cooled his advocacy of the Bill. True to his ideal of an Australian nation, he feared lest the development of manufactures in the other Colonies would be hampered under a common tariff by the competition of the established industries of Victoria ; and would have preferred a few years of State protection, in order that each Colony might enter the Federation upon terms of greater equality. This was the doubt of an honest faith ; but it did not take into account the migration of industries from Melbourne to Sydney, in order to obtain the advantage of cheaper coal and transport, which proved to be the imme-diate consequence of the first federal tariff.

[1] The effect of the Bendigo meeting was to inspire Federalists to renewed exertion. The Victorian branch of the Australasian Federation League, of which Mr. Deakin was President, arranged meetings throughout the Colony in co-operation with a sub-committee of the Australian Natives' Association. On April 5 the leader of the Conservatives, Mr. Murray-Smith, the ex-Labour leader, Mr. Trenwith, and Mr. Deakin spoke on the same platform at Essendon in support

[1] The remainder of this Chapter has been contributed by Mr. Morris Miller, of Melbourne.

of the Bill; and eight days later Sir George Turner declared the support of the Government in a very characteristic speech. He feared that Victoria would lose her Riverina trade to New South Wales, with a consequent loss to her railways of £40,000 per annum. [At this time the New South Wales 'Antis' were declaring that the Bill gave all the Riverina trade to Victoria!] Nevertheless, he was prepared to trust the inter-State Commission (which it was presumed would be appointed immediately) to act as a judicial body with fairness towards Victoria; and although he did not agree with the financial proposals, he would not on that account advise the rejection of the Bill. He was opposed still to equal representation of the States in the Senate, but would not refuse Union because he could not get it on his own terms. Besides, it must be remembered that Federation was a union of separate States in respect of common interests; and that the Parliament to which they would hand over some of the affairs was not a foreign body, but would be chosen from amongst themselves, and he had the utmost confidence and trust in them to do what was right and just to all the States. In expressing these views Sir George Turner was the spokesman of *The Age*, which in a leader on April 14 approved of his speech and recommended electors to vote for the Bill, even although this required no little self-denial, if it were contemplated in the prosaic light of a business transaction. A series of articles was published, setting out the arguments for and against the Bill, and the conclusion was stated that ' in spite of its defects the Constitution would work in the direction of the progress and prosperity of all the Colonies and prove a strength to the Liberal party in each of them.' The final expression of opinion (May 31) was that the Bill was a fair instalment of democracy, and that the machinery clauses would tend to help the rule of the majority. It was undoubted that the Commonwealth would require a protective policy at its initiation, and the opposition of the New South Wales Free Traders under Mr. Reid was sufficiently indicative that this fiscal policy was secure and essential; but at the same time the tariff should have been in the Bill. In addition to Victoria's likelihood of losing a portion of the Riverina trade, other weaknesses were the refusal to transfer State debts and the failure to federalise the railways. But the leader was definitely written to press home the necessity of accepting the Bill upon the people. The large majority of men framing the Bill were Liberals ; and whatever blots there were, they were due to the Conservatives ; but the people might be trusted to work out their own destiny in their own way under the Constitution. ' For our own sakes,' it contended, ' and for the sake of the Empire, Australians may well be prepared to accept a less satisfactory union than we desire in order to play our part fittingly in the Southern Seas, and thus in consolidating and upholding the power and supremacy of our race. There is nothing within the borders of Australia to coerce us into the Commonwealth at this moment. If we had been left to ourselves, we might well wait in order to place at leisure the finishing touches upon the federal structure which we are about to rear ; but there is much beyond our control from which may spring at any instant an armed interference with our peaceful development.'

The opposition to the acceptance of the Bill in Victoria must now be considered. It came from two sections—the one led by Mr. Higgins, which was in close association with the Trades Hall party, the other under Mr. Allan McLean, which was largely composed of those who feared for the rural industries.

The debates in the Victorian Assembly on the Adelaide Draft Bill in 1897, sufficiently indicated the general attitude of the several parties towards the federal issue. The main body of the Liberals and Conservatives were generally in favour of the Bill, although desiring certain amendments peculiar to their political tastes. The Conservatives, remembering their defeat at the Convention elections, objected to the State being polled as one electorate for the Senate, because the principle ensured, as Mr. Murray-Smith pointed out, the absolute domination of one party in the State and the absolute, and not partial, exclusion of a party, which, though inferior in numbers, nevertheless had a right to representation. He supported the preferential system as a safeguard for the interests of minorities. The Labour Party were uncompromising in their opposition, fearing that the Senate would be absolutely at the disposal of wealthy candidates, in spite of the fact of Mr. Trenwith's return as a Convention delegate. Their strongest objections concerned the loss of the mass Referendum. Mr. McLean, in a memorable speech, stood for the protection of Victorian rural industries against any Federal Constitution not sufficiently safeguarding them. Mr. Higgins, then, and later, throughout the campaign itself, trenchantly denounced the principle of equal representation for the Senate. He considered that the States, as such, had no right to any separate form of representation in the Federation. He deprecated the fact that the railways had not been federalised, and that the machinery for overcoming deadlocks was cumbersome and ineffective. His difficulties were mainly constitutional. He became leader of the Anti-Commonwealth Bill League, with Sir Bryan O'Loghlen as Vice-President, and worked in close co-operation with the Trades Hall party. With the exception of Mr. Trenwith, the majority of the Labour leaders were solid against the Bill. They declared that the Bill was undemocratic in character, and demanded the mass Referendum and adult suffrage, maintaining that without them the Constitution was pernicious in application and destructive to a responsible government. Mr. Trenwith was considered a traitor to the party, and denounced as having consorted with Conservatives and other reactionaries whose sole aim was to prevent the growth of the Labour Party. At the Eight Hours' Day Celebration, the invitations were entirely confined to members of Labour organisations and Labour supporters. The subject of Federation was eschewed in all the speeches. The inter-Colonial Labour Congress, which was held at Melbourne on the following day, April 22, carried a resolution complaining of the undemocratic and injurious character of the Constitution. The combined opposition forces decided to adopt a Fabian policy and press for delay, as they did not consider that the people sufficiently understood the Bill. Opposition, they maintained, was growing, and thousands of electors were disfranchised. They proposed to lay the situation before the Premier and to ask for free railway passes for the conduct of their campaign. They met Sir George Turner on May 6, and he favourably entertained their request for railway passes, provided that they were exclusively used for the purpose of the campaign. A few days later he granted them twelve passes. He sympathised with those who were unfortunately not on the roll, but he could not himself delay the taking of the Referendum, for that had been fixed by all the Premiers. He, himself, would willingly delay the poll if the other Premiers would agree ; but this was afterwards found to be impossible.

In a final manifesto, the Victorian anti-Billites condemned the Constitution of the Senate as allowing small minorities to thwart the will of the vast majority. The financial clauses made the Federal Parliament the tax-gatherer for the State Parliaments ; and though the State Parliaments were sovereign in themselves, yet they were to be dependent on another Parliament for their supplies. Amendments could only be obtained with difficulty, and hence there was need for alteration in the direction of flexibility. At their final great meeting, held at the Town Hall, on the eve of the Referendum, an amendment in favour of the Constitution was moved by Professor Gosman, seconded by Mr. J. A. Boyd, and declared carried. This brought an element of confusion into the meeting, and it ended in comparative disorder.

While the objections of Mr. Higgins and of the Labour Party appealed more directly to the city voters, Mr. McLean's influence against the Bill was almost entirely directed to the rural centres. Mr. McLean had previously made a strong fighting speech in the Legislative Assembly against the Adelaide Draft Bill. He maintained that the rural industries were altogether neglected, and they had only been meagrely

represented at the Convention. He particularly objected to
the principle of equal representation in the Senate, maintaining
that a more undemocratic proposal was never submitted to
Australian Legislatures. If the proposal to poll the State as
one electorate for the Senate were adhered to, the rural interests
would have no chance against city voters. This was demonstrated at the Convention elections, when the country party
was outvoted by the towns. But, worse still, on the sweeping
away of all inter-Colonial barriers, such as the stock tax,
farmers would again considerably suffer, for there would
immediately take place in Victoria a general fall of land
and stock values. Mr. McLean estimated the loss in land
values alone at £25,000,000. As the people would be driven
off the land, this depreciation would react upon the cities.
Recognising that inter-Colonial Free Trade was a necessary
outcome of Federation, he advocated that the reduction of
the stock tax be gradual and extend over a term of ten years.
He, nevertheless, recognised that the gain to Victorian
manufacturers, through access to other ports of the Commonwealth, would counterbalance the farmers' losses. After the
discussion in the House, Mr. McLean lost no time in preparing
to influence the country against the immediate fall of the stock
tax on the initiation of Federation. The Maffra Agricultural
Society took up the matter, and sent a circular to some eighty
agricultural societies, asking them to delegate two representatives to attend a Conference at Melbourne, on September 21,
1897, to consider the effects likely to accrue from the removal
of the border duties. Although only some eighteen representatives turned up, a spirited discussion took place, and it
was moved that representations should be made to the
Convention that rural industries should receive more equitable
consideration. The defection of Mr. McLean, who was at the
time an honorary member of the Turner Cabinet, was considered likely to carry considerable weight in the country;
and Mr. Deakin went so far as to propose at the Convention
that the stock tax be gradually removed over a period of five
years, but the proposal was not carried. After Sir George

Turner's speech on behalf of the Government, at St. Kilda, on April 13, 1898, Mr. McLean decided to resign his position in the Cabinet. His resignation was communicated to Sir George Turner in a letter, dated April 14, in which he stated that, although Sir George Turner offered him a free hand as regards his opposition to the Bill, he considered it incumbent upon him to sever his connection with the Ministry. In his letter he objected to the State being polled as one electorate for the Senate, to the principle of equal representation, to the abolition of the border duties, and to the removal of the State's right to grant subsidies to industries. He reiterated his contention that the withdrawal of the stock tax would drive hundreds of families from their homes in the country, and create the need for additional taxation, to make up for the loss of revenue. The discontinuance of bounties would prevent the establishment of new industries, and probably lead to the abolition of the Agricultural Department itself. This letter was published on April 18, and on the following day Mr. Deakin replied to Mr. McLean at Castlemaine, stating that the farmers were already heavily mortgaged, and that it was better to reduce duties which had brought about this unfortunate result. Mr. McLean opened his platform campaign at Bairnsdale on April 21, and attempted to organise country members in opposition to the Bill. He received little support except from Messrs. George Graham and A. R. Outtrim. His manifesto was issued on May 4 to which Mr. Deakin replied. Mr. McLean was so convinced of the harm the Bill would do that he believed that, if carried, it would put back the political dial for one hundred years. Eventually, under pressure at Numurkah on May 25, in answer to a question, he said that if constitutional defects were remedied he would sacrifice even the stock tax. Mr. McLean's strongest challenger was found in the person of Mr. M. K. McKenzie, the member for Anglesey, who was ably assisted by Mr. T. Kennedy. Mr. McKenzie was merciless in showing up the fallacies of Mr. McLean's conclusions, and these two doughty Scotchmen maintained a hand-to-hand fight throughout the country centres upon the

incidences of the stock tax.   Mr. McLean's statements could
not fail to have a strong influence with the rural population,
as he had had a long practical experience in all matters relating
to land and stock.   He was also a gifted orator, with fine
persuasive powers.   Mr. McKenzie was an exceedingly clear
reasoner, and had a curt style, and an easy manner of laying
bare Mr. McLean's incorrect foundations.   It was due in no
small measure to Mr. McKenzie that the farmers rallied to
the cause of the Constitution and gave a pronounced vote in
its favour.

When the campaign was now fairly launched the triumph
of the Federalists appeared certain.   The prevailing tone of
the meetings was enthusiastic and hopeful, and, with one or
two exceptions, there were no attempts at disorder.   Though
the Federalists mainly directed their utterances towards
Australia's own immediate destiny, there were many signs
that they were not altogether unmindful of Imperial obligations.   Although this phase of the federal issue did not have
that prominence which the Imperial Federationists desired
that it should have had, still the fact of the Spanish-American
war, and the uncertainty of affairs in the Far East, impressed
several of the leaders, especially Mr. J. L. Purves, K.C., whose
speeches were invariably imperialistic.   While several maintained that external pressure was almost entirely absent in
affecting the Australian Federation, it was not overlooked
that the recent Jubilee celebrations and the growing influence
of foreign Powers in the Pacific had some share in influencing
many to support the immediate Federation of the Colonies
as a means of defence against foreign interference.   As the
election day began to draw near, manifestoes became prolific.
The Argus, which had never wavered in its support of Federation, in addition to issuing the complete text of the Bill, with
explanations by Dr. Quick, instituted a Federation forum, in
which the leading protagonists took part.   Messrs. Higgins
and Trenwith were brought into combat ;   Messrs. Allan
McLean and Deakin were pitted against each other ;   while
Sir John Quick reviewed all the points brought forward in the

controversy. Mr., now Senator, Stephen Barker stated the Labour standpoint, and was replied to by Mr. Hamilton, the member for Bendigo. In addition to the Federal Leagues, several other organisations assisted in the campaign. On May 19 an important Conference of municipalities, which had been convened by the late Sir Malcolm McEacharn, then Mayor of Melbourne, was attended by over two hundred representatives, including the Mayor of Adelaide and two Aldermen from Hobart, and motions were carried favouring the Bill, and pledging all present to active service in its support. The Council of Churches instituted May 22 as a Federal Sunday, and later, on Sunday, May 29, a memorable service was led by the Rev. A. R. Edgar at the Exhibition, at which, in an impressive speech, Mr. Deakin recited Kipling's ' Recessional,' and referred to the possibility of dangers arising in the Pacific in the future.

The Australasian Federation League, in its manifesto issued on May 25, warned the electors against delay, and upheld the Constitution as a magnificent advance in Liberal government. Everything that their opponents hoped to achieve by waiting might be better and more easily secured through the Commonwealth Parliament. The climax of the campaign took the form of a great meeting at the Melbourne Town Hall on May 31, under the auspices of the Australian Natives' Association. Patriotic airs and special Federation songs were rendered by a large choir under Mr. D. R. Davies. The chairman of the meeting was Dr. Carty Salmon, then President of the Australian Natives' Association. Each speaker was allotted some special aspect of the question and given ten minutes for his speech. The list of the speakers included Sir George Turner, Lieutenant-Colonel W. T. Reay, Messrs. Isaacs, J. H. Cook, James Maloney, W. A. Trenwith, R. W. Best, J. W. Kirton, A. J. Peacock, R. F. Toucher, J. L. Purves, and Alfred Deakin. The Convention delegates, with the exception of Mr. Higgins, issued a joint manifesto, which was published in the Press on May 31, and Sir George Turner, in closing his campaign at St. Kilda, said that the only new Convention he could suggest was one constituted by the opponents to the Bill, who might be given time to formulate a Constitution that they all could accept. He warned his hearers that, if they rejected the Constitution, it would be a national disaster and an everlasting disgrace. On the eve of the poll, Sir Wilfrid Laurier's Canadian greetings were made known at all the city meetings, which was an index that the vote to be taken on the following day did not concern Australia only, but the Empire at large. The polling day was one of mingled sunshine and rain, but the Federalists worked with patience and energy, confident of victory. The subscriptions received by the Victorian Federation League were almost entirely devoted to the printing and circulation of leaflets. It was estimated that over 200,000 of these were distributed. Early in the campaign the Government posted a copy of the Draft Constitution to every elector in the State. On the night of June 3, Collins Street was crowded to excess in spite of the drizzling rain, and tumultuous cheering occurred when the required majority had been obtained. The crowds were entertained at *The Argus* office with lantern views of the Queen, the federal leaders, and other incidents of the movement. Messrs. Barton and Deakin were greatly cheered, and the message of Sir Wilfrid Laurier was responded to by the singing of ' Rule Britannia.' The result of the polling was 100,520 ayes, and 22,099 noes.

APPENDIX II

THE STRUGGLE IN TASMANIA

Contributed by MR. JUSTICE NICHOLLS, of the Supreme Court of Tasmania.

FROM the earliest discussions of Federation, it had been held by enlightened Federalists that Tasmania was a necessary part of the hoped-for Union. No defence scheme would be complete which left the great harbours and productive lands of the Island open to occupation by an enemy ; while Tasmania, by reason of her smallness, could not stand alone. The necessities of trade and defence forbade it. The populace of the mainland, however, was little affected by the question of Tasmania's entry into Federation or not ; she was far from being a pivot.

The functions of the other territories now included in the Commonwealth are easy to understand, and their future contributions to its welfare not difficult to foretell. With Tasmania the case is different. There were many, particularly in New South Wales, who regarded Tasmania as capable of being no more than a hanger-on to the more populous and wealthy States. Yet it is well understood now that there could have been no real Federation without her, and that her cool-climate products and cool-climate people, in the long run, must influence considerably the development of the industries and the race of the Commonwealth. Tasmania also is the only one of the States which possesses water-power in such quantities and so situated as to make hydro-electric enterprise possible upon a large scale. With her many mountains, copious rainfall, and great rivers (one of them, the Gordon, gigantic in volume if not in length), it is now considered possible that almost unlimited power may be generated and distributed in Tasmania as cheaply as anywhere in the world.   To anyone who watches the rapid capture of the manufacturing world by the hydro-electric plant, it seems plain that there should be only one result from such extraordinary advantages ; because a State, which is the sole one in its Continent having this modern and eagerly sought resource, is probably destined to be a great manufacturing country.   As to shipping, she can send her goods from harbours which for depth, safety, and cheapness to shipping are praised by mariners as having few rivals, and no superiors in the world.

In the first days of the federal movement, however, the orthodox Tasmanian dreamed no such dreams as these.

In the early 'eighties' the question was so far from being practical that, with the exception of the late Hons. W. R. Giblin and N. J. Brown and the late Mr. H. R. Nicholls, the writer does not recollect anyone who spoke or wrote upon the subject.

Tasmania at that time was a despondent community, prone to deplore the departure, many years before, of the British troops, and to lament the total extinction of the great wooden shipbuilding industry; which had grown and died in Hobart, and the rapidity with which the once highly profitable enterprise of whaling was also dwindling to nothing.   In those days Tasmanians looked upon themselves as almost alien to 'other-siders,' as they called all Australians, and admitted an undefined inferiority in themselves to their more pushing and prosperous neighbours.   The nearest idea to Federation was that of annexation to Victoria, which was every now and then seriously propounded, but never reached the stage of formal submission to Parliament.

At this stage the Federal Council was accepted as a seed from which good might grow, and which, at any rate, could hardly fail to produce something capable of being turned to practical uses.

The first Federal Council sat in Hobart in 1886, and there-after its sittings were looked forward to by the Islanders with a new interest.   Probably not since the Governments of New South Wales and Van Diemen's Land (as Tasmania was then called) were separated in 1824 had Tasmanians realised so fully that they were a part of the great Australian family.

The service thus rendered by the old Federal Council to Tasmania has never been adequately recognised ; and, indeed, its operation was so subtle and gradual that it proceeded unobserved by the many, who are never analytical.   The proposals for the Convention of 1891 were accepted practically without dissent.   To this Convention Tasmania contributed one who was in many ways a remarkable man, the late Mr. A. Inglis Clark, whose work a few years later indirectly had an extraordinary influence in favour of Federation, even though the Bill which left the Convention of 1897–8 was so little to his liking that he refused to speak in favour of it.   He was devoured by passionate enthusiasms for knowledge and for liberty, and was one of those rare beings who really love their fellow-men.   His house, prior to the establishment of the Tasmanian University, was a centre of original thought for the Island, and many men from many countries visited the ardent circle, which met every Saturday night in the library of the *padre*, as his friends liked to call him, and joined in the high hopes for the realisation of the brotherhood of man, which were the basis of this informal church's cult.   Mr. Clark had visited America, where he had been made much of, at that period when the memories of the Civil War were young, but not so young as to be still bitter, and North and South were joining hands in their new and moving friendship.   He went back once or twice in later years, but never realised the rapid growth of the new America, swamped by dollars and dominated by the fierce and rapacious egoists who have organised their greed into a system which governs a mighty government. To him America was good ; its people were good ; and its Constitution was as good as the nobly rhetorical preamble to the Declaration of Independence.

His encyclopædic knowledge of American affairs gave him

a considerable influence in the Convention of 1891, and he undoubtedly did much to increase the already strong bias in favour of the American form finally adopted, and for that feeling which found its culmination in the following of American constitutional case-law by the High Court. This has been the most striking characteristic of the Court, and has made the discussion of Australia's problems, which are really questions as to how the genius of the people has been expressed in the Constitution, a mere industrious collection and citation of the decisions of American Judges, sometimes made in circumstances when the Court was driven by the necessities of the hour to conclusions whose ultimate results they could not foretell. Mr. Clark returned from the Convention of 1891 to give a brilliant analysis of the Bill, and founded the movement apparently firmly in Tasmania. After the failure of the 1891 Bill until 1895 the subject slept. But in that year the Premiers of all the Colonies met in Hobart to consider the forming of the Convention of 1897. From this time forward the Federalists kept up an educational campaign. A series of meetings, promoted by Mr. William Crooke and addressed by a number of prominent Federalists, kept together in Hobart the germs of a party whose subsequent energy was beyond question. When the time came, in 1898, to submit the Bill to the people the Island was in a strangely divided state. In the North a league, led chiefly by Mr. M. J. Clarke, Mr. J. H. Keating, and Mr. John Gunning, the latter two being of Mr. A. I. Clark's disciples, found a unanimous Press backing it, amongst a population of exporters of agricultural produce thirsting for the inter-Colonial Free Trade which would come with Federation. In Hobart and the South affairs were different. The daily papers opposed the Bill as being too democratic. The *Labour Weekly* vehemently resisted its passage, upon the ground that it gave insufficient power to the people, while the financial arrangement was condemned upon all sides. A pamphlet published by the Hon. H. S. Bird, a man of high intellect and sincerity, prophesied that, if the Bill were accepted, Tasmania would be ruined in a few years. Mr. R. M.

Johnston, the Government Statistician, whose influence was almost as great as his very unusual ability, supported this view and deluged friend and foe alike with showers of figures. It was at this stage that the Australian Natives' Association, of Hobart, deciding to fight to the finish what it believed was an already lost battle, formed a Federal League under the Presidency of the Hon. F. W. Piesse, with the eloquent and humorous Archdeacon Whitington as Vice-President.

Two Englishmen, Messrs. C. J. Atkins and W. H. Dawson, were amongst the first to join the League, and a small number of young men were got together. A member of Parliament was addressing his constituents at Bellerive in opposition to the Bill, and the League asked his leave to attend and discuss its provisions after his speech. The Rev. Mr. Woollnough, the member, as became an educated and broad-minded gentleman, consented ; and, when the meeting was over, the League left the Suburban Hall astounded to find that it had got unanimously carried the motion ' that this meeting is in favour of Federation.' Mr. Dawson at this stage rendered Federalists the tremendous service of providing them with a song, and the perfervid enthusiasm with which his ' Sons of Australia ' was sung at the League's meetings will dwell for ever in the memory of those who took part in those gatherings.

Mr. A. I. Clark had retired to his library. The Constitution for which he had laboured for years was about to be adopted or rejected in all its essentials ; but he was resolved that it should await its fate without help from him. His absence was sorely felt and furnished the provincialists with a strong argument, while his most intimate friends never quite knew the cause of his attitude. In June 1898 he was offered a Supreme Court Judgeship and accepted it. Thereafter his silence could be accounted for by etiquette. The falling away of Mr. Clark from the movement for which he had done so much was one of the most striking events of the campaign. Mr. Johnston's figures supplied the provincialists with unlimited material for argument. Their effect was invariably to show that, if Tasmania joined the Federation, she would be bankrupt. The weight and authority of the opposition in the South were too great to leave the rest of the Island unaffected; and signs were soon visible that there was danger of the North going wrong. At this stage the Southern Federal League decided to produce a paper of its own. The project presented difficulties enough, for the membership of the League had never been more than thirty, a secret now probably revealed for the first time. It consisted chiefly of young men with light pockets, and most of them were scattered far and wide about the country, making speeches. A small paper was nevertheless produced, and *The Tasmanian Federalist* was sent to every elector in the Colony. How the expenses of the paper were paid is known only to Mr. C. J. Atkins, the treasurer of the League. He announced, when all was over, that the accounts had been paid and that he had enough money given to the League to do it. Members offered contributions and pressed inquiries, but were met by a determined refusal of any further information; so they contented themselves with wringing the hand of their patriotic British-Australian brother and left the matter at that.

The Hon. F. W. Piesse was one of the original federal band, and almost the only one who saw the fight through. His love of figures was not a sufficient equipment to enable him to cope with the productions of the Government Statistician; and at first the League suffered many reverses in detail. As the campaign proceeded, however, the Leaguers learned the force of sentiment, and discovered that in every audience large numbers of people were tired of arithmetic; what they wished to hear about was the future of the Australian people. The fight was thus gradually raised to another and a higher plane. No man who is sincerely and hotly appealing to his fellow-countrymen not to destroy their country's future can fail to have some eloquence, and all over Tasmania the cause began to make way. Physically and mentally Tasmanians are more typical of England than of Australia. Broader of back and thicker of limb than Australians, they are also slower of speech and shyer of revealing their feelings. They are,

however, ' good stayers ' in the most desirable sense of that
phrase ; and as they awakened to the enjoyment of a new
national pride, those who rallied behind the leaders of the
movement did it with a solid determination.   The opposition
became incensed.   The Leaguers were derisively called ' flag-
flappers,' ' spadoodlers,' ' Clark's boys,' and other terms
intended to be contemptuous.   But no man who is waving
his country's flag can ever be quite ridiculous ; and many
followed the magic symbol.   It is now known that those who
saw visions in 1898 were wiser and farther-sighted than their
learned and able critics ; for Federation has not ruined
Tasmania ; that happy land now enjoys the greatest prosperity
it has ever known.

When the League was fairly into its stride and recognised
as a nucleus of organisation, Sir Edward Braddon, Sir Philip
Fysh, Sir Elliott Lewis, and Mr. Henry Dobson offered themselves as privates in the ranks of the little Federal Army.
They held high positions in politics, but they took their orders
from headquarters, travelled the country and spoke and wrote
when and where the Executive Committee commanded, with
a devotion that proved the inspiration of the cause.   By this
time the Northern and Southern Leagues had been almost
moulded into one ; they exchanged speakers continually, and
concentrated upon each doubtful district a continuous on-
slaught of their ablest and most trusted men.   An opposition
league had been formed with the curious title of ' The Federation with safety and advantage League.'   Its proposition
was to reject the Bill and wait for better terms.   It commanded
considerable support in and about Hobart.   But the fate of
battle was ultimately brought about by a fruit which has
already had great consequences to the world—an apple.
Southern Tasmania is rapidly turning into a vast orchard, and
in 1898 thousands of people were contemplating either
commencing or extending the planting of apple trees.   The
bulk of Tasmania's fruit is sold in Sydney, not in London,
even to-day, when something like two million bushels of apples
are sent away every season.   Orchardists and intending

orchardists used to see, hanging over their heads, the prospect of a Protectionist Government returning to office in New South Wales and shutting out Tasmania's produce. Gradually they were brought to realise that Federation would actually mean a free Sydney market for ever. There is no man shrewder than the simple farmer, and no one slower to believe assurances from a public platform. In the end, however, he always sees very accurately what it is that will suit his pocket, and so he came to understand Australian Free Trade, even if he did not grow enthusiastic about the great national interests and principles connoted by it. There was a speaker at some League meetings who was claimed to have put the whole case in one gorgeous combination of sentiment and practicality which completely captivated the country mind. 'Gentlemen,' he would say, 'if you vote for the Bill you will found a great and glorious nation under the bright Southern Cross, and meat will be cheaper; and you will live to see the Australian race dominate the Southern seas, and you will have a market for both potatoes and apples; and your sons shall reap the grand heritage of nationhood, and if Sir William Lyne does come back to power in Sydney he can never do you one pennyworth of harm.' This, delivered in one level sentence, invariably won high applause; and, indeed, as a farmer remarked to one who derided the quaintness of the mixture, 'It was a dam good speech; every word of it was true.'

While the apple-growers of the South were being captured, the Northern League, supported by a friendly town and country Press, was making an absolute conquest of the potato-growers of the North. Their markets lay in Melbourne and Sydney, and perpetual Free Trade meant much to them. Indeed, now that the whole matter may be regarded historically, it is clear that, had Tasmania stood out, her condition as to exports would probably have been like that of Ireland in the eighteenth century, and that she would ultimately have been driven to beg leave to enter the Federation upon any terms, however humiliating, which the other States chose to grant. As it is, she has her six Senators, and New South Wales has no more;

while the Commonwealth Parliament has made her a grant of £500,000 to compensate for the losses occurring in various ways in the course of the change from a separate to a universal tariff.

Although the result of the Referendum was regarded in 1898 as being uncertain, it proved that the people of Tasmania, when faced with the problem of deciding great national issues, were capable of ignoring those nervous prophecies which are and always have been a leading form of criticism upon every new proposal. The Referendum is a potent weapon in the hands of a party proposing that which will stir the hearts of a people. To those who have to force mere practical measures through the bog of public apathy, it everywhere tends to be a formidable and disheartening obstacle, whatever may be the merits of the proposal.

In Federation, many lovers of Tasmania found a new inspiration, and a wider hope for that sweet and lonely little sister of Australia. They were prepared to vote for Union even if it meant ruin, confiding securely in the belief that no Australian Parliament would, or could, let one of its component States remain bankrupt. At one suburban polling place a gentleman of high standing addressed the loiterers outside the booth. He was, he said, about to exercise the highest privilege of his life, in recording a vote which would have its direct influence in making his native country a great united nation. He entered the booth, and in a few moments emerged in tears. His name was not upon the roll, though it should have been, and he had no vote. No doubt, upon reflection, he was consoled by the thought that he had induced hundreds of others to vote for the Union. Many instances of similar enthusiasm were visible. To say that a cause, which could make men feel thus, triumphed over an opposition based upon the troubles of future State Treasurers is to insult the intuition of all readers of history. The Referendum of 1898 resulted in a huge majority for the Bill in the North and in a bare victory in the South. From that day opposition ceased. The financial clauses of the Bill were not regarded as the best possible by anyone ; but it was seen by all that the people had determined to be Australians ; and when the poll upon the amendments was taken in 1899 the majority in favour of Union was overwhelming, being somewhere about 13 to 1.

What the effect of Federation has been upon Tasmanian trade and politics it is difficult to say.   Twelve years is a short time in history, and there are reasons why these subjects should not be discussed in this chapter.   But its influence upon the people has already been remarkable.   The realisation of their oneness with their brethren all over the great continent across Bass Strait has given Tasmanians an outlook so broad and tolerant as to frequently cause astonishment amongst new arrivals.   The phrase ' other-sider ' has disappeared.   The past is no longer lamented ; the man in the streets of Hobart (once called ' Sleepy Hollow ') now talks of the future, and points proudly to the hundreds of new houses which are being erected in every direction.   Country districts, where formerly shabby men drove shaky chaise carts, now hum with the motor-cars of the farmers and orchardists, and a general feeling of optimism prevails.   All British men, very wisely, take athletics seriously ; and the notable successes of Tasmanian athletes have helped in no small degree to enable the formerly despondent Islanders to realise that they are the equals of their fellow-Australians.   Not that their only victories have been in the field of physical prowess.   The Tasmanian is of a solid type in every way, and has done more than respectably in many walks of life.   He has now quite settled to the belief that any citizen of the Commonwealth is any other's equal, with a mental reservation that the inhabitant of ' little Tassy,' as he fondly calls it, is entitled to add, like Sir Joseph Porter, ' excepting mine.'

INDEX

THE END

PRINTED BY
SPOTTISWOODE AND CO. LTD., COLCHESTER
LONDON AND ETON

COLONIAL HISTORY AND POLITY.

THE FIRST DECADE OF THE AUSTRALIAN COMMONWEALTH: a Chronicle of Contemporary Politics, 1901–1910.   By HENRY GYLES TURNER. 8vo. 9s.

THE HISTORY OF AUSTRALIA AND NEW ZEALAND, 1606–1901.   By ALEXANDER SUTHERLAND, M.A., and GEORGE SUTHERLAND, M.A.   Crown 8vo. 2s. 6d.

THE RISE OF SOUTH AFRICA: a History of the Origin of South African Colonisation and of its Development towards the East from the Earliest Times to 1857.   By GEORGE EDWARD CORY, M.A., King's College, Cambridge, Professor in the Rhodes University College, Grahamstown, South Africa.   In 4 vols. 8vo.

Vol. I.   FROM THE EARLIEST TIMES TO THE YEAR 1820.   With Map, Plans, and Illustrations.   15s.

Vol. II.   *In preparation.*

THE CRADLE OF NEW FRANCE : a Story of the City founded by Champlain.   By ARTHUR G. DOUGHTY, C.M.G., Litt.D., Dominion Archivist.   With a Map of Quebec, Portraits and other Illustrations.   Crown 8vo. 6s. net.

THE IMPERIAL CONFERENCE.   A History and a Study.   By RICHARD JEBB, M.A.   With a Map. 8vo. 2 vols. 25s. net.

THE BRITANNIC QUESTION.   A Survey of Alternatives.   By RICHARD JEBB. Crown 8vo. 1s. net.

This book deals with the Imperial Questions of To-day.   What does Imperialism mean?   Should the Dominions contribute to Britain's Navy or have navies of their own?   Do the " Food Taxes " matter?   Should there be a new Empire Parliament? Or, could we have a Britannic Commonwealth without a Central Government?

A NEW GOVERNMENT FOR THE BRITISH EMPIRE.   By the Rev. F. W. BUSSELL, D.D. 8vo. 3s. 6d.

THE COLONIES AND IMPERIAL DEFENCE.   By P. A. SILBURN, D.S.O. Crown 8vo. 6s.

THE GOVERNANCE OF EMPIRE.   By P. A. SILBURN, D.S.O.   With a Map.   Crown 8vo. 9s. net.

THE PROBLEM OF EMPIRE GOVERNANCE.   By CHARLES E. T. STUART-LINTON.   Crown 8vo. 3s. 6d. net.

BRITISH DOMINIONS: THEIR PRESENT COMMERCIAL AND INDUSTRIAL CONDITION.   A Series of General Reviews for Business Men and Students.   Edited by W. J. ASHLEY.   Crown 8vo. 6s. 6d. net.

ESSAYS IN POLITICS.   By ANDREW MACPHAIL.   Crown 8vo. 6s. net.

CONTENTS.—The Patience of England—Loyalty—to what ?—The Dominion and the Spirit—What can Canada do ?—New Lamps for Old—A Patent Anomaly—Protection and Politics—Why the Conservatives Failed—The Psychology of Canada—British Diplomacy and Canada.

LONGMANS, GREEN, & CO., 39 Paternoster Row, London, E.C.

NEW HISTORICAL BOOKS.

HISTORY AND HISTORIANS IN THE NINETEENTH CENTURY. By G. P. GOOCH, M.A. (Cantab.). 8vo. 10s. 6d. net.

"This brilliant and stimulating book inspires one to ask whether the art of history in the modern sense is not the most essential contribution of our times to the world's literature. . . . No one has ever made so graphic the enormous industry, the scholarly devotion, the consecration of genius, character and self-denial which for the past century have been applied to the story of the race."
The Observer.

THE FATE OF EMPIRES : being an Inquiry into the Stability of Civilization. By ARTHUR JOHN HUBBARD, M.D. (Dunelm). 8vo. 6s. 6d. net.

"Dr. Hubbard acutely remarks that the turning-point in past civilizations has been marked, again and again, by the appearance of Socialism coincidently with a failure of birth-rate. The most striking instance is that of the Roman Empire, but the phenomena to which Dr. Hubbard refers are almost as apparent at the present day."—*The Globe.*

THE AGRARIAN PROBLEM IN THE SIXTEENTH CENTURY. By R. H. TAWNEY. With Reproductions of Plans (1590–1620). 8vo. 9s. net.

"His book ought to become the standard treatise on an intricate and much misunderstood chapter of England's agrarian history."—*Morning Post.*

THE VILLAGE LABOURER, 1760-1832. A Study in the Government of England before the Reform Bill. By J. L. HAMMOND and BARBARA HAMMOND. Second Impression. 8vo. 9s. net.

"We heartily commend this book to all students of economics and local government as a serious study of those Times."—*Land Union Journal.*

HENRY VIII. By A. F. POLLARD, M.A., Litt.D., Professor of Constitutional History at University College, London ; Examiner in Modern History in the Universities of Oxford and London. Crown 8vo. 4s. 6d. net.

STOLEN WATERS : a page from the Conquest of Ulster. By T. M. HEALY, K.C., M.P., Bencher of King's Inns, Dublin, and of Gray's Inn, London. 8vo. 10s. 6d. net.

This narrative is based on unpublished MS. State Papers, and historical trials or inquisitions. It brings to light the hitherto unknown frauds practised on the Crown and the City of London in the Times of James I., Charles I., Cromwell, and Charles II. The narrative is woven round the controversy as to the title to two great fisheries in Northern Ireland—the River Bann and Lough Neagh.

ESSENTIALS IN EARLY EUROPEAN HISTORY. By SAMUEL BURNETT HOWE, A.M., Head of the Department of History in the Plainfield High School, Plainfield, New Jersey. With Illustrations, Coloured Maps, and Frontispiece. Crown 8vo. 7s. 6d. net.

A HISTORY OF EUROPE. By ARTHUR J. GRANT, M.A., Professor of History at the University of Leeds. With Maps and Coloured Chart. Large crown 8vo. 7s. 6d. net.

* Also in THREE PARTS. Part I.—The Classical World, 2s. 6d. net. Part II.—The Middle Ages, 3s. net. Part III.—Modern Europe, 3s. net.

"This is a book which was wanted. . . . It is a book of most conspicuous merit, good for students to read, and good for the ordinary man who wishes to know, truthfully and without prejudice what men have done to make the world what it is."—*Guardian.*

THE FIRST TWELVE CENTURIES OF BRITISH STORY : a sketch of the social and political conditions of the British Islands from the year 56 B.C. to 1154 A.D. With 20 Sketch Maps and 3 Photographic Reproductions of Medieval Maps. By J. W. JEUDWINE, LL.B. (Camb.), of Lincoln's Inn, Barrister-at-Law. 8vo. 12s. 6d. net.

"This is a book which would have gladdened the heart of Stubbs. . . . He has made a contribution to historical scholarship which no future historian of the first twelve centuries of our story can ignore."—*Everyman.*

LONGMANS, GREEN, & CO., 39 Paternoster Row, London, E.C.